Community at Play

Social and Religious Dynamics in the Modern Inuit Community of
Qikiqtarjuaq

ISBN 90 5170 957 9

Graphic design, cover design & cartography:
Rien Rabbers (GeoMedia, Faculty of Geosciences, Utrecht University)

Coverphoto:
Sack race at a community festival in Qikiqtarjuaq (2000).

Community at Play

Social and Religious Dynamics in the Modern Inuit Community of Qikiqtarjuaq

Een Samenleving in het Spel

Sociale en Religieuze Dynamiek in de Moderne Inuit Gemeenschap van Qikiqtarjuaq
(Met een samenvatting in het Nederlands)

Proefschrift ter verkrijging van de graad van doctor aan de Universiteit Utrecht
op gezag van de Rector Magnificus, Prof. Dr. W.H. Gispen
ingevolge het besluit van het College van Promoties in het openbaar te verdedigen
op woensdag 11 mei 2005, des ochtends om 10.30 uur

door

Anja Nicole Stuckenberger

geboren op 18 februari 1971 te Bochum (Duitsland)

Promotores: Prof. Dr. J.G. Oosten
                Prof. Dr. D.A.N.M. Kruijt
Co-promotor: Dr. S. M. Van Londen

Contents

List of Illustrations

Maps

Acknowledgments

This book is based on fieldwork that I conducted in Qikiqtarjuaq (Nunavut, Canada) from December 1999 until January 2001. I would like to thank the *Municipality of Qikiqtarjuaq* and the *Nunavut Research Institute* for permitting this project to take place (Nunavut Research Licence # 0100100N-A).

Many people contributed to this study. I owe my greatest dept to the people of Qikiqtarjuaq, their generosity, openness, and patience. For their warm hospitality that made me feel at home in a very literal way, I would like to thank Lizzy Anaviapik, Ragalee and Silasie Angnako, Taiviti Nuqingak, Imona and Uluta Kuksiak, Jaypootie and Susie Alikatuqtuq, Peter and Jeannie Kooneeliusie, John Fisher and Trudy Hutchings.

I wish to thank the elders and elderly who took the time to talk with me and who generously shared their recollections and insights. *Qujannamiipaaluk*, William and Nellie Allen, Simo Alookie, Silasie and Ragalee Angnako, Ipeelee and Yukipa Audlakiak, Markoosie and Leah Audlakiak, Mary Oonga Audlakiak, Mialia Audlakiak, Eliyah Kakudluk, Aka Keyootak, Jacopie and Leetia Koksiak, Joanasie and Leah Q. Kooneeliusie, Koalie and Igah Kooneeliusie, Geela and Loasie Kunilsuie, Pauloosie Kunilusie, Leah T. Kunilusie, Martha and Peteroosie Kopalie, Ipeelee and Saila Nauyavik, Jacopie and Leah Newkingnak, Leah Noah and Jukie Nookiguak, Aitaina Nookiguak, Martha Nookiguak, Levi and Peepeelee Nutaralak, and Peter Anilnik Paniluk.

Among the younger generations I especially want to thank Lizzy Anaviapik, Tapisa and Lucy Angnakok, Geela Angnako-Kunilusie, Billy and Daisy Arnaquq, Danny Audlakiak, Lena Audlakiak, Rosie Audlakiak, Stevie and Mary Audlakiak, Roy and Annie Bowatt Lizzy Etuangat, John Fisher, Trudy Hutchings, Jassie Keyooktak and Seleena Nookiguak, Yukipa and Noah Keyooktak, Matthew Kilabuk, Mary Killiktee, Nora Killiktee, Pauloosie Killiktee, Benjamin Kooneeliusie, Lisa Kooneeliusie, Monica Kooneeliusie, Nadia Kooneeliusie, Rosemary Kooneeliusie, Susan Kownirk, Elisapie Kunilusie, Grant MacDonald, Daisy Mosesie, Martha Newkingnak, Gamailee Nookiguak, Jaypatee Nookiguak and Leesee Natsiapik, Monica Nuqingak, Neevee Pitsulak, Ian Ross and Eunice Ejangiaq, Ena and Sami Qappik, and Lootie and Jeannie Toomasie. And, children of Qikiqtarjuaq – always kind, cheerful, and full of ideas – it was very nice to have you around.

I also owe much to John Ayaruaq and Lavinia Curley who were not only excellent translators but also provided me with a great deal of help and assistance. And so did Taiviti Nuqingak, whose help and friendship I will always cherish.

I am very grateful for the extensive and generous support that I received from Qikiqtarjuaq's institutions, especially from the municipality, and in particular from Mayor Lootie Toomasie, Recreation Director Adam Smith, and Senior Administrative Officer Don Pickle. I would like to thank the staff for their cordial reception while I worked in the building. The *Community Recreation Committee* supported my research in many ways and opened its doors to me as a visitor. I learnt a lot this way! The Qikiqtarjuaq *Arctic College* institute kindly provided me with space and facilities to set up interview sessions with elders. I did much of my writing and some interviews in the *Inuksuit* school, thanks to Principal John Fisher and Office Manager Daisy Arnaquq. I also tremendously enjoyed to have coffee with the staff in the teachers' room during school breaks. It became a second home. The *Hunters and Trappers Organization*, the

Housing Agency, and *Social Services* always had an open door and provided me with insights into their work. And last but not least, I want to express my gratitude to the Anglican and the Full Gospel Churches for making me feel welcome. I would like to thank Anglican lay-reader Loasie Kunilusie especially for taking me to a youth healing camp that he had organized – it left a lasting impression. I wish to thank Billy Arnaquq, pastor of the Full Gospel Church, for the time, openness, and patience dedicated to our conversations. I always felt very welcome to participate in the Anglican *Women's Auxiliary Group* though I have two left hands. I especially loved the games. The participants of the *Bible Study* meetings, hosted by Imona and Uluta Kuksiak, I want to thank for their confidence and their prayers.

The project was financed by the Faculty of Social Sciences, Utrecht University as a cooperative project of the Dutch Schools of Advanced Study *CERES* and *CNWS* and *Arctic College*, Iqaluit (Nunavut, Canada). I would like to thank Jarich Oosten, Selma van Londen, Arie de Ruijter, and Susan Sammons who made this possible. I also owe much to Cathleen Knötsch, Julai Papatsie, Xavier Blaisel, Louis-Jacques Dorais, Michelle Therrien, Bernard Saladin d'Anglure, and Susan Sammons who provided me with invaluable support in preparing my research proposal. And to Julai Papatsie in particular for his advice and practical support in finding a research location.

I wish to thank my *Doktorvater* Jarich Oosten for his intellectual guidance and his encouragement never to consider the next step to be the final one. I would like to thank my *co-promotor* Selma van London for her insightful comments and sympathetic advice, and Dirk Kruijt for taking it upon him to act as my official *promotor* at Utrecht University. He was drawn into the project at a later phase, but his enthusiasm made a big difference in the final stages of the work.

I also would like members of the *Research Group Circumpolar Cultures* (especially Barbara Miller, Wim Rasing, Leah Zuyderhout, and Nellejet Zorgdrager) and of the *Research Group Pentecostalism* of the *Hollenweger Institute*, (in particular André Droogers and Peter Versteeg) to know how much I appreciated their comments on various versions of this dissertation. Furthermore, I wish to thank Louis-Jacques Dorais for his never-tiring willingness to provide detailed translations and interpretations of complex Inuktitut phrases. Thank you, Nola Caffey and Barbara Miller, for doing an excellent job in editing the English.

My colleagues at the Department of Anthropology had their share in the completion of this book. I give thanks to Jan de Wolf for wise advice and keeping his door wide open; to Rieke Leenders for friendship and direction; to Geert Mommersteeg for ingenious and inspiring experiments in particular with blowgun and spinner; to Kootje Willemse-van Spanje for getting things going no matter what; to Yvon van der Pijl for thinking in different ways and for her friendship. Another person who offered me her friendship is Sonja Leferink. Sharing an office for a while was sometimes an 'surprising' experience. I want to thank her for teaching me about writing and for introducing me to the world of the *Lone Kimono* and *Scraping Hoofs*. The inspiring conversations with Christien Klaufus, my office-roommate for the last years, turned even the more difficult phases of writing into an intellectual pleasure. I hope that our shared weakness (and humor required) for organizing exhibitions will lead to some joint future projects. With Christien Klaufus and Katrin Dominik I had the perfect *paranimfs*.

I would also like to thank my friends for never wondering and unwaveringly keeping in touch. And my partner, Lennard Pisa, for taking care. And last but not least I want to thank my parents, Alois and Marion Stuckenberger, and my sister, Verena Gansler, for their confidence and never tiring support.

All of you together made this study an experience I feel deeply grateful for.

Map 1 *Qikiqtarjuaq, in the Province of Nunavut.*

Chapter 1
Theoretical background and methodology

1.1 Introduction

The population of Qikiqtarjuaq ('Big Island'), situated in the Canadian Eastern Arctic on Southern Baffin Island, is comprised of approximately 500 Inuit and 15 *Qallunaat* (that is: 'Caucasian, non-Inuit') inhabitants. It emerged in the 1960s due to the involvement of the Canadian Federal Government. The object was to replace nomadic Inuit camps by a permanent residence with direct access to health, school, government, police, and (Anglican) church facilities. I conducted thirteen months of fieldwork in the hamlet of Qikiqtarjuaq between December 1999 and January 2001 to study Inuit religious and social life. My intention was to examine how living in a modern community shapes Inuit conceptions of their own identity. My research was guided by such questions as: To what extent do Inuit identify themselves with the community? What social identity do they derive from community life? To what extent do rituals contribute to a sense of communal identity? What part do hunting and related activities play in these processes of identification?

My research initially emphasized how the principles of globalization and localization affected the formation of Inuit identities. I wondered how Inuit connect the various identities of being

Picture 1 *Qikiqtarjuaq in summer. The community is seen from the Inukshuk hill (see stone figure to the left) located north of the settlement (courtesy of Don Pickle).*

inhabitants of Qikiqtarjuaq, being Inuit, and being Canadian. In the field, I found that Inuit do indeed formulate an encompassing identity of being Inuit as opposed to being Qallunaat ('Caucasian, non-Inuit'). This identity is, however, not formulated in reference to social or political constructs, but in cosmological terms of relationships to land and animals. Inuit still identify themselves as hunters living off the land, whereas Qallunaat are perceived as strangers to the land and its inhabitants. The land and animals remain cosmological agents in forming modern Inuit identities.

At present, the dominant cosmological framework for Inuit is the Christian religion. This framework is not fixed, but it is subject to ongoing dynamic discourses[1] on proper ways to express Christianity. Since the 1980s, discourses deal in particular with the integration of Pentecostal ways into established Anglican beliefs and practices. The relevance of such practices is not confined to the religious domain, but also affects aspects of social life that are often formulated in terms of Christianity. The question, then, emerged of how the cosmological perspective connecting Inuit identities to land and animals is shaped in the context of today's Christian beliefs and practices. Therefore, I shifted my focus from general principles of globalization and localization to, first, specific issues of Inuit perceptions of the community, second, practices of social life in the community and out on the land, and third, Inuit religious life.

This study combines a synchronic research perspective with a diachronic one, focusing on Inuit recollections and perceptions of the past. Inuit frequently refer to ideals of a 'real' Inuit way of life as embodied in the *inummariit* ('the real Inuit') who are imagined to have lived before Inuit had contact with Qallunaat.[2] The people who come closest to this ideal are Inuit elders, who experienced life in nomadic hunting camps. Their recollections, knowledge, and skills are highly valued by Inuit. Perceptions of 'real Inuitness' inform modern Inuit identities. This is expressed in the phrase *inuit inunnirarnirijangat* ('identity', or literally, 'what is considered as being said by the Inuit themselves concerning the fact of being Inuit') (Therrien 1999: 33). The concept of *inuit qaujimajatuqangit* ('Inuit traditional knowledge') is used to construct a historic identity, connecting the past to the present.

Therefore, I will first briefly discuss the 'traditional'[3] Inuit way of life, of pre-contact culture referred to by Inuit as the 'traditional' times. Secondly, I will give an overview of the history of contact between Inuit and Qallunaat.

---

1   In this study, 'discourse' merely refers to ways of thinking and talking about and of dealing with certain issues.

2   See for a discussion of the notion of *inummariit* Omura (2002). The notion of the *inummariit* also has important political implications, which has been demonstrated by Jean Briggs (1997), Keiichi Omura on Pelly Bay (2002), and Nobuhiro Kishigami on Akulivik (2004). The image of the *inummariit* is distinctive in political settings or contacts with 'others' – notably Qallunaat people and institutions. The Inuit are the true owners and inhabitants of the land that is now Nunavut, and therefore they should be its main beneficiaries. The important thing in daily life is to live as an Inuk – to have an *inummariit* way of acting and thinking (Kishigami 2004: 84). Kishigami defines the notion of *inummariit* as involving "the distinctive ways that Inuit establish in their relationship with people, animals, the land, and the whole universe" (Kishigami 2004: 84). Like Dorais (1997) and Lanting (1999), Kishigami stresses that Inuit cultural identity is reproduced through daily socio-cultural practices (Kishigami 2004: 81).

3   I am following here Oosten & Remie's (1999: 2) notion that 'tradition': "is best viewed as a dynamic concept referring to ideas, practices and institutions that are handed down from one generation to the next and change in the process".

1.2 Historical perspective

1.2.1 The times of 'inummariit'

The ideology of the *inummariit* refers to the image of the ancestors as very strong, skilled, and knowledgeable, who lived entirely from the land and the sea prior to contacts with Qallunaat (Brody 1976; Matthiasson 1992). These features also correspond to the Western stereotype of Inuit living in igloos, traveling with dog sleds, and hunting seal.

Archeological evidence (see, for instance, Schledermann 1975) suggests that before contact with Qallunaat, Inuit of the Thule Culture[4] inhabited Southern Baffin Island from the 13th century onward.[5] Thule people specialized in hunting large baleen whales. Around 1200 A.D. until about 1500 A.D., the climate started to cool down. The summers became cooler, the ablation of snow and ice decreased and their retention increased. This cooling trend continued in the period between 1550 until 1850, culminating in the 'Little Ice Age' (Schledermann 1975: 33). Before the Little Ice Age, Thule Inuit lived in sod-houses in relatively permanent winter settlements along the coastlines of the Eastern Canadian Arctic. Due to the prolonged cooling trend and associated changes in ice conditions, the maritime Thule Culture gradually declined as Inuit adapted to the changing climatic conditions. Many groups gave up the whale hunt and focussed their foraging on smaller sea mammals, caribou and fish. As a consequence of the changing hunting patterns, Inuit could not accumulate enough food to maintain their earlier permanent winter settlements and they started to live in snow houses on the sea-ice to hunt seals at their breathing-holes (McGhee 1970; 1996). The Little Ice Age period also saw the advance of Caucasian explorers, whalers, and traders into the Arctic.

In fact, little is known of Inuit ways of life before the arrival of Qallunaat. In the 19th century interactions became more frequent and intense, and ever since the initial contacts, Qallunaat products and ideas continued to reach Inuit. Our images of Inuit social life, religious beliefs and practices are based on documents written by Qallunaat authors (such as Parry 1824; Lyon 1824; Hall 1865; Kumlien 1879; Boas 1888). They construct the image of a society based on hunting seals, fish, and caribou with a social life that was loosely organized and had weak leadership patterns.[6] Hunting was more than a technical, social, or economic enterprise, as Inuit believed that not only humans, but also animals and other beings shared spiritual qualities. Relations between humans, animals, and other non-human beings were subject to rules of proper conduct, the observation of ritual injunctions, and ritual practices. If these relations became strained, it was the shaman's task to re-establish proper connections between humans and these entities. Inuit cosmology was inseparably connected with the social domain.

The image of the *inummariit* refers to the life of hunters in a mixed sea and land based economy. This way of life actually developed at the same time that Qallunaat were arriving in

---

4   The term 'Thule Culture' was used by Therkel Mathiassen during the Fifth Thule Expedition (1922-23) for a set of distinctive archeological excavations. See for an extensive discussion of Thule culture the work of Robert McGhee (for instance of 1970).

5   Schledermann (1975: 275) recognized three major settlement periods in the Cumberland Sound area:

   I. A.D. 1370 – A.D. 1650

   II. A.D. 1650 – A.D. 1750 with more sporadic occupations

   III. A.D. 1750 – A.D. 1850

6   See for a discussion of these social features the sub-chapter *Inuit social life and its connection to cosmology in the past* further below in this chapter.

the Arctic. In the 19th century, Qallunaat technology and economy already had a heavy impact on Inuit society and culture. Kumlien's descriptions of Inuit social and religious life (1879) in particular reveal that Inuit ways of life were already then deeply influenced by modern western technologies. The time of the *inummariit* was, thus, already marked by Inuit-Qallunaat contacts, but in the Inuit perspective the Qallunaat are still regarded as peripheral.

1.2.2 Interactions with Qallunaat

After the famous travels of Martin Frobisher (1578 [2001]) in search of the Northwest Passage in 1576-1578, the Canadian Arctic was the destination of several expeditions during the 17th and 18th centuries. Early voyagers only sporadically interacted with Inuit. Contacts between Qallunaat and Inuit of Southern Baffin Island and Hudson Bay became more frequent and intensive with the flourishing of commercial whaling in the mid 19th century. Dutch, followed by Scottish, British and American whalers visited Cumberland Sound and the Hudson Bay regions on a regular basis between 1860 and 1915 (Damas 1988: 104). As foreign whaling ships operated in the Arctic, politics responded. The Canadian Government felt moved to assert its sovereignty in the region and consequently, in 1897 Captain William Wakeham made the formal declaration of sovereignty over Baffin Island and surrounding islands (Purich 1992: 32).

Inuit began to participate in the market economy as employees of European and American whaling fleets and many Inuit families moved to live close by the whaling stations. Inuit always stood open to western culture, specifically western garments, materials, and technology, and readily integrated new items they considered to make life in the Arctic easier, safer, and less season dependent. Through their employment they had access to such commodities as wooden boats, rifles and ammunition, knives, pots and pans, and needles.

Integrating the new technologies, Inuit adapted their hunting practices and leadership requirements. For instance, a wooden whaling boat in combination with the use of a rifle facilitated hunting expeditions of several men who could then hunt at the floe-edge rich with animals during winter, instead of the laborious seal hunt at breathing holes of previous days (Ross 1975: 136). Compared to the former foraging techniques the use of a whaleboat required the coordination of a larger number of hunters, on the other hand the newly introduced rifle, net, and iron trap facilitated hunting expeditions by a smaller number of participants (Stevenson 1997: 114f.).

The contact situation changed when the profitability of whaling gradually declined in some areas at the end of the 19th century. As whaling stations were abandoned on Southern Baffin Island, Inuit moved back to their former hunting areas (Damas 1988: 113). Replacing the whaling business, trading enterprises, such as the *Hudson's Bay* and the *Sabellum Companies*, became more active in the southern Baffin region around 1911. Inuit economy gradually shifted towards a market oriented fur trade of white fox and sealskins (Damas 1988: 107-108, Goldring 1986: 171). Earlier the Qallunaat managers of the whaling stations had decided over much of the whaling season activities of the Inuit, now the trading companies now hired the most productive Inuit hunters as middlemen. The middlemen distributed the trading goods to the camps and transferred skins to the trader. In these transactions, they had to consider the interests of the trading institution as well as the interests of their followers to maintain their position (Blaisel & Knötsch 1995: 9; Stevenson 1997: 117-120).

The late 19th and early 20th century not only brought an intensified involvement of southern Baffin Inuit in the market economy, but also the introduction of Christianity by Anglican missionaries. In1894, Reverend James Peck established a mission at Uumanarjuaq

('Blacklead Island', Cumberland Sound). After years of unsuccessful efforts to win Inuit for Christianity, the process of conversion accelerated with the baptism of the first three Inuit, women from Uumanarjuaq, in 1901 (Oosten, Laugrand & Kakkik 2003: 32). While hunters were busy with whaling, women and children remained in their camp in the vicinity of the mission. This proximity was apparently one of the reasons why Christianity was more readily accepted by women and children (Laugrand 2002:116). Another reason may have been that women were attracted by the fact that most ritual injunctions were lifted by their conversion to Christianity (Stevenson 1997: 126).

The acceptance of Christianity was not uncontested among camp inhabitants. The younger people readily accepted the new religion, but elders resisted the new teachings for a longer time (Laugrand 2002: 117), as did prominent camp leaders who often were also famous shamans in the Cumberland Sound area. Most men did not convert before influential shamans finally turned to Christianity and the leading functions, for instance celebrating services in the camps, were in their hands (Stevenson 1997: 90, 126). By the time the mission on Blacklead Island was aborted (in 1913), most Inuit of southern Baffin Island had converted to Christianity. The leading men had become preachers, and women were teaching children about the Bible (Laugrand 2002: 136f.).

Due the gradual decline in trading in the 1920s and the reports from the *Royal Canadian Mounted Police* (RCMP)[7] patrol of epidemics and famine among Inuit, the Canadian government wished to provide assistance. The state started to play a more prominent role in the Arctic having taken the responsibility to provide Inuit with relief. But whose money to invest? But their status was precarious.[8] The Supreme Court of Canada decided in 1939 that Inuit could be considered equivalent to Indians who stood under the *British North American Act* of 1867. This intervention proved to be just in time, as the fur trade on the world market again collapsed in the 1940s causing further deterioration of living conditions in Inuit camps (Kublu & Oosten 1999: 57).

Actually, little is written on southern Baffin Island Inuit societies between the 1920s and 1950s, which is the time of the onset of Government initiatives for sedentarization programs for Inuit. In conversations with Inuit adults and elders on community life, however, it was pointed out that it was relations between camps that continued to shape the social atmosphere and, to an increasingly lesser degree, determine the establishment of social relations (e.g. of marriage) in Qikiqtarjuaq. A person's association with a former camp (e.g. by kinship) continues to be relevance for the choice of the camp location during the spring and summer camping seasons, when people move from the settlement to their camps. Inuit, however, disapprove of emphasizing social distinctions while living concentrated in the settlement during other times of the year. They perceive that it would be detrimental to the well-being of the community.

I had thought that I could learn a lot in conversations with elders about the present day situation by looking closely at the relationship patterns of 1920 – 1950 period. However, in this

---

7   Canada's first Prime Minister, Sir John A. MacDonald and the Dominion Parliament established a paramilitary force of mounted police in 1873. Though the troop was trained and equipped for plains warfare, its primary responsibility was civil, namely "to advance guard of settlement, establishing friendly relations with the Indian tribes and maintaining peace as settlers arrived" (E-document by RCMP: http://www.rcmp.ca/history/origins1_e.htm).

8   Inuit were formally Canadian citizens after the transferral of Rupert's Land and the Northwest Territory by the *Hudson's Bay Company* to the government of Canada in 1870. However, the federal government, for some time, refused to live up to its responsibility for the inhabitants.

pursuit, I met with a number of difficulties. Firstly, only two of the elders in the community were born during the early years of that period, in 1915 and 1916 respectively. Most elders living in Qikiqtarjuaq in 2000 were born between 1933 and 1942 and thus experienced only their childhood or early youth in the camps prior to sedentarization. In interviews, they preferred not to speak about issues they knew about only from hearsay.

Secondly, while I had collected archival materials on the composition of camps for particular years, my data on nuclear families composed of husband, wife, and children, lacked information on seasonal variations in camp compositions and on other kinds of social alliances in and between camps.

Thirdly, interviews conducted by the *Freeman Research Limited* in the 1970s for the *Inuit Land Use and Occupancy Project* (1976) showed that people frequently moved from one camp or employment-opportunity to another, as well as crossing regions by, for instance, moving from Cumberland Sound to Davis Strait. A person's perception of belonging to a certain camp was not an issue of those interviews.

Fourthly, though elders gladly and in detail talked about camp life, they preferred not to talk about strained relationships. Fifthly, during my first interviews on elders' experiences of relocation, I was faced with the prolonged suffering that some of my interview partners had undergone. When one elder women had to cry in reminiscence, I decided to postpone conversations on this issue until I was more knowledgeable in Inuit ways of communication and comforting.

Sixthly, several elders participated in a relocation compensation claim against the Canadian government, under the guidance of Alan Angmarlik. As this claim was still in process, he had advised people not to talk about certain issues, such as camp composition. Based on these considerations, I decided not to stress the historical dimensions of the constitution of the modern community, but to focus on the present situation. I will deal with the past primarily as a feature in discourses on community life. Lacking information particularly of the period prior to the constitution of the settlement of Qikiqtarjuaq, I am unable to determine, from a historical perspective, how issues of change were chosen to talk or not to talk about and in what ways they were talked about.

In the 1950s and 1960s, the Government wanted to further facilitate the 'development' of Inuit society and to support Inuit more efficiently. Therefore, it started the process of concentrating and sedentarizing the nomadic Inuit hunting camps in newly constructed permanent settlements.[9] The official policy was:

> That the Eskimos should be drawn into Canadian national life but at the same time be encouraged to retain their cultural identity and integrity. These may be incompatible ends, but assuming that they are not, they might be attained through a long-range program of education and through the encouragement of factors that would strengthen their identity as Eskimos (L. H. Nicholson[10] in: Oswalt & VanStone 1960: 157).

---

9   See for a detailed, ethnohistorical account of the policies and developments that led to the establishment of Inuit settlements during the 1950s and 1960s David Damas (2002).

10   L.H. Nicholson, member of the Northwest Territories Council , at the Council opening in Ottawa in January of 1959 (Nicholson 1959: 20-24).

Anthropologists at that time, for instance Wendell Oswalt and James VanStone (1955), were optimistic that the enforcement of a culture-sensitive process of acculturation[11] would prove to be successful, on the condition that Inuit would gradually be involved in local administration and formal leadership.[12]

The new form of settlement went hand in hand with the introduction of new technologies. The permanent concentration of a large number of people at one site required longer journeys to reach hunting areas. The introduction of the snowmobile, which would gradually replace the dog-teams as the main means of transportation, provided Inuit with the necessary technology for fast travel to more distant hunting regions. The costs involved in this mode of transportation – the machine, gas, parts – however, made success in hunting seal for the sealskin trade, or employment in one of the few job-opportunities, almost mandatory.[13]

After a prize boom of sealskins in the 1960s, this market completely broke down with the implementation of the *U.S. Marine Mammal Protection Act* in 1972. The Act bans imports or sales of all marine mammal products. The anti-sealing campaigns of *Greenpeace* bolstered these developments which reached its climax when the *European Economic Community* also banned the import of sealskin products in October 1983.[14] Inuit again had to increasingly rely on welfare payments. To improve the family's income, men and women often engaged in the production of art, such as carvings and prints. Since the 1960s the government supported these initiatives and Inuit artwork became a sought-after commodity on the world's art market.

The government and local organizations have had little success so far in creating employment opportunities by economic development. The difficult economic conditions frustrate the establishment of self-reliant households and communities. Though most Inuit do not consider going back to live on the land year-round as an attractive option, they also perceive that most of the present notorious psychological and social problems a community has to deal with, such as domestic violence, drug abuse, property misdemeanors and suicides, are connected to modern community life. Kublu & Oosten (1999: 57-58) wrote: "Social problems such as alcoholism and suicide rapidly developed in the villages and Inuit began to organize themselves to face the disintegration of their society."[15]

During the 1960s, Inuit started to implement interregional organizations to strengthen their political impact. These initiatives resulted in 1971 in the founding of the *Inuit Tapirisat*. Inuit of the Northwest Territories, Quebec, and Labrador formulated their claims for their own land and government. They thus managed to establish themselves as an 'ethnic' group in the context of national and international political and land rights.

The *Tungavik Federation of Nunavut*, founded in 1981, conducted negotiations which would eventually result in the establishment of the new Canadian territory of Nunavut in 1999. Inuit of the Eastern and Central Canadian Arctic and the Canadian government agreed on the

---

11   For instance, by planning dog-team areas in the layout of the modern Inuit settlements (Williams 1965: 12). See also Thomas & Thompson (1972).

12   There has been an extensive debate on the concept of the rural community as formulated, for instance, by Redfield (1971), Cohen (1985), Bauman (2001), and Amit (2002).

13   See for a detailed description of Inuit community life in the 1970s McElroy (1977). She conducted research on Inuit strategies of adaptation to a modern community setting in Pangnirtung.

14   See for a discussion of the effects of the sealskin boycott Wenzel (1994: 299, 301-304, 307) in Clyde River, a community to the north of Qikiqtarjuaq.

15   See also Rasing 1994.

implementation of a new Canadian territory – Nunavut ('Our Land').[16] Of the 25,000 people living in Nunavut, about 80% are Inuit. The territory covers a fifth of the Canadian land and sea mass reaching from the Atlantic coast far into the interior of the Canadian Arctic. The territory is composed of three distinct regions: Qikiqtaaluk, Kivalliq, and Kitikmeot. They provide regional administration to 28 communities; one of them being Qikiqtarjuaq in the Qikiqtaaluk region. Formerly administrated by the Northwest Territories, Nunavut now provides Inuit with territorial self-administration. Associated rights, for instance in respect to resource management, were granted in exchange for aboriginal rights and claims to land and water (Remie 1989; Dickerson 1992: 101; Kublu & Oosten 1999: 58-59; Nunavut Land Claims Agreement: Agreement between ... Ottawa: 1993).

1.3 Christian discourses on the difficulties of the community

The difficulties that communities have to deal with play a central part in the religious discourse. The rapid integration of Pentecostal movements reaching the North in the mid 1980s illustrates the relevance of religious perspectives on social and psychological difficulties.[17] Whereas Pentecostalism was at first accepted by only a few individuals and fiercely rejected by most Inuit, in the 1990s it became increasingly established in southern Baffin Island. The new beliefs and practices have not only been integrated into the Anglican Churches, but in many communities new Pentecostal Churches have been established. In Inuit discourses on Christianity, the improvement of a person's personal life and of community life are central.

The former nomadic hunting camps have been integrated into permanent and institutionalized structures of modern communities, and into the world economy. But social life continues to be perceived and practiced in connection to cosmological beliefs. In the past, the cosmological context was provided by shamanism, today, it is formulated in terms of Christianity, so that today both the ideal of the *inummariit* of the past – nomadic hunters who lived entirely off the land – as well as proper ways of Christianity are central issues in the discourses on ways to improve modern community life. In this study, I will deal with the question how the interaction between these two traditions shapes daily life. I will approach this problem by looking at the ways in which Inuit perceive and shape community life.

---

16   Cor Remie argued that:

Originally, Inuit had no uniting perception of being a people. [...] The new educational system created a young elite, who, because of their knowledge of the functioning of the Canadian bureaucracy, took the initiative to organize Inuit to resist the increasingly pressing Canadian society and industry. (Remie 1990: 54; translation by author).

Land claims, first formulated in the early 1970s, were "actually the first clear reaction from Inuit on the process of incorporation into the Canadian state" (Remie 1990: 51; translation by the author). The Nunavut Land Claims Agreement was ratified by Inuit in November of 1992, signed by the Prime Minister of Canada on May 25, 1993, and passed through the Canadian Parliament in June of the same year. Nunavut as a political unit was stipulated and established as Inuit organizations wanted self-administration, bringing the government closer to the people – geographically and culturally. On April 1999, Nunavut finally received the territorial status in Canada.

17   I will deal with this issue in more detail in the chapter *Christian life in Qikiqtarjuaq*.

1.4 Inuit social life and its connection to cosmology in the past

The organization of social life has been one of the most debated issues of anthropological research among Inuit, ever since Mauss & Beuchat's (1979 [1904]) influential study of Inuit social morphology. Mauss & Beuchat suggested that the -*miut*[18] group was the important level of Inuit social organization. Attached to a place name,[19] the postbase -*miut* indicates a relation to a place as well as a plurality. Inuit names for places often derive from marked features of the landscape. The designation of a group of people inhabiting a place is usually composed of the postbase -*miut* attached to the place's name.[20] *Qikiqtarjuarmiut*, for instance, translates as 'those people inhabiting a place called the Big Island'.

The -*miut* postbase, in combination with a place name, indicates a link between people and the place they inhabit; it does not specify social relations between the inhabitants of the camp. The main problem in defining -*miut* groups as cohesive and formal social units is the flexibility of membership and locality. The -*miut* groups formed temporary camps that seasonally dispersed and then concentrated again in winter camps. Before the development of modern Inuit communities, the winter camp was the largest agglomeration of Inuit families throughout the year. In southern Baffin Island these camps usually had between 40 to 70 members (Stevenson 1997: 71). Furthermore, the membership composition of the concentrated and the dispersed camps changed annually. Groups did not necessarily settle at the same location each year. Thus, the groups were always changing in composition and location.

Kinship has been a central element in the organization of the group. Damas (1963, 1964), and later on Stevenson (1997), extensively studied the composition of local groups over long periods, trying to establish the organizational principles over time. They demonstrated that agnatic linkages, especially those between fathers and sons, and those between brothers, played an important part in the composition of the group. But the social organization was quite flexible as sisters and their families, as well as more distant relatives, could form core-groups or attach themselves to such groups (Stevenson 1997: 225-233).

Two marked features formed the basis for Damas' and Stevenson's interpretation of the cohesion of Inuit communities. They argued that, associated with kinship relations, attitudes of *naalaqtuq* ('respect-obedience') and *ungayuq* ('affection, closeness') constituted principles of group formation or strategies of affiliation.[21] "While the former provides 'order' to society, the latter provides the 'glue' that holds it together" (Stevenson 1997: 249). Damas and Stevenson argued that the combination and dynamic interactions of these principles of bonding could explain the dynamics in group composition. Damas and Stevenson were well aware that apart from kinship, ritual partnerships and other organizational features were also decisive factors in group composition. In a publication of 1969, for instance, Damas suggested the 'band' approach for dealing with the -*miut* configuration. He argued that, in addition to kinship, the composition of bands, ecological and social factors also played a part. For instance, local factors of the game population had an influence on the size of the band. However, he presented the association of

---

18   -*miut* is grammatically a postbase.

19   See Müller-Wille (1987) and Collignon (2004) for an examination of Inuit place names.

20   The postbase -*miut* can be attached to names of various geographical scales thereby denoting either small dispersed camp groups or the larger winter aggregation. It can also be used when referring to Inuit groups of a larger region, such as Baffin Island.

21   See also Wenzel (1981).

kinship and principles of bonding as the key to understanding Inuit social organization (Damas 1969).

Guemple focused more on the issue of alliance – relations based on cooperation and usually on a shared locality.[22] He examined betrothal, spouse exchange, namesake or *saunik* ('little bone') relations, ritual sponsorship, and adoption among Belcher Islands Inuit:

Betrothal

A betrothal took place when two co-residing families pledged their children to marry when they would reach maturity. Small gifts were exchanged between parents and children to validate this alliance. Betrothal established kinship ties. Children addressed each other with the terms for spouses, however, adding the particle *-qautik* ('contains'). The parents of the betrothed were addressed with affinal kin terms. The parents' relationship with each other was more openly defined and shaped in such a way as was useful to them. A betrothal was handled flexibly and could be invalidated by the parents taking care that "one does not break off a relationship; one merely moves away so that the relationship becomes dormant". Even when no marriage followed the betrothal, the affinal terms of address and reference continued to be used (Guemple 1971b: 57-59).

Spouse exchange

Spouse exchange could occur between two couples that closely cooperated. The exchanged spouses cohabited usually for an extended period. The offspring of the couples were placed in close ties of kinship. The links established by this alliance strongly resembled the links established by polygamy. The same term used for co-spouses was applied to same sex exchange partners. The opposite sex exchange partners applied the terms for spouses. The particle *-ngua-* was added to indicate that it was an exchange relationship rather than an ordinary marriage, when the partners did not live together in a camp. Apparently, exchange relationships were based on cooperative efforts, joined ownership of valuable property, such as a whale boat, and, as Guemple speculated, there might have been also religious reasons involved. The offspring of the exchange relation were identified by the 'regular' children of the couples as siblings, but might also be differentiated from 'real' siblings by inserting *-ngua-* in the kin term. They might also be addressed as 'cousins' (Guemple 1971b: 60-61).

Ritual sponsorship

The parents of a newborn child chose a person to whom they felt close who would dress the child in its first clothes after the child was named. When gifts were exchanged, the sponsor became the *sanariak* ('one who builds [the child]') and the child became the *angusiak/arngnaliak* ('becoming a male/female [adult]') of each other. The child and the sponsor entertained a close relationship and they engaged in reciprocal sharing. For instance, a young boy would bring his first kills of the diverse animals to the sponsor who then distributed them in the camp. The sponsor provided the child with all necessary equipment, food, and the like, as required by the child. One sponsor could be replaced by another one; the reason could be a serious illness of the child, an indication that the sponsor did not fit the child's 'personality' (Guemple 1971b: 65-66).

---

22   See also Graburn's (1964) study of Ungava coast Inuit groups for the relevance of locality in the formation of relationships.

Adoption

When a child was transferred to its adoptive parents, its biological parents did not loose their parental claim over it. The child acquired relations of support in its adoptive family, but also retained relations of support in its old family. The reasons for adoption were manifold; for instance, adoptions took place when a household broke up or a family had too many children. It could also be that parents wanted to establish social connections with another person or because a widow felt lonely. Usually the adoptive and offering parents were closely related. The adopted child was addressed by the adoptive parents with the kin terms for son and daughter, to which the particle *-saq-* 'potential' was added. This modifier was dropped once the child was well-integrated into the new family. Marriages between biological siblings, as well as between biological and adopted siblings were prohibited. The involved parents referred to each other as *tiguvik* ('child givers') and *tiguvak* ('child takers'), respectively (Guemple 1971b: 67-68).

Namesake/saunik relationships

On Belcher Island, a person is approached to share his/her name with a newborn child.[23] A name was said to be chosen in the world of the spirits as well as by the parents and relatives after consultation with a living namesake. Usually, a person of high standing and reputation was chosen. Living namesakes addressed and referred to each other as *saunik* ('bone').

Other people with the same name were the child's namesharers. They called each other *atia ualugit* ('little big name'). Inuit believed that the name would hold what we could call 'personality', which the child received with the naming. A name could be shared by a number of people. "In some sense the [namesharers] were separate individuals but representatives of only one ['personality']." The namesharers were connected to each other in such a way that the actions of one could have consequences for the well-being of the others. They, more or less casually, observed reciprocal obligations. The relationship between namesakes was more strictly defined. Namesakes engaged in reciprocal sharing until the child reached adulthood. All holders of a name were interchangeably addressed by the same kin term: for instance, a namesake of a relative was addressed in the same terms as the relative.

Individuals could be renamed. Renaming served to protect a person against dangers. Adults changed their names when they felt endangered by cosmological agents. In that case, former name-based relationships were replaced with the new network. Changing the name meant changing one's fortune (Guemple 1971b: 62-65).

In summary, Guemple suggested that the articulation of alliance relationships in kin terms made:

> Kinship [...] the idiom of social relatedness but one that is sufficiently flexible to permit a reallocation of existing kinsmen into new social roles, even when these violate genealogical criteria (Guemple 1971b:73). Kinship [...] is not the underlying skeleton of the social system, but rather a kind of rhetoric of social relatedness in terms of which crucial social and economic connections based on locality are expressed (Ibid: 92).

---

23   Among many other Inuit groups, a name is transferred from a deceased person. The social and cosmological nature of the name and the principle of the continuation of names Mauss & Beuchat (1970 [1904]: 28) referred to is not affected by the Belcher Islands variation.

In Guemple's model, shared locality constitutes the basis for Inuit social organization. Social relationships are temporal and, in principle, continuously established anew between the people who share a locality.

Leaders and shamans

Decisions to join a camp were not only a matter of kinship and alliance relations, but also of the acceptance of the authority of the camp leader. Camps were composed of two or three extended families. Whereas nuclear families were led by the father as the head of the family, the *isumataq* ('camp leader'), and his helpers, were selected on the basis of a combination of various criteria, such as age, wisdom, experience, hunting skills, personality, ownership of hunting equipment, and support from kin (Stevenson 1997: 64). The core-group of the leader usually consisted of his sons. The privileged relations between father, sons, and brothers were discussed by Damas and Stevenson as hierarchical relations of respect. The father had authority over his sons, and the *angajuq* ('older brother') had authority over his *nukaq* ('younger brother').

Men and women made decisions regarding their fields of occupation, however when involved, men tended to have the final say on most issues. Nonetheless, individuals were perceived to be their own masters making their own decisions (Stevenson 1997: 233-238). The social positions of the leader and the followers were not strictly circumscribed. Some camps were led by strong charismatic leaders whose position was not disputed (Ibid: 234). Other camps were organized by a more subtle hierarchy. Usually, they were composed of a leading family, and social positions were further determined by age, gender, and skills.[24] Leadership positions evolved situationally from the requirements of the task at hand.

The well-being of the camp members was perceived to be linked to a cosmological order within which the camp would deal with social and economic difficulties. While the *isumataq* was a leader of the camp, the *angakut*, ('shaman') was the mediator between humans and non-human beings. During pre-contact time, social and religious leadership were closely intertwined. Not seldom, camp leaders had both functions or close relatives took over one of the tasks (Stevenson 1997: 89, 127, 130). After adopting Christianity as a framework for articulating cosmological relationships, the connection between the social and religious domains continued to be perceived and practiced. The connection was represented, for instance, in the continuity of the combination of social and religious leadership. Leaders apparently adopted Christianity, after initial fierce resistance, when they came to the conclusion that Christianity would be a powerful way to deal with situations of acute distress, such as death due to epidemics (Blaisel & Knötsch 1995: 22).

Leaders in the social and in the religious domain were often those who also occupied leading positions in the context of economic transactions with Qallunaat in whaling and trading (Stevenson 1997: 125). Qallunaat whalers and traders employed 'camp bosses' as mediators between Qallunaat companies and camps. In this position, the middlemen usually became

---

24   Stevenson emphasized leadership as shaping the modes of production. Members of a winter camp with a strong leader remained together longer than those with a weak leader. Strong leadership also had its drawbacks. When a leader was too forceful, people felt restricted in their own decision making. Weak leaders permitted more men to gain positions of status. This was apparently attractive, as these camps were often bigger, though less stable, than the camps with a strong leader. If a strong leader died, or the campsite lacked prosperity, the camp often split up. New members were recruited, or people aligned with members of other camps (Stevenson 1997: 233).

owners of boats and other expensive hunting technology and means of transportation. This meant that the already influential families got an extra advantage. Lack of ownership and a limited access to these sources marked a group as less fortunate. Resentment was a frequent reaction to this increasing inequality (Ibid: 121-123). In order to be able to fulfill their responsibility towards the camp and to maintain their position, these leaders had to take care to evenly distribute the payments among their followers. Examples of the concentration of leadership tasks in Cumberland Sound were Angmarlik and Keenainak – both camp leaders, recognized as excellent hunters, owners of whaleboats, shamans and later preachers, and tradesmen in Cumberland Sound. Angmarlik coordinated whaling and trading at Kekerten, and later, after initial fierce resistance to Christianity, converted and became a preacher himself (Ibid: 92, 125, 126, 147).

We may conclude that whaling, trading, and the introduction of Christianity did not so much introduce new structures of leadership but strengthen existing leadership positions. At the same time, whalers, traders, missionaries, and the RCMP also exerted authority over Inuit ways of life in their demarcated domains.

1.5 Social change

Did Inuit have a more stable social organization in the past, before contacts with Qallunaat were established? Were the dynamics and the flexibility in Inuit social organization side effects of the contact situation? Some authors think so. Boas had already speculated that social categories among Inuit groups from the Cumberland Sound and Davies Strait regions were destroyed by the arrival of the whalers who introduced fatal epidemics (Boas 1888: 424f., 464, 466). Colin Adams (1972) argued that, due to contacts with Qallunaat, acculturative processes tended to dissolve Inuit social organization:

> It appears most unlikely that Eskimos might acquire consistent complexes of values from transactions with Caucasians, for the latter are themselves diverse, inconsistent, and variable as transactional partners, and incomplete as representatives of a total value system which might serve as a model (Adams 1972: 15).

Stevenson, after reviewing these arguments with his empirical data (1997: 105-140), concluded that "there was no significant structural transformation in Cumberland Sound Inuit social organization during the historic period" (Ibid: 139) as far as social and economic factors are concerned.[25] He suggested that, despite its apparent flexibility, there was great continuity and resilience in Inuit social structure. A similar conclusion for present day Inuit society was expressed by, for instance, Rasing (1994) addressing Inuit social order and by Dorais (1997) addressing continuity in social life and values. Concrete illustrations of resilience of Inuit 'traditional' ways from my own field study are the continued relevance of sharing and kinship relations in daily life and value orientations, the high frequency of 'traditional' adoption, and vital 'traditional' naming practices. These examples suggest that the same high degree of continuity of some of the principles of camp life of the past, indicated by Stevenson, can be observed in present Inuit perceptions of their social life and in their handling of the relationship between social and cosmological domains. It will be assessed in this study if this is indeed the case.

---

25   See also Goldring 1986 on Cumberland Sound.

1.6 The ritual constitution of society

Guemple was well aware that the strategies that he suggested were part of a wider system. He pointed out that future research should take the Inuit perspective into account as: "our inability to explain the system is traceable to the fact that we have not yet taken the native's own implicit philosophy sufficiently into account in deciding how his social organization is to be viewed" (Guemple 1971a: 8). He argued that by looking at this 'philosophy' we would find that: "underlying the whole social organization is a cultural metaphysics which fosters the native view that all social relations are to a large degree negotiable" (Guemple 1971a: 1; 1971b: 56). Guemple's description of Belcher Islanders' naming practices was a case in point, as in these practices, social relationships were connected to cosmological ones. Guemple's hypothesis is interesting for modern Inuit society, considering the relevance of a Christian framework in discourses about present community life, not the least because similar naming practice are still practiced today alongside practices of Anglican baptism and the dedication of infants by the Full Gospel Church.

For the pre-settlement past, Mauss & Beuchat argued that the recycling of names was an essential feature of the continuity of a -miut group as both a social and cosmological unit, since the name of the last person to die was given to the first child to be born thereafter (Mauss & Beuchat 1979 [1904]: 28). A society could therefore be considered a continuum of names. But Inuit children often have received several names. Kublu & Oosten argued that: "it was especially the name, which made a human being into a social person and distinguished him from other beings [which had no] social identity" (Kublu & Oosten 1999: 64). Depending on the context, different names might be used. When a child, for example, received the name of its maternal grandfather and the name of the deceased wife of its neighbor, the latter would refer to the child with his wife's name, whereas the child's mother would refer to the name of her deceased father. In this way, the child is considered to be part of both households.

Alexina Kublu described her and her family's name relations extensively (Kublu & Oosten 1999). Her account clearly illustrates how the terms of address still evoke the relationships between the deceased namesakes, or between the deceased namesake and the living namesake, and place the namesake in a complex network of connections (Kublu & Oosten 1999: 64-68). "Relations between people [...] derive meaning from the relationships between their ancestors" (Ibid: 69). Kublu's description also shows that the naming system has been dynamic and always could be used creatively, as relationships could be arbitrarily established or interpreted idiosyncratically (Ibid: 74). Kinship terms and terms of address can only be understood in the context of various forms of alliances and partnerships, particularly the naming practices.[26] By connecting people to their ancestors, the establishment of naming alliances contribute to the ritual foundation of society.

Rituals played an important part in the constitution of society in the past. The Sedna festival is a point in case. According to Laugrand & Oosten (2002), Christmas took over the functions of the Sedna festival, in the converted camps. During fieldwork, I found that Christmas continued to be of high relevance to the inhabitants of the modern settlement of Qikiqtarjuaq. Christmas is the major celebration of the year and is both a social as well as religious event. Virtually the

---

26   See also: Nuttall (2000: 39) who argued that kinship in Kangersuatsiaq (Greenland) is basically a matter of choice, but that there are definite prescriptions of conduct associated with specific kin. And Bodenhorn (2000) on the transformability of kin relations among the Iñupiat of northern Alaska.

entire community participates in the ten day celebration, filled with games, but also with feasts, dances, and community church services.

The games particularly attracted my attention. Firstly, because of the sheer quantity of games played and time spent (during ten days about eight hours daily). And, secondly, because of their atmosphere. In November and early December I noted an increasingly tense atmosphere in the community, which developed when people returned from their camps. It appeared to enliven old and new grudges. I anticipated under these conditions that Christmas would not be very cheerful. I was, however, entirely wrong. By Christmas, all tensions seemed to have disappeared. When I mentioned my surprise to Inuit acquaintances, they all told me that during play all quarrels should be forgotten. To Inuit, play has always been a prominent and effective means for socialization and for dealing with conflicts, as well as being entertaining and fun. Jean Briggs observed, concerning its use in socialization:

> In Inuit society a great deal of the serious business of life is conducted in the playful mode, and this play contains processes essential to the creation, maintenance, and internalization of the central values of the society. Play helps Inuit to manage interpersonal and value conflicts and thus to maintain smooth human relationships (Briggs 1979: iii).

In Oosten's words: "Play was a strategy to master fundamental problems within Inuit society" (Oosten 2001: 24). A case in point were the famous song contests. The opponents made satirical songs ridiculing each other. The one who gained most support was the moral victor. Importantly, the outcome of a competition was not fixed, but open to the dynamic developments of the interactions of the players and the audience involved.

Mauss & Beuchat pointed out that winter in pre-Christian times was the period of great feasts and an increase in shamanic activities. These feasts, and especially the ritual that concerned human relations to the mistress of the sea-game (or mistress of the underworld, as Boas called her) Sedna, were apparently important in the ritual constitution of the winter camp. Franz Boas provided an extensive description of the Sedna festivity in late fall/early winter among Inuit of Cumberland Sound (Boas 1888: 604-606).[27]

The Sedna festival took three days, during which the future hunting success of the camp was negotiated between its inhabitants, the dead, and Sedna, the mistress of the sea game.[28] At the end of November, traveling was difficult because the sea-ice started to freeze-up and success in hunting was very precarious. It was also a period when there was a heightened activity of spirits, as Boas vividly described:

> The spirits of the dead, the *tupilaq*, knock wildly at the huts, which they cannot enter, and woe to the unhappy person whom they can lay hold of. He immediately sickens and a speedy death is regarded sure to come. The wicked *qiqirn* pursues the dogs, which die with convulsions and cramps as soon as they see him. All the countless spirits of evil are aroused, striving to bring sickness and death, bad weather, and failure in hunting. The worst visitors

---

27 See Blaisel & Oosten 1997; Oosten 2001; Laugrand & Oosten 2002 for interpretations; Saladin d'Anglure 1993 for the comparable *Tivajuut* festival from Igloolik.

28 For an extensive analysis see, for instance, Blaisel & Oosten 1997: 22, 41; Saladin d'Anglure 1989, 1993; Laugrand & Oosten 2002.

are Sedna, mistress of the under world, and her father, to whose share the dead Inuit fall (Boas 1888: 603f.; italics by A.N.St.).

It was the task of the shamans to protect the camp from Sedna's anger and from the spirits of the evil dead. The harpooning of Sedna was a central feature of the festival. Inside a hut, Sedna was lured with a magic song, and, as she emerged through a simulated seal's breathing hole, she was harpooned. Struggling hard, she finally managed to free herself and disappeared. The shaman showed the audience the harpoon head dripping with blood. According to Bilby, the amount of blood foretold success in hunting (Bilby 1923: 214). The following day, people wore amulets for protection against the dangers still impending from Sedna, and the ritual continued. The men assembled early in the morning in the middle of the settlement, ran and jumped around all the houses of the camp screaming loudly, playing an attack of the spirits. The women waiting at the houses threw little gifts to the crowd and the men scrambled to get them.

Then people assembled for a divinatory tug-of-war game. One team represented summer, the other winter. Depending on which team would win, good or bad weather was expected. After the competition was decided, women brought a large container with water. In the order of their age, every person of the camp[29] stepped forward, took some water with his/her cup and sprinkled some water on the ground. Then s/he faced his/her place of growing-up and pronounced the date and place of his/her birth. The presentation of each person was commented on by the audience. Old people and well-respected hunters were dealt with respectfully and appreciatively. Younger ones received less attention and some were objects of ridicule, indicating their low social position in the group.

While everyone participated in the drinking round, two disguised *Qailertetang* figures, representing spirits of the dead from Sedna's realm, had approached the assembly. They were dressed with huge clothing and women's jackets and carried equipment for the seal hunt, as well as women's scrapers for cleaning the skins. They matched pairs of men and women to live together as man and wife in the woman's house until the following day. After they completed their task of pairing, the Qailertetang figures went to the shore to invoke the favorable north wind that brings good weather. After the incantation, the men of the camp attacked the figures and pretended to kill them. The Qailertetang figures made believe to be dead, but came back to life after everyone left to get a cup of water. Individuals approached them, offering a drink of water and asking the figures about the future.

The festivity was concluded with *ajuktaqtung*, a ball game. This game was believed to be played by the *Ullormiut* ('people of the day', 'souls of the dead'). In contrast to the *tupilait* (souls of the dead that could not find rest at first), the *Ullormiut* were thought to have a happy life. In this game, the players represented their deceased relatives and namesakes, the *Ullormiut* who entertain themselves in a game in the land of light. The violent relations between Inuit and the anonymous spirits of the dead that marked the onset of the festival were gradually transformed into play, general sharing of goods, and the matching of women and men by members of the community who represent the dead (Oosten 2001: 23; Laugrand & Oosten 2002: 208).

A recurrent feature of the ritual is its divinatory nature: the blood on the harpoon, the tug-of-war, the Qailertetang – all predicted hunting results. The whole ritual appears to focus on good hunting. It does so by involving all members of the community; even the deceased who

---

29   Small children were represented by their mothers. Only parents with babies born during the last year do not participate in this part of the ritual.

at the beginning of the ritual attacked the camp. At the end, relations improved and everyone engaged in playing the game of the dead. The ritual gradually developed from men behaving abnormally, (like children or the dead), through the naming procedure, where all the members of the community identified themselves as social beings in terms of time and space (name, place, season of birth), to a stage where the community created good relations with the spirits (Qailertetang) and the deceased.

The camp was involved as a whole, but throughout the community organized itself in different ways: Men made the rounds of the houses and the women reciprocated with gifts; people pronounced their names and place of birth in order of their time of birth; in the tug-of-war, the season of birth determined the order of the parties; and finally, women and men were almost randomly ordered in pairs that would have sexual intercourse with each other. All these different orders encompassed and involved the camp as a whole and reorganized the camp in its internal structure. This feature expresses a moral element, namely that only through cooperation and organization into parties could hunting success could be achieved – given that good relations with animals and spirits were established (Blaisel & Oosten 1997).

In ritual play humans, spirits, and humans presenting spirits were engaged. In the processes of play, the future was foretold and/or relationships were improved and re-established. I want to illustrate these processes by two examples, first the harpooning of Sedna, and second, the impersonation of spirits by men.

Shamans lured Sedna to appear and then tried and managed to harpoon her as if she were a sea mammal. When sea mammals were hunted, they were met with great respect. Bringing them into the community was accompanied by the ritual of giving the killed animal water, as its soul was thirsty. Providing the animal with a drink meant to welcome it to the camp. Its meat supported the hunter and his family with food, and the animal's *tarniq* ('soul') would reincarnate in another animal or in a human. In analogy, the harpooning of Sedna suggested that the relationship between Sedna and the humans of the camp would be transformed from hostility to a relation of exchange. The relationship of exchange was expressed in the amount of blood spilled as a divinatory sign for the future hunting success.

The second illustration, the play of the men visiting all the houses of the camp, started with the enactment of the hostility of the spirits of the dead in a playful way, reminiscent of children. In the context of play, the camp could interact with these spirits. Women participated by giving gifts to the men; and the men cooperated in the exchange by scrambling for the objects given. From then on, the hostility of the spirits ceased to threaten the camp. The element of play was present in the divinatory tug-of-war game, in the raillery involved when people took a cup of water and announced their names and places of origin, in the mock killing of the immortal Qailertetang figures, and in the final ball game.

The ritual system concerned with Sedna was already in decline when Boas conducted his fieldwork, and disappeared in South Baffin Island with the introduction of Christianity at the beginning of the 20th century. Instead of celebrating the Sedna festivity in late November during the freeze-up, Inuit of southern Baffin Island began to celebrate Christmas at the end of December. When Peck started his mission on Blacklead Island in 1894, he, and all following missionaries elsewhere among Inuit, immediately introduced the celebration of Christmas. Its main features were a church service, a Western-style meal for the missionaries and provisions of country and Qallunaat food for the Inuit, the exchange of gifts, and the organization of games. At the games, missionaries often provided prizes for the winners, a feature that rapidly gained in importance. In a comparative study, Laugrand & Oosten (2002) explored to what extent the new ideas replaced traditional ones. They approached this problem of continuity and change by comparing the winter festivals of the pre-Christian Sedna ritual to the celebration of Christmas in Christian Inuit camps of the past. They found that: "Many old ideas and practices did not die as easily as missionaries or Inuit assumed, but returned in a new guise.[30] [...] Many features of pre-Christian religion returned in the Christmas celebrations, but in a new context and provided with new meaning" (Laugrand & Oosten 2002: 203). With respect to play, they suggested that:

> It seems fair to assume that [in the feature of play] the ideology of the community has not changed at all in the winter celebrations. In playing games, the community shows its capacity to deal with [...] tensions and to dissolve them in a general atmosphere of friendly competition (Ibid: 221).

Thus, they suggested that the social and cosmological effects of the Sedna festival were largely taken over by Christian rituals, notably by Christmas. But what happens in modern settlements with their changed social modalities? How do participants perceive community and how does the Christmas festival shape community life embedded in seasonal variation?

1.7 Development of the research in Qikiqtarjuaq

In late November of 1999, I left the Netherlands for a period of seven months of fieldwork. After arrival and settling in the household of a cousin of Julai Papatsie who had helped to set up my research project, my first move was to introduce myself to the hamlet council that only knew of my project through the application procedure for a research permit issued by the Nunavut Research Council. I presented once again my project and invited people to comment. I was welcomed and the further steps were completely left up to me.

Christmas was quickly approaching and the community was preparing for it with decorated houses and the organization of Christmas dinners for institutions and business staff. The community celebrations started on December 24th. During the coming ten days of celebration, the unity of the community was strongly emphasized, for instance in the community festivals and the many hours of games. My first impression of Qikiqtarjuaq was that of a rural Canadian community. As Christmas passed by, I had planned to conduct a household survey to get an overview of the population and their relationships, but I very quickly learnt that this is virtually an impossible task as the household compositions are quite dynamic. Most households are based on close kinship relations, but also on more distantly related people who are attached temporarily. In addition, close family members, such as children, may temporarily live somewhere else for pragmatic reasons. My first impression of Qikiqtarjuaq as a rural community became increasingly problematic.

Movement was not only a pronounced feature of households, but also of the seasonal cycle of Qikiqtarjuaq. In spring, Qikiqtarjuaq families started to move to their hunting camps for a few days or weeks. For many, living out on the land was as close as is presently possible to the 'real' Inuit ways of life. They perceived that living off the land affects people's well-being positively.

Becoming gradually aware of the relevance of movement in Inuit life, I approached the municipality of Qikiqtarjuaq to discuss the possibility of extending my stay for another six

---

30   See for a similar evaluation Stevenson 1997: 126.

Picture 2 *Girls going for a visit to the author.*

months to experience a full annual cycle, including a second Christmas celebration. Mayor Lootie Toomasie readily agreed and pointed out that if I would like to learn about community life, I should participate in all its different forms and observe people's activities.

1.8 Fieldwork methodology

My field methodology focussed on gathering data on Inuit perceptions and practices of social and religious ways of life. My main methods were conducting open and semi-structured interviews and various forms of participant observation.

Most adult and elder people consented to being interviewed. Most younger people were less enthusiastic, feeling bashful in such a situation. Inuit traditionally learn by means of observation and practicing in various kinds of situations (see, for instance Briggs 1979, 1998; Oosten & Laugrand 1999). It is the young who learn from the old. In Qikiqtarjuaq, you will rarely see older people asking younger ones for knowledge. Asking questions is in itself a rather problematic method of gaining knowledge, skills, and insights. Just as one rarely sees older people asking younger ones, one rarely sees younger people asking older ones, especially elders, questions. To ask a question indicates that one demands an answer. It would be perceived as a lack of respect toward the elder to ask questions.

Still, most elders readily agreed to participate in an interview and demanded to be asked questions in the course of it. They said: "You have to ask me questions, otherwise I cannot answer you. When you ask me questions I start to remember." An interview was a situation of exchange. In exchange for money, as well as a part of an ongoing process of socializing me, elders provided me with the opportunity to learn what I wanted to know. As most elders are monolingual, I

Picture 3 *Cleaning sealskins during an Arctic College course on traditional sewing (courtesy of Don Pickle).*

conducted interviews in cooperation with a translator. The translator was either a close family member of the interviewee with a good command of the English language or otherwise, I employed a local professional translator, often John Ayaruaq, a middle-aged man originally from the Rankin Inlet area, or Lavinia Curley, a middle-aged woman originally from Hall Beach. I discussed the topic of the interview with them beforehand. In addition to translating the questions and answers they reformulated the questions to make them more meaningful to the interviewees, and asked their own questions. Afterwards, we discussed the interview.

Participation took different forms during my field research. I mostly combined observation with an imitative learning strategy or by asking practice-embedded questions. I applied this strategy, for instance, when people taught me Inuktitut words or when I followed a class on sewing seal skin boots at the local Arctic College institute. Through staying in Inuit households and camps, I participated in domestic life and land related activities. I occasionally cooked a meal, helped clean the house, spent some time with the children, accompanied people in their travels out on the land, and took the first steps to learn hunting and the processing of hunting products.

Later on during my fieldwork, I experimented with more autonomous ways of participation to acquire skills of planning, and decision making from a more involved perspective. I was, for instance, invited to take part in the municipal organizing committee for the community Christmas celebration. Moves on my part to participate as a provider or initiator of social activities were usually unsuccessful, though instructive. Whereas my contribution of a Christmas game to the community festivities in 2000 was generously welcomed (though I had the feeling that my acting as a provider of a game was somewhat out of place), an attempt to set up a student course on the history of the community was met with mixed feelings; some people felt that I acted 'on my own' being neither a teacher nor an Inuk[31] who would have sufficient insights into issues of the local history. In this way, I learned how leadership is granted and operates, and about the ways in which cooperation develops.

Whatever way of participation I used, I not only gathered data on Inuit practices, discourses and perceptions, but by participation I was also socially positioned according to the activities I conducted. For instance, I was accepted by most people without difficulty when an observer, however, some explained that conversations on matters of belief would be rather impossible with somebody who does not know 'the truth' in 'her heart'. Participation required one to take a social (and spiritual) position in relation to others. Progressing in fieldwork meant learning how to participate.

1.9 Design of the book

This study records the ethnographic richness of Inuit religious and social life as well as of the Christmas festival. I hope to show that the distinctions between these categories are highly problematic for Inuit. Therefore I am writing this study in the following way: first, I give a description, then I elaborate on the Inuit perspective on the described activities, and finally I add my own interpretation in the section called discussion.

A focus of my interest is the position of the Christmas celebration in this for Inuit relatively new kind of settlement. The chapters preceding this part of the dissertation have prepared the ground for an extended description and analysis of this ritual. Following this introduction into the *Theoretical background and methodology*, the second chapter *Life in Qikiqtarjuaq* will address the history of the community and I will elaborate on how Inuit deal with and perceive community on various levels of village life – special attention will be given to the work of institutions and to the ways of life in houses and out on the land. Chapter three, *Christianity in Qikiqtarjuaq*, deals with local Churches – Anglican and Full Gospel – as places for establishing social relations and creating social positions. And it will discuss the emphasis Inuit place on Christian beliefs and practices for addressing and solving social conflicts. Chapter four, *The seasonal cycle of Qikiqtarjuaq*, concentrates on the temporality of social life associated with the seasonal movements of Inuit to and away from the community and camps. The chapter addresses to what extent nomadic patterns have disappeared or are transformed. In chapter five, *Quviasuvik – Christmas, 'a Time of Happiness' in Qikiqtarjuaq*, I will look more closely at the major community celebration of the annual cycle. The concluding chapter six, *A community at play*, will draw together the most important discussion points raised throughout the study.

---

31   Singular form of 'Inuit'.

Chapter 2
Life in Qikiqtarjuaq

2.1 Introduction

Qikiqtarjuaq[32] is a fairly young community, established in the 1950s and '60s by the government of Canada. Various Inuit camps either moved on their own initiative, or were relocated under pressure of government agencies, to Qikiqtarjuaq. Presently, Qikiqtarjuaq has about 550 Inuit inhabitants. A small minority of about 15 English or French speaking Euro-Canadians, called Qallunaat[33], constitute the only group of strangers with a permanent presence in the community. Most of them work as teachers, government agents, nurses, and business managers with contracts of from one to four years. Some stay longer and have married Inuit. Outside of professional contexts, Inuit and Qallunaat have little interaction. Since this study is focussed on Inuit perceptions and practices of community life, I further deal with Qallunaat ways only in so far as their discussion is relevant for the description of Inuit perceptions and practices.

Qikiqtarjuaq is a semi-nomadic community following seasonal patterns of concentration in the settlement and dispersion to hunting camps. Inuit often contrast their life in the settlement with being 'out on the land'. Whereas living in hunting camps, associated with 'traditional' Inuit ways of life, is perceived to be beneficial for the individual as well as the community, living in the settlement is perceived in ambivalent terms. Perceived to be detrimental to people's well-being, Inuit, at the same time, emphasize the high value attributed to the community in particular in festivals, such as Christmas. The Inuktitut name for Christmas, used in Qikiqtarjuaq, is *quviasuvik* ('time of happiness') stressing the prosperity of a well functioning community on this occasion. However, the proper way of life in the community and the proper way of life out on the land are issues of an ongoing dynamic discourse in the social and the religious domains. Often, these issues are related to the ideal of past camp times and to the changes in social conditions that took place with the establishment of the modern settlements.

2.2 History of Qikiqtarjuaq

In 1606, James Baffin, traveled along the east coast of Baffin Island on the *Discovery* and was caught in heavy pack ice. Drifting along the coast to Cumberland Sound, he reported the existence of many Inuit camps. In 1840, William Perry sailed along the coast and spotted large numbers of whales. Whaling was soon booming. Whaling stations were set up, such as the Scottish station of Kivitoo,[34] and Inuit settled near these stations. Contacts with the British

---

32   Till 1998, Qikiqtarjuaq was officially called Broughton Island, but changed its name to its Inuktitut designation.

33   The Inuktitut expression *qallunaat* designates non-Inuit people, and more specifically people of Euro-Canadian descent. Most Qallunaat residing in Qikiqtarjuaq in 1999-2001 were Canadian. One was Australian and another was British.

34   It was abandoned in 1924.

Whaling Fleet changed Inuit seasonal, social, and working patterns and led to the extension of contact between the Inuit of Cumberland Sound and of Davis Strait. The history of Cumberland Sound and Davis Strait developed along different lines. The wintering of whalers in Cumberland Sound, after 1851, led to the centralization of the local population, while the camps of Davis Strait remained non-sedentary and engaged in trading with the Scots at Durban Harbor and Kivitoo.

As the whalers withdrew around the 1870s, having hunted the whales almost to extinction, the land-based fur trade expanded (Stevenson 1997: 81f.). Traders, such as the *Sabellum Company*, established small trading posts in the area, which operated with varying success. When they closed, the small Inuit camps attached to them dispersed. Inuit camps frequently and flexibly grouped and regrouped to make use of attractive economic and social opportunities (Stevenson 1997; Williams 1965: 3-1; Baffin Regional Health Board's community profiles 1994, 1998; Goldring, Payment & Preiss 1989: 10-4).

Christianity spread in the area after Franz Boas conducted his research on Baffin Island at the beginning of the 1880s. The Anglican Church sent Reverend Peck to open a mission on Blacklead Island in 1894. The population of Davis Strait was only occasionally visited by missionaries, and there it was the Inuit lay preachers who spread the new belief.

Between 1880 and 1920, the hunting region of Davis Strait stretched from Kivitoo to Durban Harbour and up to the Home Bay region. The region was inhabited by a locally migratory but regionally stable population, though seriously reduced in size by imported epidemics, such as ship's flu, syphilis, and diphtheria (Stevenson 1997: 123; Boas 1888: 426). After the *Sabellum Trading Company* on Kivitoo Island closed in 1924, people once or twice a year crossed the Cumberland Peninsula to trade in Pangnirtung.

With the introduction of U.S. and Canadian military bases, settlement patterns at Davis Strait changed. A U.S. Coast Guard weather station was constructed at an Inuit campsite on Padloping Island during World War II.[35] Around 1955, during the Cold War, an intermediate *Distant Early Warning* (DEW) station, called FOX-D, with a short airstrip was installed at the former whaling station of Kivitoo. Then, in 1956/1957, the DEW-Line site FOX 5, a runway, and maintenance facilities were built on the island of Qikiqtarjuaq, a camp location for several Inuit families.[36] These installations provided new opportunities for wage labor, which attracted families from Pangnirtung, Padloping Island, and Kivitoo.

During the same period, programs for the sedentarization of Inuit were implemented by the Canadian Government. An administrative office was opened (1958); the *Hudson's Bay Company* opened a store (1960); and a school was set up (1960). The Anglican church was opened in 1967,

---

35   It was used by the Canadian Department of Transportation after the war until 1956, when it was abandoned.

36   Larry S. Wilson, a retired Life Cycle Material Manager who worked at the Northern warning System Office, informed me that the DEW Line was built by both Canada and the U.S. He writes: "Overall control of the tremendously huge project was by the United States, but because the majority of the DEW Line sites were located in Canada there was a great deal of Canadian involvement. [...] The DEW Line was operated and maintained by the same civilian contractor (Federal Electric) for almost the entire existence of the line from when it opened until it transitioned to Canadian control becoming the North Warning System in 1987/88. [...] There was a small contingent of Canadian Military personnel [...]. Quality control of the entire DEW Line was provided by American Military personnel. The 'day to day' operation [...] was looked after by civilians under contract to the United States government. [...] There were large numbers of Canadians employed" (personal e-mail communication 24.09.2003). See also: http://www.lswilson.ca

Picture 4 *Remains of the Qikiqtarjuaq DEW line site.*

the same year that the planning and construction of the modern settlement of Qikiqtarjuaq was initiated by the governmental Rental Housing Program. The program offered courses for modern household techniques, which accompanied the project to enable the acculturation of Inuit.

The development of the new settlement required Inuit from different areas to live together and create a new community. The families already living on the island in a camp were joined by a family from Cumberland Sound.[37] Subsequently, other families from the Cumberland Sound area, the Home Bay area and the settlement of Clyde River arrived. The populations of Kivitoo and Padloping[38] were relocated to Qikiqtarjuaq in 1962 and 1968 respectively. Their former camps were closed down by government agencies. The death of three hunters in a storm was the official reason for the relocation of Kivitoo.[39] The community of Padloping, which was moved to Qikiqtarjuaq in 1968, was serviced by the government, but when the government withdrew, the settlement had to be given up. Its inhabitants refused to relocate on two occasions but finally gave in having felt intimidated by the police (see also Lawson 1984: 2). The process of relocation is remembered very well by the elders, who experienced the transfer as young people and they remain distressed by these recollections. People from Kivitoo and Padloping have initiated a legal

37   The families of Audlakiak and Kakudluk were the first inhabitants of Qikiqtarjuaq in the 1950s, followed by members of the Kunilusie family of Cumberland Sound.

38   Kivitoo lies 64 km to the North and Padloping 96 km to the South of Qikiqtarjuaq.

39   Kivitoo is famous for its religious upheaval in the winter of 1921-22, in which Neahkoteah was the most prominent figure. Several people were killed. Alivaktuk Kownirk, a former resident of Kivitoo, stated that there is still a unhappy and dangerous spirit around there, because "someone lost his mind and killed three people." (see Blaisel, Laugrand and Oosten 1999 for a discussion of the case). Because of this spirit "many people have lost loved ones" (Payment 1996: 155).

Picture 5 *Qikiqtarjuaq in spring.*

action for financial compensation with the assistance of Allen Angmarlik[40]. In 1999, Angmarlik also organized healing camps at Padloping and Kivitoo to support people in dealing with their relocation experiences.

The process of community construction took place all over the Eastern Arctic in Canada. Remie (1990) identified several difficulties common to these communities: First of all, the new settlements were much larger than the former winter camps. This led to an increase in hunting pressure on the local animal population and a decrease in hunting success (Wenzel 1994: 298f.). The Inuit had readily integrated the snowmobile into their hunting practices. To travel the longer distances, they needed money to purchase gas for their machines. As unemployment was widespread, dependence on social welfare – administered by Qallunaat – was an inevitable consequence of these developments. Secondly, leadership and social control, based on small groups, failed to work adequately in larger communities. Thirdly, with the introduction of schooling for Inuit children, the time and opportunity to learn about elders' and parents' knowledge and skill was considerably reduced. Younger and older Inuit perceived the emergence of a rift and an increasing distance between the generations and their ways of life. With the establishment of modern Inuit communities, Inuit have to deal on a daily basis with an all-regulating Qallunaat system (Remie 1990: 52).

---

40   He is known in Nunavut for his work for the CBC (Canadian Broadcasting Cooperation) as well as other organizations in Iqaluit and Baffin. He died at the end of June 2000 in a crash of an ultra-light aircraft. The process of acquiring compensation is resumed by others.

2.3 Approaching the community

Most Inuit and Qallunaat travel by airplane to and from Qikiqtarjuaq ('Big Island'), and a few will travel by snowmobile to Pangnirtung in spring and winter. Air service from the neighboring community Pangnirtung (225 km) and from the capital of Nunavut, Iqaluit (483 km), operates on a daily basis. When traveling in early summer from Iqaluit to Qikiqtarjuaq, the route covers vast expanses of ice-speckled open sea, steep mountains, and meadows with moss and lichens, low shrubs, fragile flowers, and berry bushes. In spring and winter, the landscape is saturated with shades of white and black when snow covers the land and mountains and the sea is frozen solid. Along the shores, hunters have left snow-scooter tracks resembling a net of 'highways' on the sea-ice, which disperses into single tracks in the distance.

As the plane dives and takes a sharp curve for landing, Qikiqtarjuaq comes into view on the east shore of an island which measures 16 km in length and 12 km in width and is located off the east coast of Baffin Island in Davis Strait, 67E33'N and 64E02'W. The settlement presents itself in orderly arranged lines of wooden houses along gravel roads. Little shacks are attached to the houses or are built along the shore. Community garbage sites and water reservoirs are located

Map 2 *Qikiqtarjuaq settlement (courtesy of Municipality of Qikiqtarjuaq).*

just outside the residential area. During my flights to and from Qikiqtarjuaq, this sight reminded me of the "satisfactory visual order" aimed at by the consulting engineers for community construction, F. J. Williams Associates Ltd., in their report to the *Department of Northern Affairs and National Resources* in 1965 (2-4).[41] Later during my fieldwork, I often climbed up hills to recapture this scenery.

After arrival at Qikiqtarjuaq's tiny airport building, passengers and goods are picked up by people waiting outside the airfield. They welcome family members, mothers with newborn babies coming back from Iqaluit hospital, guests from other communities, a group of lay and ordained ministers for a Bible conference, a few tourists, Japanese business partners, visiting managers, doctors, dentists, or the new nurse and teacher. One enters the community proper on the main gravel road that leads from the airport to the settlement. The road passes the grey Government buildings and the residences of employees. It leads along the dark red, green, brown, or pastel painted municipal buildings, businesses, school, and one or two story detached or semi-detached wooden houses of the residential areas,[42] up to the little hill that has an *Inukshuk* stone figure on its top. From there the road goes past the most recently built houses and the satellite TV and telephone installation and finally reaches the garbage dump, the water reservoirs, and a filling station used mostly during winter.[43]

Neither the main gravel road nor the sideroads were named and houses were simply numbered according to the sequence of their construction. As the community grew, the hamlet suggested systemizing house numbers with reference to the layout. In the year 2000, it was agreed to name the streets and to re-number houses. The naming commission, including elders, decided not to use names of famous people. Their work resulted in names designating physical or functional features of the road, such as *Alaniq* ('Shade Side') Drive, *Sanaviit* ('Garages') Road, *Ungammut* ('On the outward journey') Road, *Qiggut* ('Boulder Bed') Drive, or *Nattiq* ('Jar Seal') Drive. A number of people are still unhappy with the naming, as they perceive applying street designations to be a Qallunaat custom. Each of the about 150 house is now formally identifiable by the combination of a street name and a number. Most of the houses are owned by the Housing Association; a few are owned by the Co-op, and others by the Government. Inuit increasingly become private home owners.[44] This trend is encouraged by the government, and financial programs are offered to facilitate private ownership.

Due to permafrost, all houses are built on stilts about 50 cm above ground. The interspace is used to store bulky materials, such as pieces of chipboard, which is used for repairs, for building a cabin out on the land or a sled and a transport box. When it is warm enough, men do their

---

41   The community was planned according to western models of sedentary life. However, the layout of the settlement aimed to combine formal aesthetic and practical considerations in respect to the Arctic conditions and Inuit economic life. A dog compound and a central skinning and cleaning center are examples of this. The report of the consulting engineers explicates: "The plan provides a central skinning and cleaning center, to discourage the indiscriminate scattering of offal throughout the settlement" (Williams 1965: 2-4). This example shows how sedentary modern Inuit settlements were meant to fulfill their acculturative function.

42   All of these houses were imported with the annual sea-lift as prefabricated sets.

43   A second filling station is located near the little harbor.

44   According to the Community Census 2001 of Statistics Canada (www.statcan.ca) 110 houses are rented and 30 are privately owned. The 1996 community profile does not give figures for house ownership (See: Broughton Island, NWT). The increase of ownership was referred to in conversations and can be deducted from the new construction of houses for private ownership.

Picture 6 *The house of a successful hunter in late spring. Sealskins are stretched in frames and are exposed to the sun for bleaching.*

woodwork, machinery repairs, and stone carving outdoors. Otherwise, they work in the little shack attached to most houses. Large items, such as boats, snowmobiles or old furniture is stored around the shack. Women usually work inside, but in spring place their stretching frames – with cleaned and dried sealskins and occasionally a polar bear skin – outside leaning against their houses.

Although there are only a few dog teams in operation, most households keep a dog. While most of these dogs are chained at the side or the back of most houses, puppies and sometimes small dogs are kept indoors as pets; but people quickly grow tired of them and place them outside. Bands of escaped dogs roam around the community to look for food. Since these packs are a potential danger to people, and as they often rip sealskins from the frames to eat them, by-law officers shoot them. Dog-teams for sleds are stationed in the vicinity of the community. When the fire brigade siren sounds each day at noon, all dogs join in an enthusiastic howling performance.

2.4 The house and its inhabitants

Noon is also the time that schoolchildren, employees, and others go home to have lunch. To enter a house, one has to climb a short staircase. On the landing of many houses, one can find a large freezer used to keep sealskin boots and other fur garments from losing their hair due to the warmth in summer, and to keep meat from becoming frost-burned in winter.[45] The front

---

45   Keeping meat at the entrance to one's home was already practiced in the times of camp settlements.

door leads to a porch or corridor. Boots, sport shoes, and slippers are neatly lined up underneath a coat-rack. Accessory outer garments are kept in a box or shelf. Jackets and shoes are taken off when entering a house. In many of the more recently built houses a door leads from the corridor to a small furnace room.[46] Its good ventilation and warmth makes it a much appreciated smoking retreat, where one often finds a cozy arrangement of a small table with a scented candle and an ashtray, with a chair waiting for a comfortable cigarette break. If no such room is available, people take a cigarette break on their landing. Though most Inuit are dedicated tobacco users, smoking in the living quarters is commonly perceived to be a nuisance. Neatness and cleanliness are highly valued in all parts of Inuit houses. Not only dust and dirt removed regularly, many women also use room fragrances to freshen up their furniture, carpets and the air.

In most houses, the hallway opens to a combination of living and dining room with an attached kitchen. The bedrooms are approachable either through the living room or the hallway. A bathroom completes the interior of a house. The living room is furnished with a sofa and comfortable chairs, a TV, a VCR, a high-fi tower, a shelf with porcelain figurines and other collectibles. Dark or pastel curtains, often decorated with flower motifs, are arranged at the windows. Some Inuit living rooms are soberly decorated with a showcase, a calendar, and a few photographs. Most also display pictures with Christian motifs and proverbs. Other interiors are more elaborately furnished with, for instance, prints of Christian and other motifs, artificial flowers, decorative lamps and plants. The living/dining/kitchen area is the most frequented space for socializing and women's work. Visitors are welcomed in the living/dining room, where women also do much of their work and children play their games, while others watch TV or listen to music. In the evening, refreshments, candies, and chips are consumed there and overnight visitors fetch a blanket and sleep in the living room.

The dining area features a table and chairs. It is mostly used for paperwork and to have lunch. Food bought from the supermarket is usually served for lunch. It is the only meal of the day the household takes together. While eating, everybody listens to the local radio station that broadcasts local news, announcements of events, and provides the facility to transmit birthday greetings from in and outside the settlement.[47] People can also phone in or get on the air with special requests, invitations to share a seal, and the like. In between, the station also broadcasts the BBC news programs.

The kitchen, resembling that of average Canadian households is equipped with the usual modern appliances. The refrigerator-freezer unit is often the only place in the kitchen for rich decoration. They feature magnets that display proverbs,[48] stickers, and children's art work. The marked difference to an average Canadian kitchen are, firstly, the *ulu*, a fan-shaped women's knife, in the drawer, secondly, that there is always coffee or tea ready for visitors who are expected

---

46 In older houses, the noisy furnace is in the living room.

47 See Briggs (2000) on the use of the radio for making social difficulties public in conveying seemingly neutral messages.

48 A few examples for worldly wisdom are sayings, such as: "Of all life has to offer, of all that's great and true, that which means the most to me is being friends with you" or "Life is simple but men insist on making it complicated". Examples of religious sayings are: "What we are is God's gift to us – what we become is our gift to God"; "God's promise: God didn't promise days without pain, laughter without sorrow, or sun without rain. But God did promise strength for the day, comfort for the tears, and a light for the way. And all who believe in His kingdom above, He answers their faith with everlasting love."

to help themselves, and, thirdly, that cardboard is placed on the floor serving as a table for the consumption of such country food as seal, caribou, or fish.

The parents' bedroom, usually the largest, is fitted out with a built-in closet, a bed, and often a small dressing table. The room is usually not further decorated, except for a nice bedspread and plates with Christian proverbs. Children's bedrooms are kept sober, whereas teenagers have started to decorate their rooms with posters of pop or film stars. Many of them also have their own hi-fi set and television equipment. Children and teenagers also use their bedrooms to have visitors, and overnight visitors stay there as well.

I want to complete the tour through the house with the bathroom, that is elaborately decorated in most houses. Ornamental shower curtains and mats are chosen and pictures with Christian and other sayings decorate the walls. Often, a Bible, magazines and catalogues are kept in an open shelf or under the sink for everyone to read. So far, most elements of Inuit houses may appear familiar to a Western reader – probably with the exception of how country food is served and consumed. The way in which people lived in these houses, however, reminded me more of their camping practices than of Western ways of living in a house.

2.4.1 Life in a house

Houses are often crowded, occupied by people who live there permanently, people who stay there temporarily, and others who are just visiting. While there is little privacy in Inuit homes, it is usually quiet and people take care not to disturb each other in their occupations. The following situation, which I observed in a house of an elderly couple toward the end of my fieldwork, shall serve as an illustration.

I went to the house of the elders to pay for a pair of gloves their daughter had made for me. When I went in, after taking off my shoes and jacket on the porch, I saw the elders sitting on the couch in the living room watching television, with the volume turned very low. A middle-aged man, apparently a nephew of the old man, was quietly sitting on a chair. Their eldest daughter, the one I wanted to talk to, lived in their house together with her husband and a young daughter, sharing a bedroom. As both she and her husband were working, her parents as well as one of her sisters and sometimes also her parents-in-law took care of the youngster. As I came in, she sat on the floor cutting out parts for a *kamik* ('sealskin boot'). Her husband was out hunting with his father and the child was taken for a walk by a young girl who liked to babysit and was especially fond of this youngster. We greeted each other and I addressed her parents who nodded at me. She told me to fetch some tea. Hot tea, bread, and jam stood ready in the kitchen, as well as a large assortment of variously decorated and souvenir mugs. I refilled her and her parents cups, took one for myself and settled down beside her. We talked in a low voice about the latest news and the gloves. I watched her sewing for a while, without further conversation.

When a boy came out of one of the tiny bedrooms to go to the bathroom, I saw, through the open door five or six teenagers settled on the bed. They visited the old couple's adopted son and were watching a video. The phone, which was within reach of the elder woman, rang frequently, and most of the time, it was she who picked it up. She briefly listened to the caller and then summoned the required person. The callers exchanged a few words in a hushed voice and soon hung up. About half an hour later, another visitor came. Inuit visitors never knock or ring the door bell. A young man opened the door to ask if his cousin, the adopted son, was present. The daughter of the house said: "*iii*", ('yes'). He left his shoes and jacket on the porch and disappeared in his cousin's room. The elders continued to follow their program on television and the daughter continued to work on the *kamik*. After a while, I cleaned my cup, paid for my gloves, and said goodbye. The couple and their daughter said: "*takuniaravugut*" (we will see each other soon').

2.4.2 Social relationships in a house
It is usual for two or three generations to live together in a house. The actual composition of the household dynamically changes as people move in and out. The social position of people living together in a house depends on their gender, age and kinship relation.

Being a baby or infant
Babies and infants are coddled a lot by everyone and their needs immediately attended to. Visitors also pay much attention to them, holding and entertaining them. Most babies and infants are brought up at home and at their grandparents' or their parents' siblings' homes. A few stay for a few hours per day at the newly established day care and later attend kindergarten classes.

Name relations
Relatives usually address each other with kin terms. Kin terms, however, apply not only to consanguine, affinal and adoption relations, but also to name relations. The name relation provides the child with social as well as with cosmological relations, as discussed in the introduction (see also Mauss & Beuchat 1979 [1904]: 28). Usually, the baby's grandparents have a say in the choice of names, but there are also other options for naming. For example, someone who knows that death is near will sometimes ask that the baby of a (usually related) pregnant woman be named after him/her. At other times, people may observe that a baby cries a lot. They call it with various names until the baby stops crying considered that the appropriate name

Picture 7 *A baby of a few months old (courtesy of Taiviti Nuqingak).*

Picture 8 *Little girl playing with her two puppies. One of them sits in the back of her jacket like a baby in the mother's amauti.*

has been found. Names of deceased highly respected elders from other communities may also be chosen. A baby usually receives several names. After naming, people search for resemblances between the child and its main deceased namesake. Do they look alike? Does the baby also tend to snore?

Baptism

Naming practices perpetuate the community by transferring names from one generation to the next. However, new names are also integrated. For instance, parents may chose James for their son's baptism and various other names of deceased men and women at other occasions. If James is the name that is usually used to address the boy, it would be given to babies born after his death. It is said to be comforting that the name of the deceased is carried on and one can still relate to it. These names provide the child with networks of name relations expressed in kin terms and are of relevance in daily life. The relatives of the deceased act toward the child as if it is the deceased person. For example, a woman whose daughter is named after the woman's own mother treats the child as respectfully as she would treat her own mother, but also appropriately as a child of a certain age.

Being a child

While small children get much attention, older children are expected to become more self-reliant. They are taught to control their emotions and not to complain about difficulties. Inuit rarely scold or beat their offspring, but parents expect that they will continuously improve their capabilities and self-control. As an illustrative example of education, a ten year old girl insisted on playing with her older brothers who refused to take her along. She burst into tears and ran to her mother for support. Her mother reproved her for making such a fuss. The girl sat crying on the floor for a while; people passing by ignored her. As she calmed down, her mother sat down with her on the sofa and combed her hair to make braids.[49]

Around the age of five, children are also expected to take over chores and run errands. Girls start with easy household tasks and boys are taken out hunting. The boys' first kills are a special event and are celebrated within the family or camp. At five or six years of age, children also start to attend school. They spend increasingly more time with their peers, visiting and playing outside with each other. Most girls will go for a walk, visit newborn babies or play inside the house. Boys usually can be seen, for instance, playing hockey on the street, riding bikes, balancing on ice-floes during the period of break-up of the sea-ice, hunting lemmings, and watching a snowmobile being repaired or a sled being built. They are supervised up to about the age of ten by their parents, by older siblings or older girls who want to babysit. At this age, boys and girls easily come into contact with Qallunaat. It is not unusual to see a teacher, or another of the children's Qallunaat favorites, surrounded by a flock of youngsters, who are telling stories, asking for candy or for the permission to visit.

Adoption

Adoption is very common among Inuit and frequently a couple has one or two adoptees. Most children are adopted immediately after birth by close relatives, friends, and occasionally by non-related people. Inuit adoption practices are not necessarily related to difficulties the biological parents may be experiencing. More often, a child is given into adoption because a related couple

Picture 9 *Three boys experimenting with a sea-ice floe using it as a float.*

---

49   Women often engage in combing each others' hair or in removing white hair (which is considered to itch) when socializing at home or in camps.

is childless, or a family with older children, or grandparents, desire to take care of a baby. The biological as well as the adoptive families use kin terms to address the adoptee and vice versa. The child is part of the social network of both families, but the family of his adoptive parents is usually more important.[50]

Siblings and closely related peers

The distinction between biological, adopted or step siblings is of little relevance in household life. On the average, about three to five children, siblings and sometimes cousins, live together in a household. Children are expected to assist their parents and to cooperate with each other. Thus, for instance, younger children are taken care of by their older siblings, especially by their sisters. In turn, later on it is expected that the younger ones will help out the older siblings. Relations between siblings are also shaped by age and gender. Boys tend to be assertive towards girls, and older siblings towards younger ones. The most explicit relation of dominance is that between the *angajuk* ('older brother') and *nukaq* ('younger brother').

Being a teenager

Children at about the age of thirteen reach puberty and are expected to take on responsibilities at home and when out camping. At the same time, teenagers spend much of their time with their peers. Commencing with puberty, many girls have their first boyfriend. Usually, boys are two or three years older when they have their first relationship. In the settlement, teenagers increasingly become more independent from the directives of their parents making their own decisions, however when being out camping they are expected to instantly follow the orders of older people and in addition they have many tasks. The transition from adolescence to adulthood is also marked by the participation of teenagers in community games[51] and teenage dance events. However, most of the thirteen year old boys and girls feel too socially insecure to participate and only start to frequent these occasions a few years later.

Many teenagers drop out of school at the tenth grade, making a step into an adult life and giving priority to establishing themselves in the community. They maintain relationships with peers outside of school; they 'hang around' till late at night; they earn some money with jobs at e.g. a supermarket; they support family members in hunting and in other activities; they spend time with a boy/girlfriend; and more and more they make their own decisions.

Being an adult

Many young women have their first child around the age of nineteen. A young woman receives her own *amauti*, a jacket in whose large hood babies and young children are carried, with her first child. Being a mother is perceived to be an important part of being an adult woman. There is no such marked event for young men, who with their first kills and by increasing their competence in hunting and social skills, more gradually gain the status of adults. Usually, the young family stays at one of their parents' places for a while before finding a suitable house and setting up their own household. They will also start to establish their own campsite, either by adding a new tent to those of their parents or by building a cabin close by.

---

50 The biological mother has the right to see the child, and in case of hardship, she is supported by the adoptive parents.

51 Depending on the number of people who are attending celebrations, admission to games may be at thirteen but frequently the ages of sixteen or eighteen are applied.

Picture 10 *Nora Killiktee celebrates her graduation from highschool.*

Grown-up children maintain close contact with their parents and take care of them in old age. They pay high respect to their elders and follow, to a variable degree, their advice. Parents also support their adult children with money, food, and household assistance, such as babysitting. People who have lost their parents early or who have felt neglected by them told me they feel like 'nothing'; living without parents, who take care of one's well-being, is considered to be very hard.

Husband and wife
Husband and wife are the core of most households. Married in church or by common law, they are expected to stay together for life. A widow or widower is free to choose a new partner. Having a partner and children is considered to be indispensable for a successful life and those singles often talked about painful feelings of loneliness and incompleteness. A couple divides the work and responsibilities of the household. Men usually hunt and take care of the household equipment. Women run the household and take care of the children. The division of labor is not strict. Men occasionally participate in household chores and there are a number of women who are known for their hunting skills. In addition to these occupations, men as well as women may opt for paid employment. Men are perceived to be the household heads, but women have their say. In case of severe domestic problems, elders, or one's parents, and occasionally also Social Services are sought for help to deal with these difficulties. The couple is counseled; a divorce is usually not approved by elders, who rather advise them to stay together and tackle the problems with patience. They think a partnership grows from overcoming difficulties rather than from feelings of affection. Young people often have different views on this issue, advocating relationships based on love.

Being an elder

Elders are much respected by all younger people. Their advice is sought and their demands and wishes are taken care of. Elders, in turn, participate as much as possible in the daily tasks of a household and help out with babysitting. Older women do much of the sewing for the household. Older men support the household with hunting or lending their equipment to younger members. Their old age pensions contribute considerably to the monetary income of the household. A number of elders attend the *Elders' Committee*, where they discuss community life and entertain themselves with games. They are also members of various committees and institutions, such as the school, the *Justice Committee*, and the street naming committee. Their knowledge and skill is considered to be valuable to the younger generations as well as beneficial to the community.

Elders and youth

Discourse on the relationship between elders and youth reflects the change that has taken place in the Inuit way of life. Many elders and young people perceive a gap between the generations and notice that they have difficulties in understanding each other's point of view. Ever fewer girls and boys acquire the skills and the knowledge their grandparents obtained by living in camp settlements. From the point of view of elders, lacking this kind of knowledge is to lack the necessary qualifications to live like a 'true' Inuk – out on the land by hunting and fishing. Young people like to experiment with both Inuit and Qallunaat ways. Having been taught basic hunting and sewing skills, they have also received a modern education, are skilled and knowledgeable in dealing with technical equipment, and prefer some modern ways to the old ways. Instead of, for example, spending several weeks out camping with their family, teenagers prefer to stay for a shorter period and then return to their peers in the community. While elders are increasingly concerned about a perceived disrespect of younger people towards the older – for example by staying in their peer groups, by talking back, and by getting drunk – young people frequently mentioned that it is difficult to satisfy many elders.

According to my observations, Inuit young people were very attentive to the wishes of the elders. They were appropriately shy when addressing elders. Elders still have a considerable influence on younger people, but it is difficult for both groups to share their experiences and perceptions. Hunting and camping are still most relevant issues for young people, even though young men know considerably less about being out on the land and young women less about sewing and the use of game-products. Women still gain status being good seamstresses. And the first kill is always an important step for a boy, as acknowledged by his family and the camp. This practice continues to be of high relevance. If asked, almost every young man readily talks about his own first kill of any species.

An Inuit household is composed of people who are related to each other as described above. The household is not organized in a fixed pattern of membership, however, but marked by dynamic movements of people. Though placed in the sedentary context of a wooden house, it is therefore problematic to speak of Inuit households as corporate units.

2.5 Being out on the land

Most Inuit live in Qikiqtarjuaq during the coldest months of winter and during the surrounding periods when there is a freeze-up and break-up of the sea-ice. The rest of the year, Inuit disperse

Picture 11 *Spring camp north of Qikiqtarjuaq*

to their camps that are spread over about 120 km of coastline to the north and south of Qikiqtarjuaq. Many Inuit adults and elders choose locations for their camps considered to be their place of origin or their former camps.[52] These choices indicate that the artificial nature of Qikiqtarjuaq is still recognized. The relationship to places of family origin is often transferred to grown-up children, and many, as adults with their own families, continue to choose their parent's camp locations if the hunting, fishing, or berry-picking conditions should still be favorable.

Camps are set up by several generations of a family, their siblings and their families, and are usually located at some distance to other camps in the area. Some families have wooden cabins at their favorite places, while others use canvas tents. These constructions are for sleeping, cooking, receiving visitors, and for shelter during bad weather. If the weather permits, people cook, work and socialize in front of their tents or cabins. Men and women complement each other in their tasks, as they had in the community. It is usually the men's task to prepare the sled for traveling, to hunt and fish with nets; women keep the camp, supervise the children, work on the skins and other animal products, and go fishing or pick berries.

Children and especially teenagers are expected to contribute their share of work, for instance cleaning the bedstead, emptying the urine cans used by elders during the night, fetching water, and helping to clean the skins. Hard and sophisticated work is valued in teenagers and elders know many stories which emphasize the benefits of enterprise and the drawbacks of laziness. Though teenagers usually acknowledge the value of work and of being out on the land, several

---

52   Families originally from the Cumberland Sound area often camp at Davies Strait. Still, they continue to occasionally visit their former camps in the Cumberland Sound region. The family of Silasie Angnako, for instance, not only occasionally visits family in Pangnirtung but also organized a family meeting at the family's former camp in Cumberland Sound.

Picture 12 *Little boy helping with chores – emptying the dishwater – during spring camping.*

Picture 13 *Having a meal of boiled seal in a spring camp on Pilaktuak Island.*

of them chose to stay in Qikiqtarjuaq and to withdraw from the strict authority of their parents and elders in camp. Still, as soon as they become a bit more independent by owning their own equipment and having their own family, most young people resume practices of long-term camping.

Each tent/cabin household in a camp cooks for its members, especially when the meal is prepared from store-bought food. Frequently, however, everyone from the camp comes together to share a meal when there is fresh seal, fish or caribou. When the men return from hunting, one of the wives, usually the oldest, prepares the game. The hunter or one of the women shout "*mikigaaq!*" ('there is raw meat!') which is the invitation to share it with them. Sometimes, people are also invited to share a meal of boiled meat. Close kin serve themselves first; guests modestly wait a bit before participating. People do not visit other camps frequently, but visitors are always welcome and travelers usually stop to have a cup of tea and exchange information.

Distinct from the seasonal context of camping are the so-called 'healing camps'. Such camps are organized to deal with a variety of traumatic experiences: relocation or otherwise difficult memories of the past; to deal with experiences of violence, as well as with other troubles specifically perceived to be caused by community life, such as drug addictions and criminality among teenagers. Those teenagers I went to camp with and those I talked to were usually enthusiastic about this camping experiences – the company of peers probably made camping more enjoyable than being under the authority of one's elders. Camps organized for women and elders were also spoken about as positive experiences. Problems which arose in the context of community life are dealt with in the healing-camps by being out on the land, practicing hunting and camping, as well as by talking openly and by prayer.

Picture 14 *Learning how to build an igloo during a youth healing camp in winter.*

2.6 Income and employment

When out on the land, many Inuit wear garments made from seal, caribou or polar bear fur in combination with insulated rubber boots, water-proof trousers, or thick parkas. In the settlement, a few people use seal-skin boots, but most prefer to wear sport shoes – Nike being the favorite brand of young people. Garments are either bought at the local stores or ordered from catalogues. The supermarkets also sell snowmobiles and equipment, household and sewing supplies, hunting and camping gear as well as the assortment of food comparable to the smaller supermarkets in southern Canada. Prizes up North are high, because everything has to be transported from the South.

What cannot be purchased in a store is game hunted locally.[53] The production of meat through hunting requires costly equipment, such as a boat and a snow scooter, rifles of various calibers, ammunition, gas, and camping gear. Hunting provides the family and the community with food, but it requires a considerable financial investment.[54] A cash income has become indispensable for participating in present day community life.

Employment opportunities are provided by local and regional institutions or businesses, such as supermarkets, hotels, the telephone company (*Northwesttel*), the airport, the power cooperation, the post office, the reopened sewing and tanning center, and seasonally, building contractors. Young men also take the opportunity to work for several month for a commercial shrimp fleet. Inuit are employed at all levels, from management to tasks of unqualified labor. Most people prefer not work for extended periods in another community or down South. In the Inuit community, recognition does not primarily depend on the formal rank or the nature of one's responsibilities, but rather on the quality of one's accomplishments and one's way of interacting with others.

Employment contracts are often inflexible with respect to work-schedules. Men especially experience employment as a restriction to their hunting practices, which are planned according to the weather conditions and the migrations of animals. The acquisition of money through employment is a high priority for teenagers as well. Even though they still live with their families, teenagers want money to purchase fashionable garments, music, refreshments and snacks, as well as hunting equipment. It was my impression that their parents expected the teenagers to participate financially. Teenagers work as cashiers or stock boys. Those who finished high school are also employed by the day care center, offices or the municipality.

Those who are interested are offered further professional training, but as this usually means having to leave Qikiqtarjuaq for a while, only a few make use of this opportunity. Opportunities for further professional training are also offered to adults in the form of upgrading or training courses in and outside of Qikiqtarjuaq. Courses are usually well attended.

About 25% of Qikiqtarjuaq's inhabitants 15 years of age and over were unemployed during the period of my fieldwork and lived on welfare money and rent subsidies (Statistics Canada Community Profiles 2001). These payments barely cover the living expenses of a family. Skilled men and women increase their income by producing arts and crafts, such as stone and

---

53　The Northern Store frequently offers minced caribou meat from other Inuit communities, but this is not a favorite item among Inuit.

54　Hunting as a source of monetary income lost its relevance to a substantial degree as a consequence of the European seal skin ban in 1983. However, about 35% of the daily caloric intake is from country food in Qikiqtarjuaq (Kuhnlein, Receveur, Chan & Loring 2000, 372f.).

bone carvings, prints, drawings, and garments. These are mainly sold to resident and visiting Qallunaat.

To deal with unemployment, the government supports the establishment of private businesses. In 2000, a hotel, a hostel, outfitting enterprises, taxi and transportation businesses, a garage, three convenience stores, and a pool-hall including a snack bar were offered by local enterprises. Most private businesses are owned by members of two related extended families of Cumberland Sound origin. Members of this extended family also occupy leading functions in church life, and formerly, leadership positions within the municipality. More and more members of other families are starting their own enterprises, mainly in art, translation and outfitting.

Picture 15 *Charly Alikatuqtuq with his new economic enterprise: clam diving (courtesy of a clam diving colleague).*

2.7 Local institutions

Local institutions[55] are involved in many domains of modern community life. They administrate the community, they participate in social, legal, health, educational, religious, and economic proceedings, and they connect Inuit to the systems and politics of the Canadian state. Inuit perceive these institutions as basically a Qallunaat undertaking, though indispensable for modern community life.[56] Inuit work for and profit from these institutions. I want to illustrate how Inuit work within institutional contexts by two examples, the municipality and the school.

2.7.1 The municipality

The municipality is housed in a large green building in the centre of the settlement. Two separate entrances lead to the lower and the upper levels of the building. The old gym and community hall[57], the post office,[58] and the offices of the recreation director and of Economic Development are on the lower level. A stairway leads to the upper floor, with a spacious hall, administration offices, the mayor's office, and the council chamber. The comfortably furnished hall, with a seating arrangement, a shelf with books and magazines, and a coffee maker, is used by employees and visitors to drink coffee and chat. The wall is decorated with an aerial photograph of Qikiqtarjuaq taken several years ago that envisions the continuous expansion of the settlement and the increasing efforts required for its administration and maintenance.

The municipality is administered by six elected community councillors and the mayor. Inuit and Qallunaat are eligible to run as candidates for council membership. There are no political parties. In 2000, one out of six councillors was a Qallunaat. The council, chaired by the mayor, meets twice a month to discuss and to decide on municipal affairs. The council is supported by five specialized committees, such as the *Works, Public Safety & Health Committee*.[59] These committees consist of councillors, selected community members, and representatives of relevant institutions or work places. The *Works, Public Safety & Health Committee*, for instance, is composed of two councillors, two community members, the mayor, the foreman, a secretary,

---

55 List of local institutions and facilities:
Uunicipality, hamlet maintenance sites, *Hunters & Trappers Organisation* with community freezer, *Social Services*, office of the wellness councillor, *Department of Sustainable Development, Economic Development Office, Housing Association, House Owner Association*, fire brigade, health center, R.C.M.P. station with cell bloc, *Alcohol and Drug Education Center*, community radio station, *Ayuittuq National Park* Office (Parks Canada), post office, *Alcohol and Drugs Committee, Youth Committee, Elders Committee, Canadian Rangers, Search and Rescue*, day care center, *Inuksuit School, Arctic College, Department for Education* (before July 1st, 2000 *Baffin Divisional Education Council*), *Education Council*, swimming pool, *Qikittamiiut* hockey arena, hamlet gymnasium, *St. Michael & All Angels Anglican Church, Katiqsivik ('Harvest Time') Full Gospel Church, Women's Auxiliary Group, Northern Lights* youth group.

56 Nicole Gombay (2005 forthcoming) examined Inuit (Nunvik) strategies of dealing with institutions by situationally using various sets of rules and skillfully managing various formal/institutional and 'daily' identities.

57 This hall is only occasionally used as the wooden walls dried out to such an extent that the hall is a potential fire hazard.

58 The post office was moved to the Northern Store in the year 2000.

59 Other committees are: *Finance, Legislative and Administration Committee* (FLAC), *Community Land Development Committee* (CDLC), *Community Service Committee* (CSC), *Development Appeal Board* (DAB).

the community health representative, and a local member of the *Baffin Region Health and Social Services Board*. Other, non-municipal community committees, such as the *Alcohol & Drug Committee* or the *Housing Association*, work independently. The community council sends delegates to their meetings to provide direct lines of communication.

The decisions of the community council are implemented by the municipal office, which also takes care of all other municipal administrative and executive tasks. The office has a secretary, two Inuit women as financial administrators, an Inuit man as land administrator, and three Qallunaat managers: a *Senior Administrative Officer* (SAO), a financial manager, and a recreation director. The office staff is complemented by executive workers, whose task is the maintenance and construction of community facilities and infrastructure.

To show the style Inuit use in dealing with community issues in the context of a council meeting, I will relate part of a council's discussion (meeting of April, 3rd, 2000), which dealt with a snowmobile accident due speeding and also the stricter handling of speed limit by-laws.[60] The councillors took their seats in heavy leather chairs at tables arranged in a circle. Delegates of the community and myself took seats in a second row at one side of the room. The SAO and I were provided with headsets for simultaneous translation. The agenda for the meeting was set up by the SAO in agreement with the mayor. The meeting was formally opened with a prayer in Inuktitut; the minutes of the last meeting were checked, and the agenda extended on further issues of immediate relevance. One of these issues was speeding violations and the snowmobile accident. It was briefly introduced by the SAO, then councillors took the word. They were given turns by the chairman:[61]

Lootie Toomasie:	"Who wants to say something? Jukie."
Jukie Nookiguak:	"Thank you chairman. We have to make children aware of [the dangers of snowmobiles traveling at high speed]. It is scary to see them playing on the road, because of the traffic."
Lootie Toomasie:	"Levy."
Levy Nutaralak:	"Thank you chairman. At the main road there are a lot of people. Even small kids play around there all night, when the snowmobiles are going back and forth. Snowmobiles tend to get very bothersome when they are going all night. I know [my criticism] sounds bad for people, BEFORE there actually is a bad accident. Everybody should go on the [community] radio."
Jacopie Nuqingak:	"Just during our meeting somebody got hurt. Jimmy. Snowmobiles should not carry long ropes [coiled] around their backrest."
Levy Nutaralak:	Expresses further concerns about snowmobiles.
Lootie Toomasie:	"Thank you. Jacopie."
Jacopie Nuqingak:	"We all have the possibility to talk to people for the safety of the community."
Lootie Padloo:	"I am going to remove the long rope. Children unwrapped the long rope, which I use for going through water. I will be responsible from now on."
Ragalee Angnako:	"The dance at the gym is usually open till late hours. I can hear it from my house that there is very loud music. We should think about our children.

---

60 Compliance with snowmobile speed limits is dealt with in the community by by-law officers who patrol the streets. Breaking the speed limit is fined.

61 Simultaneous translation from Inuktitut to English by Ena Qappik, secretary and translator at the municipality.

The Recreation Committee is responsible for this. I want to bring it up as an ordinary person, because I didn't know I will be a councillor.[62] Even small kids are around. Recreation people are responsible."

Jacopie Nuqingak: "We have the responsibility as councillors to ensure that laws have to be kept. We have to remind people of the by-laws. That is the responsibility towards the people who elected us."

As this discussion drew to an end, the SAO informed the council of how the speed by-law is implemented and on the financial and administrative scope for possible modifications. A decision was taken that each council member would work to increase public safety, and that the SAO would support the by-law officers in reducing speeding violations.

This fragment of a council debate shows that decisions are reached by consensus. Each councillor is given the opportunity and the time to make his/her contribution. The problem under discussion is presented from different points of view. Then one of the councillors suggests a solution by formulating a workable compromise. The suggestion is discussed and re-shaped until a solution is found that is supported by most of the councillors. The content of the discussion emphasized putting the problem into a social context. For instance, in the case of the speeding violation, councillors opted to alter the public awareness of the effects and the dangers of speeding. By providing the public with good arguments and examples, they carefully tried to influence the social climate without openly condemning the wrongdoer.

2.7.2 The school

The Inuksuit School is centrally located on the main street. It is a modern, spacious, and well-equipped building which includes a gym, two classroom tracts, an administrative and teachers' area, a library, a computer room, and craft rooms. The walls of the hallways and the rooms are colorfully decorated with children's artwork, educational materials and trophies won by students at sport events displayed in a large showcase in the entry-hall.

The school's name is represented in an Inukshuk sculpture standing in front of the building, built of piled stones of different shapes from the nearby mountains. This kind of stone figure is used for, among other purposes, signposts and information boards. In the context of the school, the figure emphasizes the combination of Inuit skills, values and knowledge with modern education as crucial for the future of Inuit children. This ideal is implemented in the school's teaching curriculum as well as in the teaching methods.

From kindergarten to highschool grades, Inuit students are trained in *inuit qaujimanituqangit* ('Inuit knowledge') in an Inuit teaching setting mostly based on observation, imitation, and the telling of stories. For instance, elders are invited to share their life experiences and stories with the children to teach them about the old times as well as about Inuit values. They also demonstrate 'traditional' crafts, such as the construction of a kayak from sealskins or sewing gloves. These courses take place in school, but also during day trips to different locations out on the land. The school owns, for example, a *qamaq* ('grass sod house') in the vicinity of the community. Students are expected to take the initiative to closely observe what teachers do and to afterwards practice it him/herself. Education in Western scientific knowledge usually is based on Western teaching methods that make extensive use of the spoken and written word, as well as question and answer communications.

---

62   She had been sworn in as councilwoman the same day to replace a council member who had moved away.

Children are educated through grade four in Inuktitut by Inuit teachers. From grade five on, they are educated in English only. These classes, except for courses on Inuktitut language, are usually taught by Qallunaat teachers who, in contrast to most Inuit staff, hold the required diplomas.[63] High school students often express feeling bored by the lessons, and a number of them do not attend school any further. As written above, teenagers are busy with creating their position in the community. Competencies acquired in school education and relationships with other students and teachers in the context of school are of little relevance to their relationships and activities outside of school. Furthermore, many teenagers want to stay in Qikiqtarjuaq. Most of them do not have ambitions to pursue a career somewhere else or to extend their education at college or university. Qikiqtarjuaq does not offer many job or career opportunities which would make higher education more relevant or attractive.

The curriculum and the work of teachers are supervised by the local Education Council that reports to the District Education Authority. The council is elected and consists of Inuit elders and middle-aged men and women. They look after the quality of education and they stimulate the further integration of Inuit knowledge and skills at school. The integration of *inuit qaujimanituqangit* in the formerly basically western curriculum is indeed not only a concern of the community of Qikiqtarjuaq, but also for Nunavut governmental institutions. In the report of the *Nunavut Traditional Knowledge Conference* in Igloolik in 1998, the *Nunavut Social Development Council* (NSDC) defined *inuit qaujimanituqangit* as encompassing all aspects of traditional Inuit knowledge, including beliefs, values, perceptions, language, social organization, and life skills (e-doc Nunavut Social Development Council, 1998).[64] It is perceived to be crucial for the improvement of living conditions in Inuit communities. The concept is widely used in designs of educational, health, and scientific programs and policies. For example, the *Department of Sustainable Development* (DSD) summarizes its institutional tasks to be:

> Managing environmental conditions and biodiversity through good science and *Inuit Qaujimanituqangit*. Building healthy communities through our programs. Developing and supporting sustainable economies. [Related programs are designed to] provide the support needed for people and Inuit organizations to develop and use their capacities to enable them to participate fully in decisions on development (e-doc Department of Sustainable Development, 2000).[65]

Inuit traditional knowledge is perceived to be a crucial ingredient in the establishment and operation of modern Inuit communities. Western scientific knowledge is seen as useful, but it is not valued as facilitating the way Inuit want to shape their present and future. As children do not grow up in camps anymore and many 'traditional' skills are not practiced on a daily basis in the settlement, the school is perceived to be a place where this knowledge should be taught.

---

63   Students with special needs are specifically trained in addition to their participation in regular classes. Deaf children, for example, are intensively trained in sign language. All other children also receive basic training in sign language in order to facilitate communication among all inhabitants of the settlement.

64   http://pooka.nunavut.com/~research/docs/TK%20Conference.htm

65   http://www.gov.nu.ca/Nunavut/English/departments/DSD/

2.8 Discussion of Life in Qikiqtarjuaq

This ethnographic introduction to life in Qikiqtarjuaq showed in various cases that the material and institutional Western-style appearance of Qikiqtarjuaq is misleading when taken as a representation of the Inuit ways of life. We saw that houses were planned according to the format of Western-style stable domestic units and Inuit were trained in the first years of the community accordingly. Looking closer, life in Inuit households resembles Inuit camping more than Western ideas of functioning domestic units. Furthermore, residence in a household is frequently only temporary; as some members leave and others enter. The ongoing dynamics of social formation and re-formation are also part of the seasonal cycle of concentration in the settlement and dispersion to camps. Movement continues to be a marked feature of Inuit society. When we looked at two local institutions we found a similar situation there. Inuit make good use of the available facilities; while at the same time, their style of operational procedures and content emphasize Inuit values and knowledge. We can draw the preliminary conclusion that, although planned as a sedentary community, Inuit manage to maintain nomadic ways of life in Qikiqtarjuaq.

Chapter 3
Christianity in Qikiqtarjuaq

I study the Bible, because the Bible is alive and unmoveable.
Pauloosie Angmarlik

3.1 Introduction

In pre-Christian and Christian Inuit camp times, cosmological relationships were relevant for the establishment of social relations. The purpose of this chapter is to explore how the modern Inuit community of Qikiqtarjuaq has been established within its present Christian framework. The first part of this chapter deals with the institutions of the Anglican Church and Full Gospel Church of Qikiqtarjuaq and the church leaders. The second part discusses religious beliefs and practices in Qikiqtarjuaq.

3.2 Anglican and Pentecostal: Churches and leaders

3.2.1 The Churches
History, perceptions, and recollections of recent developments in religious life:
Just like the school and the municipality, the Anglican Church was introduced and run by Qallunaat. However, the Anglican Church differed in two relevant aspects from other institutions. Firstly, it emphasized a Christian framework in dealing with religious and social issues. Secondly, it has been present on Baffin Island for a considerably longer time than other institutions. Christian beliefs and practices have become integral parts of Inuit-life and most Inuit viewed their local Anglican church as 'Inuit'.[66]

The Anglican reverend James Peck established a mission at Blacklead Island (Cumberland Sound) in 1894. He and Julian Bilby translated the Bible and hymns between 1895 and 1905 (Laugrand 1997: 838-840). They transcribed the books using the syllabic system which Peck had adapted from the syllabics introduced among the Cree. These syllabics were to become the standard for Inuktitut writing. The population of Davis Strait was only occasionally visited by missionaries.[67] However, the availability of the Inuktitut Bible and hymns and of traveling Inuit preachers, facilitated the distribution of Christian ideas (Harper 1983b: 29).

---

66 Almost all inhabitants of Qikiqtarjuaq are members of the Anglican Church. Only ten individuals are formal members of the Full Gospel Church and a very small minority of Inuit, all of them originally from other communities, are Catholic. These numbers are approximations based on data from interviews and on data from community and church files. The community profiles of Statistics Canada do not differentiate between Anglican and other protestant groups (e-doc: http://www.statcan.ca) or between Inuit and Qallunaat members.

67 Church files documenting baptisms, weddings, and funerals during the period suggest that no missionary visited the Davis Strait area between 1913 and 1925.

After years of unsuccessful efforts, the process of converting Inuit to Christianity accelerated after the baptism in 1901 of the first three Inuit women from Uumanarjuaq (Blacklead Island) (Oosten, Laugrand & Kakkik 2003: 32). Within the first decade of the 20th century all Inuit of the Cumberland Sound and Davies Strait regions converted to Christianity and became members of the Anglican Church. The process of Christianization was not forced upon Inuit. Saladin d'Anglure (1989), Sonne (1990), Stevenson (1997), Laugrand (1997), and Blaisel & Oosten (1999) found that Inuit actively integrated and shaped the new religious beliefs and practices to fit the particular context of their ways of life.

Anglican missions were led by Qallunaat ministers, who were assisted by Inuit helpers. Outside the immediate reach of missions, Inuit took over religious leadership. The elders of Qikiqtarjuaq recalled that one or two men were in charge of celebrating the Sunday services. For example, Peter Anilik Paniloo, an elder man born in Kivitoo in 1930, spoke about the practices in his camp: "We heard people talking about Uqammak,[68] who visited Kivitoo before I was born. He left some Bibles and pictures. Naujavik and Paniloo, my father, were reading the Bible [celebrating the service]." Martha Nookiruaq, born in Sauniqtuajuq[69] in 1916, elaborated the practices of her camp:

We had prayers in the sod houses[70] and during spring, we had our prayers outside. For the Sunday evening prayer, we shouted to the small community to come and attend the services. Everyone invited everyone else by shouting. Iqalik, my stepfather, and his brother Moses held the services. [...] One white person used to preach to us, but he is buried in Pangnirtung now.[71] Those who preached never were taught. They taught or preached by their own experiences and understanding. These were my uncle Kisaq, Tulugarjuaq, Unuqsaagaq, Keenainnaq, Eevik, and others. I remember those men. They were never taught. We thought they were ministers.

With the establishment of modern Inuit communities, various camps were brought together. At first, services were held in the home of a religious leader. It appears that from early on, the community celebrated services together. With the construction of a small church in 1964 (Laugrand 1997: 818), an alternative space for the congregation was established. Special services, such as for Christmas, were held in the community hall as the church was too small to accommodate all attendants at such an occasion. Some communities, such as Qikiqtarjuaq, had no resident ordained minister but were served by lay-readers and helpers and visited by ministers or the bishop about three or four times a year. During such visits, baptism and wedding ceremonies were performed and the local church volunteers received instruction and supervision.

The Anglican Church implemented formal leadership structures in the local churches that fit the institution's hierarchy by developing educational programs. At first, Inuit lay-readers and later Inuit ministers were trained at the Anglican mission in Pangnirtung and sent to other communities to support the churches there.[72] The proportion of Inuit ordained Anglican

---

68   Uqammak is the Inuktitut name for Rev. E.J. Peck. It translates as 'the one who talks a lot or well'.

69   A camp in the Pangnirtung area.

70   These houses were made of a driftwood or whale bone frame in a conical shape. The outer layer consisted of sod and plant material, the inner layers were made of skins or, later on, newspapers.

71   Probably Rev. A. Turner, called Quinijuq ('the one who is fat').

72   The establishment of the *Arthur Turner Training School* in Pangnirtung in 1970 implemented the education of Inuit to become ordinands.

Picture 16 *Church goers are leaving St. Michael & All Saints Anglican Church after a Sunday morning service.*

personnel has continually increased in the last years and leadership positions are increasingly filled by Inuit. In summer 2002, Andrew Atagotaaluk, became the first Inuk bishop of the Anglican Diocese of the Arctic.

When the first church was constructed in Qikiqtarjuaq lay-reader Pauloosie Angmarlik[73] moved there to run the church and to provide associated services for many years to come. He was one of the first to receive an education for becoming a lay-reader in Pangnirtung. The Church had requested him to become a lay-reader, and he believed that this took place because God also wanted him to do the work of a lay-reader. He recalled:

> Elijah Keenainak, Anilniliak, and I were the first three students in Pangnirtung. Once, we had a big conference in Iqaluit. Ministers and Women Auxiliary groups from all over Baffin came there. They voted for me to go to Qikiqtarjuaq. I was happy and I went. Quinijuq was a minister at that time. They were going to give me an education. I went [from Kivitoo] to Pangnirtung to study. [Becoming a lay-reader] was not up to me, it was God. He needed help. I told them that I will help till I retire. I like being a minister. I worked hard on that, because it helped many people following the Lord's words.

Pauloosie Angmarlik stayed in Qikiqtarjuaq for the next 24 years. He described his broad array of tasks as a lay-reader and as a community member:

---

73   Pauloosie Angmarlik was born in 1911 in a camp of Cumberland Sound.

I did what a minister has to do and communities tend to have difficulties within themselves. From day one, there were always problems within the community. If there is a problem between partners, husband and wife, I had to counsel them. If I was asked to counsel [...] I did what I was asked to do. I worked in different organizations. I have worked at the Northern store to provide for myself and my family. I was a council member of various bodies. The Bishop did not provide me with money, no funds. Therefore I had to work. I was ministering. I was a councillor. I worked with the court, assisted the R.C.M.P., and I helped by counseling those who needed help. I helped according to what needed to be done.

Canon Don Whitbread and his family moved from Spence Bay to Qikiqtarjuaq in 1968 to stay for two years. His task was to serve the communities on the east coast of Baffin Island north of Cumberland Sound (Arctic News Oct. 1968). He built a bigger church in Qikiqtarjuaq, the new *St. Michael & All Angels* Church, which still serves the community today. Pauloosie Angmarlik was his assistant, as were other helpers such as Julai Nuqingnak and Atamie Nookiruaq. Several ministers visited or served in Qikiqtarjuaq after Whitbread left.[74] The last ordained minister appointed in Qikiqtarjuaq was Rev. Loie Mike. She took up her position in 1998 and left a year later to go back to Pangnirtung.

Pentecostal[75] Christianity entered the North when Rev. John Spillennar started his evangelical missions in Northern Quebec in the 1950s.[76] He established the *Arctic Mission Outreach,* which has organized a number of Bible Conferences[77] and has since built five churches. Among them is a church in Pangnirtung whose construction was supported by members of the Full Gospel Church of Qikiqtarjuaq. Kayy Gordon was another evangelical missionary. As a member of the *Glad Tidings Tabernacle* in Vancouver, she established her mission in the Western Arctic in 1956 and gradually extended her work eastward. Pentecostal evangelic missions reached Baffin Island by the 1980s when Kayy Gordon held Bible Conferences. Pauloosie Kunilusie[78] attended one of her meetings in Pond Inlet on Baffin Island. This experience stimulated him to establish a new Church in Qikiqtarjuaq for a Pentecostal congregation. Speaking about his career as a religious leader, he began in a traditional manner, describing his childhood experiences of hunger and misery and his wish for a life without hunger:

I was born near Pangnirtung. The place was called Nunataq. When I was growing up as a child – I want to talk about this, I want to reveal it – when I was about eleven or twelve years

---

74 See appendix 1 for a list of ministers visiting or serving Qikiqtarjuaq.

75 Inuit use a variety of phrases to talk about the new Christian ways. They use: 'the Full Gospels', 'the New Church', 'the Pentecostal Church', 'you know those new ways', 'the other church', etc. For clarity in writing, I apply the term 'Pentecostal' to designate all liturgical contexts in which an emphasis on the Holy Spirit, glossolalia, strong expressions of emotions, and baptism in the Holy Spirit are believed in and practiced. These practices are not the monopoly of a specific church, nor are they perceived and practiced in a uniform fashion in Qikiqtarjuaq. It is, for example, acceptable to receive the gift of speaking in tongues before as well as after the baptism in the Spirit.

76 Bill Prankard is another influential pastor, who from the mid 1970s followed Spillennar and Kayy Gordon with his Full Gospel ministry in the Canadian Arctic.

77 One of these conferences took place in Qikiqtarjuaq in September, 2002. See: www.arcticmissions.com

78 Pauloosie Kunilusie and his family settled down in Qikiqtarjuaq when it was still a camp settlement. He latter achieved social, political, and religious leadership positions and established his own business.

of age, my father died, and we were hungry and we had nothing to eat. We had no supporter and we were always hungry. We were really hungry at that time. As a child, as a naive child I imagined I would leave the camp and live somewhere else. I used to wish and I used to think I would leave the camp and go somewhere else. I would be able to support myself and my family and would never be hungry again. And by actually doing it when I grew up and got married, I moved to another place where I am now. I have my own business and am able to support my family and not let my family go hungry.

Pauloosie wished and worked to provide for a family and to lead a prosperous life. At some point, he realized the cosmological origin of his endeavor. He became an entrepreneur with a God-given mission:

Nowadays, I recognize that God gave me those thoughts, because he had a purpose for me, and the purpose for me was to start a church. He used me spiritually when I started up the church. He used me physically when I started up my business. And my family is not hungry, I am not hungry, because my goal was to be able to support my family and I am very well off at this moment.

At first he was a lay-reader in the Anglican Church. He was sent to attend conferences to study the Bible. He also attended conferences organized by the *Glad Tidings Mission*. He recalled: "I started to read on my own and I started to teach myself and I was able to understand what God had said. At that time nobody really understood the Bible. As we started to learn about the Bible, we started to believe in God." Pauloosie felt then that God had given him the mission to start a new Church. He did not want to polarize his enterprise with the existing Anglican Church, but setting out was difficult at first:

God has certain goals for every individual. Although I am a sinner and not a very good person he appointed me to start up a church. That is why, when the Glad Tidings Church surfaced, I had to leave the Anglican church, because God had a purpose for me to start up a different church. Before there was a church building, we had prayer services at my home and at other people's homes who welcomed us. The first church was in what is now the [Sijamiut] convenience store; that is where I started up the program.
I have nothing against Anglicans. I don't dislike them or anything like that. The only reason I left the Anglican church was to perform my duty, which God had set up for me. There were a lot of differences between the Anglican and the other church. It was quite hard, a heavy burden, because there were a lot of people who disliked the idea, and who had difficulties understanding what it was all about, whether it was for real or not. I thought of this actually before I went ahead, because I knew right away that there would be people who disagree with me and who would dislike the idea. This was a very heavy burden, trying to perform these things when there are so many people against it. My immediate family was against me; my family or my siblings didn't want anything to do with what I was doing. But other families attended the services, and they would become the followers. [...] I saw myself changing and my family didn't recognize me anymore and therefore they were against what I was doing and they assumed that it was not a real thing. Finally, my family started to accept things.

Pauloosie Kunilusie described his career in terms of maturing from a child to an adult provider for a family, and then, of becoming a religious leader. Even though he talked about his personal development, the family played an important role during the development of his career. First, the family of his childhood in which context he made up his mind for his future life. Secondly, the family he established as a successful adult man. Thirdly, the painful experience of disagreements in his family in the time of his development of religious leadership. And, finally, the reconciled family marking the passage towards the completion of his spiritual tasks. As we will see further on in this chapter, Pauloosie Kunilusie's emphasis on the family in relation to his spiritual development was not idiosyncratic, but a recurrent topic in the domain of Inuit religious beliefs and practice.

Pauloosie Kunilusie was not the only Anglican lay-reader who, inspired by a vision or an experience, left the confines of the Anglican Church to become a religious leader. Silasie Angnako, an adopted-out brother of Pauloosie Kunilusie, is another lay reader who, by a vision, felt constrained by the established ways of the Anglican Church. Silasie's wife, Ragalee Angnako, told me about his religious career, which began when he attended a course at the *Arthur Turner Training School* in 1962:

> When my husband started as an Anglican minister, he already was a helper at church. He had a dream. He felt through his dream that he was told to go to different communities to help through ministry. When he approached the head person of the mission in Pangnirtung, they transferred him to another community to become a minister. Through a dream.

He served as an Anglican lay-reader in various Baffin communities. In 1975 he moved with his family to Grise Fiord (see also: Arctic News Fall 1977: 3). Then they moved to Resolute Bay, and finally to Qikiqtarjuaq. Ragalee Angnako recalled: "We were transferred to Qikiqtarjuaq because we wanted to be with both our mothers [who stayed there]." Silasie Angnako, who joined Pauloosie Kunilusie, felt moved to support the new movement and to help others. He became a leader in the new Church. Together, they held gatherings and services at first in private homes and later in the new church. Services were held Pentecostal style. For instance, Christian soft rock music and band instruments were introduced. And people were encouraged not to hold back their emotions but to express them in public. Services also facilitated what was believed to be manifestations of the presence of the Holy Spirit, such as glossolalia and 'holy laughter'. Often, those who attended the services decided to undergo a 'baptism in the Holy Spirit' – a baptism of adults. The discrepancies between the traditional Anglican and the Pentecostal ways would appear to mark a break between the new Church with the Anglican Church. However, Inuit who followed the new ways did not make such an emphasis. Pauloosie Kunilusie and Silasie Angnako, the Pentecostal leaders, did not intend to polarize Churches, which has been recollected by Silasie's wife, Ragalee, and their daughter, Lizzy Anaviapik, now a woman in her late thirties, as follows. Ragalee made clear that:

> I do not refer myself to be this or that, Anglican or something else. I do not care what the titles of the churches are. I can go to any church where I feel comfortable, where I can follow my heart by worshiping. Follow the word of God instead of following what the minister has to say.

Lizzy Anaviapik pointed out that:

The way I grew up, dad always used to tell us: 'It doesn't matter what kind of Church you go to. It does not matter what kind of people with different religions you hang out with, as long as you believe it is in here,[79] as long as you feel comfortable. I've heard people say: 'I am an Anglican. I'll never go to any other Church. My attitude was: 'You expect the same Church to stand up in this world for all your life? Do you think you're going to be saved by that Church? By that individual building or something? It is just a church building as far as I am concerned. It will collapse eventually and when it does, who is going to save you? When my mom and dad decided to go to [the new] Church, I guess, it was difficult for them, because of my dad being an Anglican minister for so many years. Then to go to a different Church, you know – people did not understand why. People thought: 'Oh God, he lost his mind this time.' [...] As soon as the new church building was opened, all Anglican people neglected them. Some were kicked out from the Anglican Church and they were never allowed to go back again. I remember that at some evenings, some people would throw rocks at the new church.

The inhabitants of Qikiqtarjuaq dealt with the new church in different ways. Bert Rose, a former Qallunaat long-term resident and teacher in Qikiqtarjuaq, recalled that especially women in their teens and twenties together with some members of Silasie's and Pauloosie's families joined the new Church with enthusiasm. Then there were people who participated in the services a few times to form an opinion. Others refused to go there, and some openly expressed their opposition by disregarding its leaders and participants. Lizzy Anaviapik recalled the opposition very well:

There was a lot of confusion. Mostly, because people were told two different services. A lot of people in the community also said: 'We don't need another church; we already have a church.' A lot of people felt deceived. One person from out of town was very much into all this praising and all this worshiping. Whenever they were coming from out of town, even before the new church [was built], people used to go on the radio warning each other: 'Watch out, there is that person trying to confuse other people. Make sure that you watch yourself. Make sure he doesn't get to you.' Some people said that they came from Satan. They were saying that it is said in the Bible that in the last days all these people would come and try to make changes just to confuse people, take them away from the true faith. Like: 'You have no choice but to be an Anglican, because Anglican was here before anything else'.

Discourses on proper ways of being a Christian intensified, not only in the community at large, but also within families. Pauloosie already described his own experiences in this respect. Martha Nuqingak-Kunilusie, a daughter of church helper Julai Nuqingnak, also recalled the tensions that arose from her participation in the new services. She was in her late twenties when the new practices were introduced to Qikiqtarjuaq. Her parents took care that their children attended the Anglican services regularly. She recalled:

My father was an Anglican; this is the ministry I grew up in. [Then came] a new sort of religion. It kind of broke away the churches years back. [...] I attended in the beginning once, because I needed to find out what it was like. [As a result] I didn't want to hear any

---

79   She pointed to her heart.

kind of song except the religious song and I didn't agree with singalongs. It was very difficult, my father was furious. He once told us: 'Don't go overboard'. As he experienced it, it was dangerous and he didn't want anything to happen to his kids of what had happened before. Even my mother said: 'Don't go overboard.' Just because something happened before with someone and they thought it is connected to that,[80] and the same thing will happen again. We [respected] their beliefs and we had to, because they were our parents. [After some time my enthusiasm] kind of wore out.

Although the leaders of the new Church may not have intended to polarize their ways against those of the Anglican Church, the introduction of the new ways initiated a, at times, fierce discourse on proper Christian ways in the community; which also affected social relations within families and the community. What was the response of the Anglican Church to these developments? Pauloosie Angmarlik, lay reader at that time, suspected that the new ways could be considered as different than Christian practice. He contacted his bishop to learn about the new ways and to receive directions on to how to deal with them. He recalled:

> I called my bishop that I wanted to talk with him, that I wanted to understand the other church. I would not go there. I had never heard anything else than Anglican rules. If I would go to the other church, I wanted to know their rules first. That's what I talked about with the bishop. The bishop said that it is okay to go there just for listening. He said that they had 18 different rules. He did not tell me the rules, just that there were 18 different rules and that the rules were hard and that the new church did not belong to the Anglican Church. That new church was too much for some people. That's how I understand it. [...] Our bishop told me that, if the other church would want to hold prayer sessions in our church, they may not use it. I will not leave the Anglican Church. I understood myself as being Anglican, but it was getting harder.

The Anglican Church initially refused to cooperate with the new Church. Pauloosie Angmarlik was in favor of that decision because, from his point of view, the new ways were potentially dangerous. Still, people were free to decide for themselves which Church to attend. However, with formal membership in the new Church, institutionalized relations with the Anglican Church changed. As Lizzy Anaviapik indicated above, the Anglican Church withdrew the membership status from the leaders of the new church. Ragalee Angnako, Lizzy's mother, related her own experiences with the institutional regulations:

> When we moved here, I was involved with church committees, like the Women's Auxiliary group. But when my husband resigned as an Anglican minister, there was a regulation they followed: if you are not involved with the Church you cannot be involved with the committees. I am going to continue what my mother taught me to be always involved with the Women's Auxiliary group.[81] I used to be the chairperson of that group before my husband resigned.

---

80 She is probably referring to the religious movement that took place in Kivitoo in the winter of 1921-1922. See for further detail Blaisel, Oosten, & Laugrand (1999).

81 She participates in all meetings of the Women Auxiliary Group, but does not have the status of member.

After the first wave of opposition the tension gradually eased. According to Pauloosie Kunilusie, the resistance calmed down after a while because people began to understand the new ways. Furthermore positive changes in community life were, according to Pauloosie Kunilusie, attributed to, for instance, confessions or counseling practiced in cooperation with a Pentecostal leader:

> As the years went by, people started to understand [the new church] and to accept it and today there are no worries or anything, because people understood that this is for real and they accept it today. [...] Whenever an individual had been touched by words, the person started to think of giving him/herself to God. And sometimes there were quite a few people who wanted to confess and who needed guidance to solve their problems or who needed guidance with every day family problems. These people came up to me and asked to be blessed and since the church had been built the problem with the people of Qikiqtarjuaq is decreasing; this is understood more and more by Qikiqtarjuaq people. There are still some people out there who don't accept it and disagree, but it is nothing compared to the first time that it actually started to happen.

The new Church was increasingly accepted in the settlement, but it experienced obstacles within. There were questions of leadership resulting in a crisis. It was difficult to learn the details of it. Apparently, family issues and among the leaders different views on the proper Christian practice played an important role in the process. The church fell apart in the mid 1980s. Pauloosie Kunilusie, looking back, thought that, as God had used him for the difficult task to explore new spiritual ground and to integrate the new ways into the daily life of the community, God also determined that his achievements in establishing improved cosmological and social relationships would provide a foundation for others to build on:

> I was one of the first pastors to start up back in the 1980s. At that time I also had a vision that after I had built up the church and after I had been a priest for a little while, I would have to step back and let someone else take over. That was my vision. That was why everything I had seen was going to happen in time. That is why it is still happening. I don't want to say I had quit that program. I never quit my belief, but my vision was that I would have to step back and let somebody else take over, and it would be my task to watch if things were working out well and everything. [The vision] was like watching a movie. I had the vision repeatedly. Although it was the same vision, it was more understandable each time, and everything I had seen has happened and continues to happen.

After he resigned from his leadership position, Pauloosie opened a convenience store in the former church building and rarely ever went to church again until the year 2000. That year, he had to deal with difficulties in his family and business, and employed various strategies to deal with them. One strategy was to lead a service in the new Full Gospel church to fight the negative powers which he thought played a role in his situation. The other was a public meeting to discuss the situation.

Silasie and Pauloosie had both stepped back from their positions as church leaders, but the leadership position remained within the family. Furthermore, it became institutionalized when Silasie Angnako sent his son, Billy Arnaquq, to attend a three-year course at the *National Native Bible College*, led by Ross Maracle, in Deseronto, Ontario in 1985. Billy Arnaquq was finally

Picture 17 *Katissivik Full Gospel Church.*

ordained in April 1996. He took over the leadership from his father and his uncle. In 1989, he built a new church for the Full Gospel denomination, with the financial aid of the *Harvest Field Ministry*, led by Roger Armbruster.[82]

The introduction of this Church was not as tumultuous as when Pauloosie started his movement. The Full Gospel Church, however, as a small attendance during regular Sunday services. Billy Arnaquq has acknowledged the difficulties for the acceptance of the new Church in the community. In his view, the Church still has to develop: "I always use the scripture proverb: 'By wisdom is thy house built'. [...] It takes a long time to lay the foundation. Especially in this community, where things have not gone right." Together with Pauloosie Angmarlik, Pauloosie Kunilusie, and probably also his father, he perceived the improvement of spiritual and social relationships to be his task.

Although the local Anglican churches refused to open its doors for Pentecostal gatherings until the mid 1990s, it gradually changed its policy. Loie Mike, ordained as the first Inuk female Anglican minister in 1998, explained these changes by referring to her own experiences of becoming a minister:

[Becoming a minister] is no picnic. It's a picnic, but on a blizzard day. [...] I was between 8 and 10 years in Christ. I was born again about eight years ago, when I began really to

82 Roger Armbruster is the leader of the *Harvest Field Ministries*, Manitoba. His aim is to help to build the indigenous church in Canada's north, particularly among the Inuit. This ministry is based in the *Maranatha Good News Center* (Full Gospel) in Niverville, Manitoba – a church founded in 1978. Billy cooperates with them also for mission tours outside Canada, such as to Russia, Israel, and Greenland.See www. canadaawakening.com/new_page-1.htm (see also pages 2, 3)

be drawn into ministry. For four years I pushed it aside – woman, Anglican priest. But I knew who I believed in. He is my Lord and my Savior. I told him: 'My life is yours. You do whatever you want with it.' And it's still true today. I feel very privileged to have that role, to have that calling. [...] There was an old man [Noah Angakaq], who lived to see Rev. Peck. And he told me when I was going to *ATTS* [*Arthur Turner Training School*], three of us he told, that we were going to wish to do something entirely different than the other ordained ministers that had come here.

Many Inuit Anglican ministers, like her, asked for a baptism in the Holy Spirit.[83] In the first years, the Anglican bishop sanctioned this practice. According to Billy Arnaquq, those ministers sanctioned earlier have recently been reinstated and many Inuit Anglican ministers in the Eastern Arctic have been baptized in the Holy Spirit. Anglican lay readers in Qikiqtarjuaq have also all been baptized in the Holy Spirit. As the Anglican Church became increasingly open to Pentecostal beliefs and practices, evangelists, such as Billy Arnaquq and representatives of the Pentecostal Church of Iqaluit were invited to conduct Bible Conferences in the Anglican church of Qikiqtarjuaq. Pauloosie Kunilusie thought about the developments in the Anglican Church in terms of strategy rather than in terms of fundamental change:

A few years back they were really serious when praying. Nowadays it is not like that; it is fun and exciting. It is my understanding that the Anglican Church is changing. My point of view is that the Anglican Church and every other Church which has God or Jesus in them don't want to be forgotten. They don't want to be left behind and if the Anglicans had kept praying that seriously, nobody would be attracted to it anymore. Every church has to have an attraction so it can be fun. It does not want to loose its followers.

And Loie Mike emphasized other aspects:

I am reading an interesting book about [Rev. Peck] right now. He thought: 'Poor Inuk, didn't know much.' So, he did everything for them. Even gave us a written language. And you know, that knowledge of Christianity, the first Christian life grew, then he left. Then they thought whoever came in after him should be like him. So all the priests after him ever since have been like this: do this, do that, that's what you have to do. It's a tradition. [...] Traditionalism is a dead faith of the living.
For a long time, the church in this community, in Pangnirtung, and almost everywhere for over a hundred years lived by the service book. Lived with, live by that. They did everything according to the service book. And if anything else happened outside of what is supposed to happen according to the service book, it is not of the Church. They say its false teaching. [...] You don't expect a tree to be this height all the time.[84] It grows. It also says in the word of God, you will grow lots of branches that even birds will nest in it. Well, it has to start with one nest, then two nests, then three nests. All these join together.

She viewed the religious developments in terms of continuity of beliefs and of growing independence from practices fixed in writing and based on Qallunaat religious performance.

---

83   A baptism in the Holy Spirit is a Pentecostal practice of adult baptism.

84   She indicated a height with her hand.

The image she used to express change and continuity in Christianity related to Inuit ideas about growing up, from being a child that has to learn to think and to make decisions, to becoming an autonomous adult and a partner for cooperative enterprises.

The variety of positions in the discourse on the proper practice of Christianity were, to a large degree, implemented in the various forms of church services.[85] Though many people, usually in relation to their age-group, had a preference for a form of service, they were not exclusive in which practice they participated in. Most young people participated in Pentecostal style Anglican youth services and Bible Conferences. Most elders preferred to attend the traditional Anglican Sunday morning services. Middle-aged people visited the Anglican Sunday morning services as well as well as the evening services that had integrated Pentecostal elements. Middle-aged people who participate in the services of the Full Gospel Church also occasionally attend the services of the Anglican Church, though to various degrees. However, people who prefer the Anglican services, usually only visit the Full Gospel Church for special occasions, for instance a wedding ceremony.

3.2.2 Church leaders
Qikiqtarjuaq's Anglican and Full Gospel Churches are part of larger institutions, which provide them with a specific religious discourse, organizational structure, and funding. The positions of minister/pastor, lay-readers, volunteers, and the congregation are part of a formal hierarchical order of leadership. During my fieldwork, the Anglican Church operated through a team of lay-readers, members of the board, and volunteers. Most of the leading members took care of various functions. For instance, Loasie Kunilusie, Jacopie and Leetia Kuksiak were lay-readers, who celebrated services and provided spiritual counseling. Loasie also played the organ and supervised the youth group *Northern Lights*. Geela Kunilusie, his wife, taught at the Sunday school and sang in the church choir together with about fifteen other men and women. Imona and Uluta Kuksiak were members of the Church Board, led the Bible Study group, and Uluta also participated in the choir. Both gave spiritual support when required. Jacopie Nuqingak was the sexton. Leah Q. Kunilusie looked after the children during the service. She and Leah Kunilusie were also leading members of the Women's Auxiliary group. Sami Qappik and Monica Kunilusie, both in their twenties and the youngest among the leaders, were responsible for the youth services.

A similar picture emerged for the Full Gospel Church. Billy Arnaquq was the pastor. Most of the volunteers of his congregation were family members. He was supported by two musicians, Lootie Toomasie, his cousin and community mayor, and by Ipeelee Audlakiak. His parents took up the collection, spoke the Lord's Prayer, and his mother organized activities for the children during the service. Occasionally also his sister, Mary Killiktee, supported him with playing keyboard and singing. The services were prepared in cooperation with the Church's prayer and support group. Billy Arnaquq traveled a lot. If the services were not cancelled due to his absence, it was usually Lootie Toomasie who led the congregation in the service.

Just as believers moved between the Churches and the different forms of service, so did their leaders. For instance, older leaders of the Anglican Church had attended Pauloosie Kunilusie's services and underwent a baptism in the Holy Spirit. Later, they moved back to the Anglican Church. Some of the younger and middle-aged leaders, all of them baptized as adults as well, went for leadership training to the Full Gospel Church, intending to join the team there. Later, some of them resumed their participation in the Anglican Church.

---

85   See for a more detailed discussion the sub-chapter on services further below.

Inuit acknowledged the hierarchical structure of the church and the tasks ascribed to a position, but they considered adults to be their own masters in spiritual matters. When, as believers, they felt that they needed support, they approached a person of their choice, usually one of the church leaders. Leaders took up their position expressing their mission as: 'I am standing here because I want to help others.' The leader's success depended on his/her acceptance by the congregation. The acceptance was based on the congregation's perceptions of his/her capabilities and ways of assisting. An esteemed quality of a leader was the leader's credibility in view of his/her public claims of having exchanged an old, often miserable, life for a new and happy life by having faith in God. People were skeptical. They closely observed the leader's conduct and they knew him/her well enough to point out problematic issues.[86] They acknowledged that anybody can make mistakes, but people should be open about their mistakes and not present themselves as better than others. Leaders who were thought to be 'too religious' likewise lost their status as spiritual guides and supporters.[87] An ill-founded pretension of being qualified for leadership was a serious matter and was considered to point to a poor relationship with God and to cause social and spiritual harm to followers.

3.2.3 Church groups

The Churches ran several groups. The Full Gospel Church was supported by a service preparation group, a prayer group, a music group, and occasionally organized baptism preparation groups. The Anglican Church supported (and was supported by) a choir, the *Northern Lights* youth group, a Bible Study group, a Sunday school, and the Women's Auxiliary group. Participants of both of these Church's groups expressed the wish to do something for the benefit of the community, for example, by visiting lonely people, by running errands for old and sick community members, or by raising money, for instance with sales and lotteries, to support families in need. Participation in some of the groups, for example the Women's Auxiliary group, was a tradition in some families, but were still open to all persons interested. The value assigned to the group by its members did not concern a corporate identity but concerned the group's aims and avenues to support people. However, not only the wish to support others had relevance, but also the Christian framework in which it operated. Several new initiatives in the community, for instance a men's self-help group or a youth healing camp, which explicitly positioned themselves outside of the Christian framework, were welcomed by a number of people but also met with substantial opposition from religious leaders who believed that 'true healing' could only be bestowed by Jesus Christ. To my knowledge these initiatives met with little success.

3.2.4 Sunday church services[88]

The Anglican Church offered three services each Sunday: in the morning, late in the afternoon, and in the evening. These services varied in their set-up and atmosphere. On Sunday morning, it

---

86 Some leaders were thought to neglect their family, others were thought to be mostly interested in their own social and economic benefits. Others were thought to be still secretly womanizing.

87 The intensity with which people commit themselves to religious practices is an issue of ongoing discourses. People agree that 'being too religious' is detrimental to the well-being of an individual and may have detrimental effects on the community at large. But exactly where 'being too religious' starts is an issue of personal opinion.

88 I deal with the holiday cycle in the chapters *The seasonal cycle of Qikiqtarjuaq* and *Christmas in Qikiqtarjuaq*, where special attention is paid to the Christmas and New Year services.

Picture 18 *The Northern Lights youth group and its leaders (at the left hand side) during their Christmas celebration.*

was mostly middle-aged women and elders who attended the Anglican service.[89] Upon entering the church building, people vigorously cleaned mud or snow from their boots and took seats on the wooden benches. The first two rows often remained unoccupied by traditional Anglican believers as long as other seats were available,[90] however they were the first choice of Pentecostal-oriented Inuit. Most people brought their own Bible to follow the texts of the readings.

Bibles have received much attention from Inuit. Women kept their Bibles in beautifully embroidered covers and in between the pages, were pictures of their families. Many of the pages showed handwritten annotations commenting on the Bible texts or adding relevant contextual information.

The service, which was held according to the standard Anglican liturgical format, was celebrated in a composed and sincere atmosphere. The lay-readers and the church choir were dressed in habit and the Bible texts were taken from the *autamasiutiit* ('Daily Bread'), a yearly schedule for Bible reading of the Anglican Diocese. People stepped forward occasionally to share their testimony or to ask for support in a difficult situation. For example, a hunter be missed, the congregation performed a special prayer for his rescue. When the service ended, people shook hands and went home. Middle-aged and older people recollected that services in their youth had been much stricter in terms of discipline, even though the morning service was shaped according to Anglican traditions. It would have been unthinkable that children walked around in the

89   During hunting seasons, hunters can be out until late to make their catch. Youths use the weekends to socialize and go to the Saturday dances and on Sunday morning they sleep too long to attend the service.

90   John Ayaruaq explained that people probably feel uncomfortable to be looked at by all the people behind them. It is Inuit-style to be modest and not in the center of attention.

church and ate candies during the service. Most people thought that the rules had changed since the coming of new ways, which encouraged a less controlled way of celebrating services. People tolerated the more relaxed ways as long as they were not disturbed.

The morning service at the Full Gospel Church took place at the same time as the Anglican morning service. Usually, only a handful of people, mostly family members of the pastor, attended. Like the Anglican morning service, it too was held in a composed atmosphere. The pastor read from the Bible, preached, and testified to the (financial) blessings bestowed upon the Church thanks to the faith of its members. He talked about his travels to, for instance, Siberia or Israel and he provided an account of the success of the latest Bible Conference in which he had participated in another Inuit community. Occasionally, a churchgoer went forward to share a testimony or a sorrow with the congregation.

Songs played a prominent role in the service. Occasionally, they were chosen from the Anglican hymn book, but, more often, from a repertoire of modern church songs that were in part written and composed by Billy Arnaquq himself. He, apparently intuitively, would choose to sing the same verse repeatedly. On these occasions, the otherwise calm atmosphere became more excited, and some believers experienced what Pentecostal Inuit called *quviasuqtuq anirnimi ijunaitumi* ('excitement of being filled with the Holy Spirit'). Some attendants had tears in their eyes and raised their arms, swaying their bodies rhythmically to the song. It occasionally happened that someone started to talk in tongues. The excitement rarely lasted longer than a few minutes. The pastor supervised this event and after it had reached its climax he intoned a soothing song that guided people to compose themselves.

Late afternoon Anglican services and, even more so, evening services in both Churches were distinctly more lively than morning services. Modern songs were performed during the afternoon service of the Anglican Church, and most people prayed and sang with raised arms. The Anglican evening service was meant to be a youth service. Most elders left after the afternoon service, and middle-aged and younger people arrived or stayed in church, dropping in and out. The youth service often lasted three or more hours (usually in late fall, winter, and early spring, when there were many people in the settlement) and was filled with varying sequences of modern Christian music, some of it composed by Full Gospel pastor Billy Arnaquq and other community members, and included prayers, occasional readings from the Bible, and short intermezzos of preaching. Recently, the Anglican Church had received funding for band instruments which were considered more appropriate for this kind of music than the traditional organ.[91]

Usually more than one church leader was present at the these meetings, with one leading the service while others attended to individuals who asked for assistance. As the evening unfolded, the atmosphere got increasingly excited. Verses of songs were repeated over and over again, leading the congregation into an ecstatic condition. Leaders closely observed the developments and steered the singing and praying to prepare for the presence of the Holy Spirit. People sang and danced with raised arms, welcoming the Holy Spirit. The Holy Spirit often was experienced to manifest itself in glossolalia performances by several worshipers. Others received a gift of 'holy fire'[92] which they shared with the congregation. At the same time, mostly teenage or young adult individuals asked leaders for special prayers to help them deal with troubles. Individuals went to the altar and while the church leaders, often two of them together, held their hands over his/her

---

91   A few people of all age-groups expressed their dislike for these instruments in Church. According to them, people should stick with singing hymns accompanied by organ.

92   The 'holy fire' was interpreted in reference to the gift of flames by the Holy Spirit at Pentecost.

head, their clients were crying, howling, shivering, and some fell on the floor. Difficult cases were attended to in the side building. After the climax was reached, leaders intonated soothing songs that usually expressed gratitude towards God, Jesus, and the Holy Spirit. People composed themselves and, one by one, joined the singing. As the service ended, often late at night, people either went home or stayed for a while to socialize with friends.

Attendance of services and the intensity of the performances varied with the seasons and the related population size. Services at periods of community concentration in late fall, winter, and early spring were, firstly, attended more regularly and by relatively more people, and they were, secondly, often more intense than services during the periods of community dispersal to the campsites. Also community events such as visiting Bible Conferences, or peculiar incidents, shaped the celebration of services. For instance, services tend to be more enthusiastically attended shortly after people participated in a Bible Conference.

The evening services in the Full Gospel church had a similar character, although they were usually shorter and less well-attended.

Discussion

The Anglican Church has a long presence in Southern Baffin Island and it became, for many Inuit, closely related, if not synonymous to, Christianity. Once adopted, Christian ways, beliefs and practices were, as were those of shamanism before, interrelated with the domain of social life. Social issues were, and continue to be, prominently articulated in a Christian framework. About twenty years ago, Pentecostal beliefs and practices were introduced to Southern Baffin Island. Soon, a new Church was established in Qikiqtarjuaq. However, instead of challenging the Anglican Church's corporate identity, and instead of opposing the new Church as an institution, the occasionally fierce discourses centered on the issue of what are proper Christian practices. The membership in a Church was less relevant to Inuit than the beliefs and practices promoted by the various leaders. Due to the interrelation of the religious and the social domains, the relevance of proper practices was not only based on spiritual concerns, but also on social concerns.

The relevance of proper ways of social and religious life for the well-being, not only of individuals, but also of the community, can be exemplified by the practices of procuring and thesharing of country food. As discussed in the chapters, *Theoretical background and methodology* and *Life in Qikiqtarjuaq,* these practices continued to be central features of Inuit life. Inuit believed that, aside from skills and knowledge, proper social and religious conduct were a crucial condition for success in the procurement of country food. Pauloosie Angmarlik explained that: "all animals have souls. God is controlling them. We cannot control them. God has invented them. We have to treat them properly. We cannot kill an animal and abandon it. If we are not going to eat them, then we do not kill them." Even though there were different beliefs among hunters as to whether animals have a soul, people agreed that animals had to be treated with respect. Game was believed, for instance, to be sensitive to being killed without need. It would avoid being killed by an unskillful hunter. It would also disapprove of meat being spoiled and of the negligence of not covering blood spilled during hunting with snow. It would mind coarse language and humiliating remarks, such as: "What a small fish you have caught!" "This seal is not fat enough!" "This seal looks funny! Look how it is laying on the ground." And game would also reject hunters boasting of their success.

In the social domain, hunters were obliged to share meat with their family and with the community and people should in general show a proper social conduct. Should people fail in these respects, animals were believed to react by withdrawing themselves from the hunter. A successful hunt would facilitate, in turn, a good social atmosphere as, for example by sharing meat.

Church leaders wished to help people who approached them for assistance to resume and follow proper ways of life. When their claims of having a proper, maybe even a privileged relation with God, was credible, leaders were accepted and esteemed. Since the Church as an institution was not at the center of people's attention – at the center was the discourse on proper Christianity – the leader was not esteemed for his/her position within the Church hierarchy, but for his/her ability to maintain and convey proper relationships with God and within the community.[93] And this propriety of relationship was thought to be the basis for the leader's capability to help others. At the same time, by engaging in social interactions and being functional therein, the Church also provided a space for leaders and volunteers to create social positions for themselves within the community.

Adequate practices were considered to be relevant for maintaining proper social and spiritual relations and for dealing with difficulties and conflicts in the community. Therefore, rather than to focus further on the relationship between the Churches as institutions, I will focus on religious practices in the second part of this chapter.

3.3 Religious practices

Introduction
References to Christianity were ubiquitous in Qikiqtarjuaq. For example, a Bible could be found in all public buildings and posters with proverbs decorated office walls. Institutional meetings were opened with a prayer and funds from government development programs (e.g. *Brighter Futures Program*) were granted to Christian projects to support troubled youth. Most private homes were decorated with religious art and in each house there was at least one Bible and a hymn book. Most CD collections included at least a few discs with Christian pop music and many households also had video tapes of prominent evangelical crusaders, like Benny Hinn. Reading the Bible, praying, and singing hymns or modern church songs were not exclusively practiced on Sundays, but also throughout the week in the settlement as well as in the camp. Some women actually told me that they like to listen to gospel music or Christian pop music while cleaning the house, as it would improve their cleanliness. Christian practices were also thought to be highly relevant for dealing with individual difficulties and conflicts in the community. Christian practices were furthermore associated with the events of the life cycle, such as Anglican and Pentecostal baptisms, confirmation, marriage, and death.

In the following paragraphs, I will deal with these issues by discussing Christian practices from the chapter's central perspective – the contribution of the Christian framework to community formation. Firstly, I will address various religious practices that may very loosely be grouped under the heading of relating to God and the Devil. This will be followed by paragraphs on dealings with the Devil and demons. Then, I will turn to the more specific issue of dealing with conflicts by looking at practices and perceptions of confession, conversion and the life-cycle event of a baptism in the Holy Spirit. I will conclude this investigation by addressing the life-cycle event of death, funerary practices, and beliefs concerning the after-life.

---

93   Just as were shamans and other leaders.

3.3.1 Relating to God and the Devil

Prayer

Tusiartuq ('prayer') was performed in various ways and contexts. Prayer was used to ask for support for oneself and others, to deal with evil forces, and to express one's faith or gratitude. People either prayed alone by themselves, in small groups, during church services or meetings, and to open committee meetings or community events. In collective settings, situation-specific words of prayer are usually followed by the Lord's Prayer. Whereas in contexts in which a traditional Anglican framework was employed these prayers are calmly spoken, in Pentecostal contexts,[94] individuals are encouraged to also express their zeal and emotional conditions.

Inuit Pentecostal Christians stressed that only speaking the prayer is not sufficient to be effective. According to them, the spoken words have to come 'from the heart'. They have to be imbued with the person of the speaker in order to activate a 'personal' relationship with God. Billy Arnaquq, the priest of the Full Gospel Church, actually warned that prayer should not become a routine as may happen for example with the Lord's Prayer in the traditional Anglican services:

> You have to pray from your heart. Otherwise your words can become shallow and just from the mouth. Doing something again and again can be dangerous, because it becomes a routine. And with written words you do not have to prepare. It is not from the heart. It grieves my heart. Written words are good to remind somebody to be careful.

Rev. Loie Mike, now living in Pangnirtung, elaborated on the effectiveness of Pentecostal style praying in groups:

> When these people who have a personal relation with Jesus Christ get together and start praying to God in their own personal ways, things begin to happen. When you set the Spirit free, when you let him have his way. [...] And that is happening everywhere, all around the world.

According to Billy Arnaquq, prayer needs preparation. The spoken words of prayer receive their power, not from intonating the written words, but from integrating oneself into the words spoken to God. Written words provide, from his point of view, orientation, but not a relationship with God. As we will see in the paragraphs on conversion, people who shared his view experienced that words of prayer spoken in a disengaged routine way are not effective and thereby frustrate one's faith and keep one from establishing a relation with God. This lack of relationship made them, in their experience, vulnerable to influences exerted by demons as well as to a process of decreasing social skill. Considering the relevance of spiritual development for the social and spiritual well-being of the individual, falling into routine is a dangerous condition.

Pauloosie Angmarlik, former lay-reader in Qikiqtarjuaq and traditional Anglican believer, agreed that prayer is beneficial and should be spoken 'from the heart'. However, he doubted and disagreed with the Pentecostalist's claim of establishing a direct relationship with God when praying:

---

94 Note that I am not referring here to an institutional context, but to a style of practice.

Praying to God has to go through Jesus, because we are too weak to handle God's Spirit. If we ignore Jesus while praying, our prayer will not go directly towards God. In order to get to God, we have to go through Jesus' name. We could otherwise die instantly, because his Spirit is too strong for us.

Both Angmarlik and Arnaquq emphasized that prayer is effective in the relationship of an individual to non-human beings. They disagree, however, in the source of power and the kind of relations required. Exactly what these proper relationships should look like is a matter of discourse in Qikiqtarjuaq.

Visions and prophecy
There were a number of people of all age-groups and Christian orientations in Qikiqtarjuaq who experienced *takutinauniq* ('received a vision') at least once. Their visions did not necessarily have the form of images, but also took the form of sounds or internal impressions. They revealed aspects of the future,[95] provided advice or helped a person, and they gave insights into the person's relation to God. An example for a vision was told to the church congregation by the elder Martha Nookiruaq at Christmas.[96] Sitting in a plane on her way to hospital for an eye-operation, she had heard the hymn 'How great thou art'[97] in the sounds of the aircraft engine. Satan had tried to distort this song, but did not succeed.[98]

Visions were viewed as a personal message provided by God, and there was no obligation to share visions. People were free to keep them to themselves or share them only with those close to them. However, usually during services and especially during the New Year's service, older people particularly felt moved to reveal their visions as a *piviksaqaqtittiniaratta* ('testimony'). Church leaders emphasized that sharing experiences of God's support in public would be in honor of God and would make not only the speaker but also the audience happier. Experiences with God as well as issues of a properly functioning community are appropriate to present in this context. John Ayaruaq explained to me the proper ways of giving testimonies:

Testimony means sharing how you felt, what you saw in relation to God. [...] The topics of the new millennium, healing and change of life are also okay for that occasion, as well as talking about the elders. It is also appropriate to talk about young people as our future. It is important not to put people down, which would be the case, if you talk about drugs, gambling, alcohol, etc. Topics of social or economic character are also inappropriate. Talk about positive, not negative things and in a positive way. If you talk about negative topics,

---

95 *Nalautartuq* ('prophesy') was a gift often associated with older people and elders. The coming of the new millennium was an occasion with an increasing number of prophecies. Prophetic visions were also used for the purpose of counseling. Opinions about prophetic practices were mixed. Some people doubted the credibility of people who received many prophecies. They often found it scary and wondered what the source of these visions were. Others thought that a high frequency of prophetic visions was a sign of spiritual authority.

96 See further examples in the chapter on the Christmas and New Year services as well as in the chapter on the history of Christianity in Qikiqtarjuaq and on conversion.

97 http://igeb.org/spiritua/howgreat.html

98 J.G. Oosten informed me that hearing hymns in engine sounds was reported to him by several elders of Igloolik (personal communication).

you have to do it in a positive way, because people are expecting negative events from the new millennium. Gratitude is also an important topic.

A testimony, thus, had to be a thoroughly positive event that made people aware of the benefits for individuals and the community that proceeds from a good relation with God.

Speaking in tongues
Tunsangnataktuq ('speaking in tongues') was practiced by Pentecostal oriented Inuit. It was believed to be a manifestation of the Holy Spirit that could be experienced by everyone who gave him/herself over to the Spirit. As described in part one of this chapter, glossolalia spontaneously followed singing during a service. Prayer also led occasionally to speaking in tongues. When one person started others, though not all, would follow. Some people also had to laugh very hard – perceived as 'holy laughter' – or started crying. While in this condition, some people are said to have received further gifts form the Holy Spirit, for instance the 'holy fire' that played a prominent role in the Biblical Pentecost. These gifts were shared with others who were willing and in a condition to receive them. I was present at one of these occasions and saw that people reacted in various ways to these offerings. Most received them eagerly and tuned into the excitement of the giver; others looked skeptically and withdrew a bit to the background. People emerged from the condition of speaking in tongues looking relaxed and happy. One by one, they joined the still singing congregation.

Speaking in tongues could also take place in a different form. Pastor Billy Arnaquq, for example, told me that he became used to speaking in tongues silently, for instance when walking down the street. He and others said that their relation to the Holy Spirit had developed such that they were able to move in and out of the condition at will, rather than being carried away by it. The feature of giving oneself over entirely was a matter of discourse among Pentecostal Inuit. Some emphasized that one should not control the Holy Spirit in his work. Others thought it to be a dangerous practice for a Christian, as a loss of self-control and guidance by excitement would lead to an unstable development of religious relations and faith of the individual. Furthermore, there were doubts among Pentecostal Christians and even more so among traditional Anglican Christians concerning the reality of a person's practice of speaking in tongues, especially if the person was frequently and intensively practicing it in public. A person with questionable social and spiritual conduct was likely not to be taken seriously in his/her practice of glossolalia as compared to people of a better reputation.

3.3.2 Dealing with demons and the Devil
In the above paragraphs, I described and discussed various ways in which Inuit relate to God. In these practices, three issues came up recurrently. First, that the social and religious domains connected in daily life. Second, that in order to deal with the religious domain, people need to have established proper relationships with spiritual beings. Third, that Inuit are engaged in an ongoing discourse on proper forms of Christianity that emphasizes the relevance of religion in social life. In the following paragraphs, I will first deal with interactions between Inuit, demons, and the Devil that, by contrast, further clarify the relevance of a proper Christian life for the community. Subsequently, I will address in some detail processes of dealing with social conflicts and difficulties in the religious domain, as well as processes of religious conversion.

Demon possession

The human soul was believed to be the prey of demons usually associated with the Devil. These demons were thought particularly to take advantage of a person who was feeling exhausted, worried, angry, or who showed improper social conduct without making that public. Persons without these troubles were thought to be less vulnerable to the destructive influences of these spirits. Prayer and proper conduct were believed to help prevent demons from entering one's house or one's body. Demon possession of houses, besides creating an eerie atmosphere in the house, was also believed to cause severe domestic problems. Demon-possessed human beings were thought not only to suffer mentally and emotionally, but also to become dangerous due to the evolving lack of self-control and display of aggression caused by the demon, but also by emanating negative thoughts and moods. The victims were expected to be depressed, brooding over unpleasant experiences, and to become less and less social, and prone to suicide. Furthermore, the possessed person could not easily connect to God, Jesus, and the Holy Spirit anymore – relations known to be crucial for healing the person from the affliction.

The practice of expelling demons is called *anirnilumianitittuq*. Usually, specific church leaders, which could be Anglican or Pentecostal, are approached for help by the victim. One or more counselors might either visit the afflicted house or person or deal with a demon-possessed person during evening church services or at a prayer meeting. The counselors start with identifying the harming demon, each of whom is believed to have its own personality and features. Then, prayers are spoken and additional measures are employed depending on the kind of demon one is dealing with. Prayer is one measure employed either for houses or persons. In dealing with demons through prayer, success is thought to increase with strong faith, the gift of discernment conveyed by the Holy Spirit, and ample experience in dealing with demons. Though most people tend to approach a religious leader for assistance, dealing with bad spirits was not exclusively a matter for experts. Loie Mike and Billy Arnaquq emphasized that, although some people may have special abilities to deal with demons, every person could be his/her own master in dealing with the evil spirits, provided that s/he is strong in faith. Loie Mike told me that she tried to reduce her requests for help in Pangnirtung by attending only to those people who were actually possessed and could, therefore, not help themselves very well.

Devil worship

Shamanism and Devil worship were religious practices people alluded to in a Christian framework, but which most of them hesitated to talk about in detail. Shamanism was referred to as the pre-Christian Inuit spiritual ways of healing or harming, bringing hunting success or disaster to the camps. People distinguished between good and bad shamans. Good shamans are still respected today. People who were very selfish and successful at the same time; people who were perceived to act strangely; people who induced scary feelings in others; or men and women who were seen in unusual shapes – with a black face, for example – were sometimes rumored to be evil shamans, magicians, or Devil worshipers. A middle-aged man from Pangnirtung and related to a Qikiqtarjuaq family, explained to me that people who had been dissatisfied with the results of their prayers to God would sometimes turn to the Devil to gain immediate power to manipulate things according to their wishes.[99] The Devil would grant them this power and in exchange would win their souls. These people would then even be responsible for a number of

---

99　We discussed the issue of the ineffective prayer in the above paragraph on prayer. Here, we are dealing with one of the possible consequences of improper prayer indicated by the church leaders quoted above.

suicides, initiated by them for their own benefit and entertainment. In respect to Qikiqtarjuaq, Billy Arnaquq sketched the present situation concerning Devil worship as follows:

> Some people still worship the Devil in Qikiqtarjuaq, but it is not common. They are desperate. They are very much hurt. Some start to do it also through music. Sessions take place in private homes. People doing so belong to the age-group of the 20-30 years old. [Former] teenagers get older and with that the Devil worship matured as well. Some worship the Devil to gain power over demons. It has a long history. There are certain evil spirits assigned to certain people, certain weaknesses of a person. A [Christian] commitment helps break the cycle.

People known or suspected to be Devil worshipers tended to be overlooked in social interactions, as they were perceived to be dangerous. Christian intervention was thought to be indispensable to break the relationship with demons and the Devil.

A telling incident of the discomforts evolving from suspected interactions with demons and the Devil took place in 1986 or 1987. At that time, Heavy Metal music was particularly, but not exclusively, cherished by male teenagers. They listened to the music, collected tapes and CDs, decorated their rooms with Heavy Metal posters and wall-hangings, and let their hair grow long according to the fashion of that time. Parents, elders, and church leaders had difficulties accepting this behavior. They did not appreciate the music and thought the lyrics to be negative and dangerous. They observed that the young people dedicated to this style changed their ways of socializing. Some recollected, for instance, that several of the teenagers started to look at the ground while walking down the street, not greeting anybody anymore. People also observed or suspected that these young people would worship and call upon the Devil and demons.

Some of these teenagers, now grown men, actually told me about practices of devil worship in which they felt inspired by the music and songs, but also motivated by their wish to gain power to change things and have them the way they wanted them to be. A young – and from all that I heard, well-respected – man killed himself in his room that was heavily decorated with Heavy Metal paraphernalia. This, as well as a number of subsequent suicides, was thought by many people to be related to the influence Heavy Metal had on the young people.

The more northerly community of Pond Inlet experienced similar developments and leaders of the Anglican Church there persuaded the young people to burn all Heavy Metal materials together with drugs and pornographic materials in a bonfire, in order to clean the community from their influences and to prevent further suicides. This initiative was adopted in Qikiqtarjuaq. Many young people, on their own initiative or persuaded by their parents and elders, piled their things up at the beach. Many people came to see when the bonfire was lightened. Some people reported that crying and talking came out of the tapes when they were burnt; an observation that justified for many of them the drastic measure of burning their property. One acquaintance, who informed me about the event, commented that Heavy Metal was interesting to him and his friends, and they liked to listen to it together while visiting each other. Though he perceived that his social demeanor changed, he pointed out that he wanted to provoke people to see how they would react to him. Having been persuaded by social pressure and the hope of doing something to end the suicides, to burn his things, he was very disappointed when the wave of suicides continued. The actuality of the involvement of evil forces, and how religious measures had been applied, continued to be issues of different point of views.

3.3.3 Dealing with conflicts and difficulties in the community

The Christian framework was a privileged context for dealing with conflicts and the re-establishment of functioning relations in the community. In the following paragraphs on confession, conversion, and the life-cycle event of a baptism in the Holy Spirit I will explore this aspect further.

Confession

Usually, a person who wanted to confess approached a religious leader to organize a session during an Anglican or Pentecostal service, Bible Conference, or in a smaller circle. It also happened that the leader asked if anybody from the congregation would like to come forward to talk about his/her wrongdoings. Pauloosie Kunilusie thought it a useful practice and explained that it would be a social act:

> The reason why I [facilitate the confession] in front of all the people is because they are seeking for help. If people reveal themselves to all these people there are some people who have the same difficulty, but they have done something about it and they are in a different path now. They are able to help the person who is in front of the people, and because of this, they go in front of the people and the main thing is asking for help.

By making transgressions public, the wrongdoer not only acknowledged the damage done by him/her, but also placed him/herself into the social and religious processes of counseling, support, and cooperation. A confession also helped to prevent misconducts from further harming the offender:

> Everybody who holds a secret harms him-/herself. Everybody not talking about the things he/she should not have done destroys him/her from the inside. The sin grows. It does not get better, because it is being ignored. It just sits there and grows and rots and destroys the person. When this happens, the person keeping the secret makes all kinds of assumptions to him or herself. The person starts to have low self esteem due to the secret he/she is withholding. And when a person finally tells what he/she has been holding, he/she feels better about him-/herself. The person starts to get a positive self esteem and it is not going downhill anymore. He/she is climbing up and when this happens, the person changes and feels better about him-/herself. Withholding something damages or destroys the person, but revealing betters it up. It makes it better and brighter.[100]

Pauloosie Kunilusie emphasized that the effects of improper social conduct were not confined to the social domain. Employing a concept of sin, he explained its effects on the religious domain. Through a confession, the wrongdoer dealt with these effects in the social and, at the same time, in the religious domain. Not only were the deed, the effects, and the cure part of both domains, but also the public was constituted in both contexts. The public was constituted as a social group by engaging in Christian practices. Through cleaning him/herself from the improper deed, the wrongdoer re-established his/her social relationships within a Christian framework. Members of the congregation, by cooperating as the audience and engaging in prayer also perform at the

---

100 I will come back to the issue of 'brightness' as associated with proper social and religious relationships in the following paragraph on conversion.

same time socially as well as spiritually. The conflict at hand was, in this way, dealt with by encompassing both relational domains.

Confessions were already used in pre-Christian times to deal with misconduct. According to Boas, Inuit thought that particularly the transgression of ritual injunctions would leave on the wrongdoer a stain visible to shamans and abhorred by animals and Sedna, who were thought to become easily contaminated. Human beings could also be contaminated by it. As animals would withdraw themselves from being hunted by a 'stained' person, and also the land and weather would act to the disadvantage of the hunters, disaster would inevitably befall the camp. Confessions, frequently under the guidance of a shaman, enabled the community to protect itself and to deal with it. Boas thought that this idea developed into the notion that confession itself would work as an atonement of the misconduct (Boas 1901: 120f.; see also Bilby 1923: 207).

3.3.4 Conversion and baptism in the Holy Spirit

Today, Pentecostal practices are a privileged framework for discourses on personal as well as community transformation. A growing number of Inuit, mostly young or middle-aged people, perceived that they underwent a process of transformation or conversion, changing from the 'old person' to a 'new person' or a 'reborn Christian'. Many of them decided to confirm this condition by being baptized in the Holy Spirit.

Billy Arnaquq, the pastor of the Full Gospel Church, used the phrase *nutaani anirngiangujuq* ('birth of the spirit') when referring to conversion. This phrase emphasizes a spiritual transformation and a new beginning. Martha Nuqingak-Kunilusie, a middle-aged woman, I talked about her experiences of being introduced to Pentecostal ways in Qikiqtarjuaq, and used the stem *saliak-*[101] to refer to the process of conversion. She explained that it means that "you have given your life to the Church." According to Dorais, the root *saliak-* literally means 'to move, or slide' like a sled would on slippery snow or like a boat that is brought aside by a wave. He suggested that the way in which Martha Nuqingak-Kunilusie used it could best be interpreted as, "those who convert to Pentecostalism, while keeping the same (Christian) direction, slide aside and change track."[102] Martha Nuqingak-Kunilusie's description of the introduction of Pentecostalism accentuated a combination of continuity and change. Furthermore, she suggested that there was also a sense of a potential danger related to the conversion of easily impressible young people. As a young girl, she felt attracted to the new ways and wanted to see for herself

---

101   The combination of continuity and change expressed in the concept is also reflected by elder Ragalee Angnako, the wife of one of the first Pentecostal leaders of the community, Silasie Angnako. She experienced her own Christian development as gaining more freedom to express herself in worship:

I was brought up in and involved with the Anglican Church for many years, but there was never any worshiping like raising hands or clapping. It was almost like: 'Do not do it! It is not allowed.' They referred to the Bible verses from Psalms, where it says you should worship the Lord with all your might and strength. Even though they were taught that in the Anglican Church, they were never allowed, or never given the freedom, to do it. Also, many of the hymns say: praise with all your might, clap your hands, worship. That was never allowed. Today it is different. They just sing along. They go by the words of the Bible and worship. [...] I feel I have not changed inside my heart, because it was always there. The only difference today is that there is more freedom to worship. In the Bible there is a verse saying: 'before the end of the days of the world, there will be a lot of people worshiping God and praise him and there will be an understanding of worship'. In the last days. It is like that today. (emphasis by A.N.St.).

102   E-mail communication from 28 October 2004.

what was going on. Getting involved, she soon changed some of her daily activities. For example, she did not want to sing or hear songs other than church songs. In the first part of this chapter I quoted her saying that her parents had warned her back then: "Don't go overboard". Respecting her parents' concern, she gradually withdrew herself from the new movement. Taking this history into account, her choice to use the stem *saliak-* also expressed a concern about the risks of becoming too focused on religious issues and judgmental towards other ways of life.

Conversion

In stories of conversion, the contrast between one's life before and after the experience of transformation is a recurrent *topos*. Individual experiences of transformation vary within these parameters. Three stories will elucidate Inuit perceptions of the process of conversion. These are the stories of Sami Qappik, the youth lay-minister, Peepeelee Nutaralak, an older woman, and Rev. Loie Mike, a female Inuit Anglican minister. Sami Qappik told me:

> I saw my life, how I lived it and then I saw a life that was, wow, that was beautiful. In my life I used to do drugs, alcohol, little bit of gambling, sometimes break and enter. I used to do all sorts of stuff, but it is gone. I used to see dreams. They were about dead stuff. Sin is dead stuff. These were not regular dreams. My mother was a lay-reader. I told her I had these dreams to commit suicide and to pray to Satan, all sorts of stuff. When I did all sorts of drugs, my life was not happy. When you are not happy, your room seems to be very dark. There is no joy and happiness. Your body feels down, the whole house is fuzzy and grey. The house follows that person. If parents argue a lot and they don't think about their kids; [this is] one reason why young people commit suicide. If the mother is good, but the father drinks alcohol or takes drugs, his speech gets sharp. When somebody answers, it sparks a fire. It brings a thing to the house.[103]

Sami Qappik perceived that there was a connection between his affliction and the condition of the house he was living in, in particular in terms of its illumination. The experiences that the "house follows the person" and also that the house tends to get darker when the household faced serious problems, or if the presence of a demon was felt, were widely shared in Qikiqtarjuaq. The oldest member of the community, Mialia Audlakiak, for instance, was looking for a new house. She made clear that she was looking for a place where nobody had committed suicide, where no drugs were used, etc. Those kinds of houses would not provide good living conditions.

The perception that "the house follows the person" was already present in the camp times of the past, where the house was the focal point of family and social life. The comfort of the home was to a large degree dependent on the success of the hunter, since he provided the food and oil needed to run the *qulliq* ('seal-oil lamp') for light, warmth and cooking heat (see also Boas 1888: 574). Houses also had been the location of shamanic rituals, for instance to improve

---

103 For the southern Baffin Island camps in the 19th century, Boas (1901) described the belief that the wrongdoings of parents have a negative effect on the child:

In many cases the transgressions become fastened [...] to the persons who come in contact with the evil-doer. This is especially true of children, to whose souls the sins of their parents, and particularly of their mothers, become readily attached. Therefore, when a child is sick, the angakok [shaman] first of all, asks its mother if she has transgressed any taboos. [...] As soon as the mother acknowledges the transgression of the taboo, the attachment leaves the child's soul, and the child recovers (Boas 1901: 124f.).

hunting success, cure sickness, and to deal with transgressions of ritual injunctions. In many rituals, manipulations of the *qulliq* had been part of the performance. For instance, at certain points in the ritual its light was lowered or turned bright.[104] The *qulliq* also needed to be dealt with in specific ways if a death had occurred (Boas 1901: 144f.).[105] Treated in proper ways, the house was thought to protect its inhabitants not only from the cold, but also from dangerous spiritual beings, such as the evil spirits of the dead (Boas 1888: 590f.).

Sami Qappik believed in the interrelation between his house, its inhabitants, and their social and cosmological relationships. Becoming aware of his spiritual and social problems, Sami decided that measures needed to be taken to deal with his difficulties and with his house. He wanted happiness and light to return to his home and to his life:

> I said let someone go and pray to my house. There were three people, besides my mother: two lay-readers and a reverend [Loasie Kunilusie]. They prayed for me first. I prayed with them. Loasie told me that after he prayed for me, my house would be prayed for. Something unusual came out from me. I heard a noise coming out from me very fast. Like 'wwwrrrmm'. The people praying didn't hear it, but I heard it. Maybe an angel took it away from me. I never experienced something like it. That was unspeakable. There was warmth all around my body, a warmth, which made me happy. My underarms were warm. It was not me. It was different, unspeakable. My heart was warm. A small little light was going through the room, entering my heart. My heart was burning. I started crying, sitting on the couch. I rarely cried before. They started to pray on the house. Making crosses on the walls, using tap water which they spoke prayers about.

The effects of the treatments were immediately perceptible to all those present:

> After finishing praying for the house, my mother told me to see my room. The lights were on, but it was brighter than normal. It seems there were no shadows, that bright. That was the glory of God in my room. My mother told me to go to the other room, which was lit only by one bulb that was not very bright. This room was also brighter. The glory of God shone in the whole house. The same in the living room.

Having been released of his spiritual burden and the unwanted presence of dangerous spiritual beings, he experienced a sharpening of his senses and of his intellectual, emotional, and spiritual

---

104 Light and darkness were already central features in Inuit shamanic practices. Having 'light' provided the shaman with the ability to see souls. Darkness provided him with the ability to remain hidden (Laugrand Oosten, Trudel 2000: 108). Also spirits incorporated light and darkness. Rev. Peck, who established the first Anglican mission in southern Baffin Island in 1894, collected the names of *tuurngait* (shaman's helping spirits) for Boas. He interpreted the contrast of light and darkness in terms of good and evilness of spirits. This perspective was also expressed by Ollie Ittinuaq, a north-Baffin elder, who explained about the helping spirits to Henry Kablalik and Frédéric Laugrand, in 1999. He said:"They both have light, the bad and the good. The only difference is that the bad spirit's light is dimmer. The inside of the black spirit might be dark (black). The inside of a good spirit can be white although the outside can be dark." (Ibid: 94)

105 For further information on the relation between the deceased and his/her house and material belongings as well as about the spirit houses the deceased will stay in during his passage to after-life, see the work of Boas (1888: 590f., 592, 612; 1901: 144f.).

insights. The experiences of the evening not only changed his perceptions of himself and of his home, but also his perceptions of the settlement (houses), of social relations, and of religious practices and beliefs – of life in general, thus:

> I believed in God deep inside, but it was not relevant for my life. In my own experience it was 11 or 12 p.m. at night, it became Sunday. I walked out in a different community, I saw a different house. I had always walked face down. I saw perfect corners at houses, corners in windows, which were perfect. My inside was so happy, every person seemed to be happy to me. I went to the Anglican Church service. They had read the same stuff every Sunday, saying the same words every Sunday. They had never prayed for me. The sermon [had been] tiring. That Sunday, when they read the same stuff, the words became alive. They touched my heart. I just cried. The sermon was different, too. Words were sharp and full of love. [...] I started to feel for people. I know when they need help; I know their pain; I can feel it. I cried with them, not just in church. Christians are one body, one spirit. All are one person.

Looking back, Sami found that his experiences were not unique. Being a religious leader himself today, he has been involved in a number of similar situations in which people with social or spiritual difficulties called for religious treatment. He concluded: "I never experienced exactly the same, but something similar, when we prayed for a house. For example for a troubled family, suicidal youth, people, who cannot sleep, because they feel a presence or being watched."

The second example of a conversion story was told by Peepeelee Nutaralak, an elderly woman. Her conversion experiences were foreshadowed in a dream vision she had as a child:[106]

> I always had a dream when I was growing up and I was sick all the time. [I dreamt that] there is a healing spirit and that we can change our lives and become better, if we want to become a better person. I dreamt that everything is possible, healing within yourself either spiritually or mentally. I also dreamt that I would reach the river and as I reached the river I was healed of the sickness I always had. It actually happened [by that dream] and I was healed.

Like Sami, Peepeelee focussed on the moment she developed the wish to improve her life:

> Looking far back at my life right now, I have a so much better life than I did in the past. I went to church all the time as a child and as an adult, but nothing changed. I always had hardships. I always was unhappy. I did whatever I wanted to do, things which belong to the earth. I drank and I committed adultery and think about leaving my husband and divorcing him. But then I was afraid of doing all this, because when I started to see myself and started to look at myself, I was afraid of going to hell with eternal burning. I started to search how to better myself.

Like Sami, she repented and wished to 'clean' herself from her old life. She realized that she had been helped by God when she observed herself to act differently in social life:

---

106 The reference to a memorable childhood experience is a *topos* often used in Inuit conversion stories. See also Pauloosie Kunilusie's story of becoming a church leader.

When I started to seek for forgiveness, I didn't know right away that I had been forgiven. I started to notice that I had been forgiven when I began to say '*akuluk*'[107] to my sister's youngest son, to whom I had never said nice words. I started to love him. That is how I started to change and I was healed with Jesus' blood.

She concluded her story stating that there are still difficulties in her life, but that she would not feel touched by them in the same way as she was before. Her newly established relationship with God found expression in improved social relationship and increased self-control, a highly valued social skill:

Ever since I had Jesus in my heart, he keeps me happy and he keeps me company, even if I go through lots of sorrow and some days I feel hopeless. That goes away when I pray. I have a more relaxed life. Although I get angry at times and say harsh words [to my husband], it is not an ongoing thing, we solve it right away. [...] I have a soul which I don't want to be thrown to hell and I have to keep myself clean and ready for whatever had been set-up for me to do.

Peepeelee Nutaralak and Sami Qappik both chose to undergo baptism in the Holy Spirit, emphasizing that it would mark a new beginning, a new 'childhood'. Sami Qappik explained the meaning of baptism in the Holy Spirit:

The old self dies, the old person dies. If you were swearing, because of little mistakes or being mad, it slowly dies. The old self is crucified. Baptism symbolizes that the old life is dead and the new life comes. I can't say it through words.

Also Loie Mike, ordained Anglican minister in Qikiqtarjuaq in 1998/1999, was baptized in the Holy Spirit. She talked about her view on the 'old' and the 'new life':

Before Sin happened, we were like God, because we were made in the image of God. [Because of the Sin] the spirit that was able to make man live like God died. When you are born again, you are brought back into the paradise. New life begins. [...] When you are baptized as a baby you are brought back into the family of God. When you grew up, you rebelled. So you must be born again in the spirit. When you got baptized you are back in the family of God totally. [...] You can't go into the kingdom of God, not by good works. You have to be born again.

Discussion

In all three accounts, religious transformation and social restoration were combined. The close connection between the two domains was also stressed in the use of language: Religious relations were articulated in social terms. And counseling to deal with difficult social relations often referred to a Christian framework and frequently started with the improvement of religious relations before dealing with the social issue at hand.

---

107 *Akuluk* is used as an expression of intimacy. It translates as 'I care for you', 'I like you', or 'my dear one'. It is used for children, for family members, for spouses, and occasionally for good friends.

The transformation experienced by Sami Qappik, Peepeelee Nutaralak, Loie Mike, and many others in their relationship to God was conceptualized as a new beginning, frequently phrased in terms of leaving the old life behind and starting all over as a child. What was left behind, were, in particular, relationships that turned dysfunctional because of the improper conduct of the person seeking renewal. In the second chapter, *Life in Qikiqtarjuaq*, I described how infants were perceived and dealt with in the household. They were treated with much affection and ease. When they did not behave well, it was an occasion of amusement for adults, rather than a time for correction. Inuit believe that young children simply did not have the mental capabilities (*isuma*) that would enable them to control themselves and understand what was right or wrong. At the same time, children were born into a large social network of relatives and frequently of adoptive relations. These relations were functional and could not be disturbed by improper behavior of the child itself. This would change as soon as the child developed sufficiently to acquire the skills and the knowledge to negotiate relations and would then be held responsible for his/her deeds.

The child was also part of cosmological relationships. It received names of deceased persons and was thereby linked not only to the living name-relatives, but also to the ancestors. It was baptized in the Anglican Church or, more seldom, dedicated at the Full Gospel Church and was thereby placed into a relationship with God. The relationship to God was assumed to be functional, even though the young child could not be held responsible for his/her conduct. It was believed that once the child acquired the necessary capabilities of adulthood, it would not transgress the rules associated with that relationship and thereby turn away from God. The articulation of transformed religious and social relations in terms of becoming a child and making a new beginning suggest that the conduct leading to dysfunctional relations and the disturbed relations themselves were removed from the person of the proselyte. The proselyte could start over again with a new social and Christian identity.

Loie Mike associated the transformation into a 'child' with becoming part of the family of God again. Sami Qappik connected his experiences of transformation with changes in the conditions of the house,[108] and Peepeelee Nutaralak talked about how the relation to her husband changed after she went through the process of transformation. All three articulated the renewal of their religious relations in terms of or in reference to close kinship relations. In the first part of this chapter on Christianity in Qikiqtarjuaq, we also heard Pauloosie Kunilusie telling his story by repeatedly referring to issues of his family life. Furthermore, we will encounter this *topos* also in the following paragraphs on the baptism in the Holy Spirit. Household relations are the focal point in processes of social and spiritual transformations. This points to the centrality of the household formation in Inuit social organization. It is in this configuration that relations have to be appropriate in order for an individual to be a functioning community member and a potential social partner.

Is this a feature linked to Pentecostal belief and practice alone? Having a family and taking care of its well-being is highly valued among Inuit. The Anglican Church has been involved in helping when problems arose. We heard Pauloosie Angmarlik, who most clearly expressed his disapproval of the new ways, say that he perceived family and other social issues to be at the center of his responsibilities as a church leader. The relevance of the family in a church leader's life should even have priority over the leader's responsibilities towards others. Both Pentecostal and traditional Anglican Inuit became concerned if the activities of believers and leaders were to

---

108 See the relation between the house and the people living in it as discussed above.

a large degree consumed by their religious responsibilities. It was not only seen as improper social behavior but also as improper Christian behavior. Under no condition whatsoever should one neglect one's children. We saw that Loie Mike, for example, explained that she needed to reduce her call-outs in order to spend more time with her family. She did so by reviewing her beliefs and practices and found that she made a mistake by not realizing that everyone had the power to deal with spiritual mishaps. A last indication, though of a different kind, of the relevance of the family in the Christian framework is that among Pentecostal and traditional Anglican women alike it was a widely spread practice to carry pictures of one's closest family in the Bible. Though the Pentecostal framework is presently privileged to articulate experiences of transformation and dealing with social and religious difficulties, the centrality of one's household and family relations within the Christian framework is not bound to a person's religious practices.

With the adjustment of these relations, wider social relations also improve, as was described by Sami Qappik and Peepeelee Nutaralak. According to Peepeelee:

> If there were a lot of people who understood the meaning of the Holy Spirit and the flow of the spirit, people would be able to communicate now and be able to work together as a whole. If everybody understood each other and if all the people understood the meaning of the Holy Spirit people would be able to live peacefully within the community.

Baptism in the Holy Spirit

The belief of healing a person by changing his/her social and cosmological identity is not new to Inuit. Authors such as Boas (1888: 612; 1907: 494f.), Nelson (1900: 289), and Rasmussen (1931: 150) described such practices in Inuit groups from Davies Strait and Ponds Inlet, from the Bering Strait area, and the Netsilik area. One way of treating sickness and other afflictions was by changing the person's name. This made him/her 'new'[109] in respect to his/her social and cosmological identities. Although Inuit do not change their names during processes of conversion,[110] an increasing number of them restore the relationship to God implied in the Anglican baptism by a baptism in the Holy Spirit.[111]

The baptism service of January 19th, 2000

Pastor Billy Arnaquq and the Anglican Bible Study group, led by Imona and Uluta Kuksiak, had for weeks prepared a number of young men and women for their baptism. At the evening of the baptism the *upirlirtuit* (those who were sinners and became believers; proselytes' met in a side room of the church and prayed. Meanwhile the main building filled with the young people's parents, families, friends, and others until all seats were occupied and many people had to remain standing. A water basin, long and deep enough for complete immersion, stood in front of the altar and it was there that Pastor Billy Arnaquq opened the service:

---

109 See for an explicit example Boas 1907: 494 on healing practices of an Inuit group of Pond Inlet. The patient receives a new name from a spirit. Then the *angakok* says, Let us cut this child's navel-string.' [...] Next the *angakok* questions the guardian spirit as to what taboo the man is to have in the future. [...] By this performance the patient is 'made new'.

110 Though some experienced that they got to know their 'real name' mostly only known to God.

111 Names received from the deceased are not addressed in this respect. Namesake relations may be addressed indirectly in the changes converts perceive to take place in their social lives.

We had been preparing for this evening all afternoon. I want to sing a song which I translated when my wife and I separated.[112] We have to keep feeding ourselves that we will not be tempted and that we will keep our faith. My wife, Silasie Alikatuqtuq, and I were the first three people to be baptized, in 1981 I believe it was. At that time, most people were against our religion and now people say that they rejected something which is gentle, full of love, and beautiful.

Having established a sense of community-wide support for the young people's enterprise,[113] he then referred to the larger spiritual context of the work of the Holy Spirit, in which the present baptism would take part:

I bought holy water in Israel and it will be added to the water which we will use for baptizing these people. It is from Jesus' birthplace. I heard Benny Hinn at one time – and I know it is not from him, I know it is directly from God himself – he indicated that in the year 2000, God's Spirit will be working more than ever. There are seven people who will be baptized. If anyone wants to talk about his/her experience being baptized – they will all be blessed and will be happier.[114]

Four persons, Jacopie and Leetia Kuksiak, Loasie Kunilusie, and Yukipa Audlakiak accepted his invitation. We are already familiar with the first three as leaders of the Anglican church. Jacopie and Leetia Kuksiak as well as Yukipa Audlakiak were furthermore parents of proselytes. First, Jacopie Kuksiak took the opportunity to testify:

I used to pray to God seeking for His guidance and I kept praying, but He did not listen to me. I got upset at God and I asked Him why he is never answering me. After I had said that, fear came to me and fear was directed to me and to others. If I am going to be like this, upset over God, then I am nothing in front of him, I have no power whatsoever. And I started to fear God and I said: 'Do what you please to me, to my family and children.' [...] My wife was in Iqaluit and I had no plan of any kind and I heard that there was going to be a baptism service. And out of nowhere, I got up, went to church and practically jumped into the water. Baptism is very good. I've never told my children to do this and that. I just waited for them to make their own choice and now one of my children is one of the ones who will be baptized.

As in other stories of conversion, he emphasized the transformation of a dysfunctional relation to God, marked by ineffective prayers, into a proper relation. In Sami Qappik's and Peepeelee Nutaralak's stories of conversion, social relations were affected by changes in cosmological relations. Jacopie Kuksiak also refers to the relevance of his own transformation for his family.

---

112 She is the daughter of Pauloosie Kunilusie. After being divorced, they got married again later on.

113 In the first part of this chapter, we saw that the leaders of the new Church wanted to avoid polarization within the community. The community should not be divided along denominational lines. Emphasizing the unity of the community in relation to God, he tried to prevent baptism from disrupting social relations of the proselytes.

114 Note the positive value associated with the practice of sharing a spiritual experience publicly that we already saw in the paragraphs on testimony and confession.

Having transformed his own relationship to God, he made his family part of it. Though they would be autonomous in establishing their own relations, their future alliance was prepared by the father through extending the sphere of influence of his own relation to include his children.

Then Leetia Kuksiak, his wife, shared her experiences of being baptized in the Spirit with the congregation:

> I was also baptized in Iqaluit and it is such a peaceful feeling. I was baptized as a child, but I mistreated my baptism by doing wrong. I got baptized, because I was thinking to change myself and to become a Christian.

Billy Arnaquq commented: "God asks us to come to Him from childhood on. God uses children although they are just children. We have to pray first before we start doing anything. Always think of Him first." Next, Loasie Kunilusie combined his testimony with preaching:

> When I was baptized, I saw myself lifted up to heaven and I saw myself talking to God saying that he will always be my God. If we want to follow God, we have to follow Jesus' footsteps. Getting baptized is cleansing ourselves from all the dirt that has smeared our soul. When we are baptized, it is a beginning. The old us is killed and the new us arises.

The last person to speak was Yukipa Audlakiak:

> I have prayed for my children and tried to have patience, because God works in mysterious ways. And now, my son will be baptized, too. God answered my prayer. I have given God permission to do with my children as he pleases. I think of my son when he was an infant.

She, as Jacopie Kuksiak before, emphasized the giving over of her children to God as part of her own relationship with God. In this context, she visualized her grown-up son to be an infant – the age of a new beginning, as we saw earlier. Billy Arnaquq added:

> His father used to talk to me about wanting his children to become Christians and he used to say that this son is the most hard-headed and stubborn. He always said that he feared that this son will be the one who will be hardest to pray for, due to his addictions. And he is the first child who wants to be baptized and we are both surprised. This shows that God works in mysterious ways.

The testimonies were followed by songs and readings from the Bible. Finally, the service approached the actual performance of immersing the candidates for baptism into the water. The pastor explained:

> A few years back, it was really scary to do any of this, because people were so against this and doors in their hearts were not open. But now it is different. People are starting to understand God. If we say that we were baptized as infants and we will not be baptized again, we shouldn't say that. We could harden our hearts and it will be difficult for Jesus to enter our hearts and we should listen to God. If we feel we should be baptized, it is coming from God.

Having emphasized once again the unity of the community in reference to the Christian framework, he concluded the preparation of the baptism with a last testimony of the healing power of the baptism connecting also a person's physical being to the processes of doing wrong and renewal:

> Being baptized, God heals. My father-in-law, Pauloosie, used to have major rash and mucus would come out of that spot and it was gross, it couldn't heal. After he had been baptized, that same evening, he was healed. He did not notice right away, but he noticed when he went to bed. This problem was a problem from his teenage years and it was gradually getting worse over the years, but it healed within hours after he had been baptized. That problem never occurred after that again. The old lives will decay and new life will surface.

Then the candidates for baptism were called forward, one by one. The congregation sang gospel songs and Billy Arnaquq spoke the baptism formula. He and Lootie Toomasie stood at the left and right of the candidate supporting him/her when he/she fell backward into the water. A moment later, the two helpers took him/her out again and the young man or woman emerged with raised hands, gleaming face, screaming and crying with joy, laughing, and praising the Lord. The congregation appeared to be touched by this sight and some joined the expressions of joy of the candidates or applauded. The baptized person was taken by helpers to a side room to dress in dry clothes. After all of them had gone through the process, the service was closed and people went home.

The assessment of the baptism was the issue of various opinions in the community; and not all people were as enthusiastic as the participants of the service described above. Whereas a few people were still outright against this practice,[115] others supported it even though with doubts about the quality of the preparation of proselytes in the context of the Churches and related activities. These doubts were generated by observations that some people fall back into their 'old ways' soon after their proclaimed conversion. A middle-age woman explained:

If they were getting the right message, why would they want to go back to drinking and doing drugs again? The biggest problem is that they felt really good about themselves for a little while you know, after being cleansed or whatever, but they have all these issues inside their head that they have to deal with.

3.3.5 Death, funerals, and spirits

Proper ways of Christian and social life were perceived not only to be relevant for one's existence as a living person here on earth, but also for one's existence after death. A person's way of life was thought to determine his/her after-life. And again how a person exists in the after-life was thought to have effects on those living in the community. I will elaborate these issues in the following paragraphs on death and funeral.

---

115 Pauloosie Angmarlik, former Anglican lay-reader in Qikiqtarjuaq and decidedly against the new Christian ways, commented rather dryly on the baptism practice:

It is quite dangerous, from my point of view, when they push them inside the water. It could be dangerous, if the person was not ready. He could inhale water and that is very dangerous. Anglican Church does not do that, so I do not really have an understanding about the way [of the other Church].

Death

In Qikiqtarjuaq, most Inuit agreed that when a person dies the *timi* ('body') and *isumatak* ('mind') perish, whereas the *tarniq* ('soul') enters the after-life. Some added that people also have the *anirniq* ('spirit, breath') which belongs to the soul and survives death as well. The *atiq* ('name') of the deceased is perpetuated when babies receive the name of a deceased. Pastor Billy Arnaquq addressed the features and relationships between *tarniq* ('soul'), *anirniq* ('spirit'), *isumatak* ('mind'), and *timi* ('body'):

> The soul is our own spirit, spirit of God, your real you. Our personality is located there. The real Nicole is a 'spirit woman'. [...] It is important to have respect for others. Be careful with being pushy. It is a spirit matter. God created spirits because he is spirit. Everything we do starts in the spirit, then it manifests. We are living in a spirit world. We are spirits, too. There is good and bad in the spirit world. In the spirit realm there is order and life. When we change toward our spirit being we change from corruptible into incorruptible, imperishable. Like Jesus did after rising from the dead. The spirit is God's breath. It is of eternal being. It responds to the decisions of the soul. The spirit does not make decisions. The soul is will, emotions, intellect. It makes decisions, it controls. The soul allows the spirit to respond to God. Soul and spirit belong together. The mind is part of nature. It is where our thinking and decision making is located. The mind is like a door: you can open and you can close it. The body is a corpse when soul and spirit are not there.

People pointed out to me that there are individual differences in thinking about body, soul, mind, and spirit. These differences are not perceived to be a problem. Billy Arnaquq's view is one among various others. His basic assumptions, however, that individuals received a unique soul, a unique 'true personality' from God, and that all human beings have that relationship to God in common, are shared by most Inuit. In social life, people place high value both on the individuality of a person as well as on a basic sameness – everybody is different and nobody should pressure others, and one should not be judgmental about others. The relationship to God through the soul and the spirit is innate to the human person. At the same time, the relationship generated in this way has to be maintained by proper conduct and can be damaged by improper conduct. In case of damage, the relationship has to be renegotiated. Besides this widely shared model, pastor Billy Arnaquq pointed to the necessity of conversion in order to maintain the relationship with God.

It is a widely shared view that the personality of an individual is also influenced by the names received as a baby from recently deceased people.[116] Many Inuit believed that a name, besides transferring kin relations, also somehow carries characteristics of the deceased that could influence the child's personality. Although people of Qikiqtarjuaq had various opinions about this matter, they agreed that the transfer of the name is a consolation for the bereaved who can visit, look at, talk to, and touch the namesake baby. Some babies were named at the expressed request of the deceased who had made the arrangements before his/her death.

After-life

The name remained with the living and connected them to the ancestors. The soul of the deceased, however, moved on. Beliefs about life after death were diverse in Qikiqtarjuaq. Some

---

116   See for a description of naming practices the chapter *Life in Qikiqtarjuaq*.

believed that when a person died, his/her soul would leave the body to go to paradise or hell to await Judgement Day. Some souls would be granted access to heaven and others were eternally lost. Others were convinced that everyone, including victims of suicide, believers and unbelievers, would go to heaven. Suicide victims were thought by some to reside in a special space in between earth and heaven. A woman who had attempted suicide told me about her near-death experience of being in a passage. On one side, separated only by an invisible wall, she saw carousels with people on them. Looking closer, she observed how suicide victims endlessly repeated their death while the carousel turned round and round. Deeply scared by these pictures, she prayed to return to her body and woke up in hospital.

A person's manner of death and social conduct were believed to have an influence on the deceased person's after-life. Deceased persons who could not find rest and desired to continue the social relationships of the living were believed to be dangerous. To see apparitions or to engage in conversation with the deceased was thought to be dangerous. A middle-aged woman told me about the fateful encounter of her son with the apparition of his friend who had committed suicide a few moments before. The young man saw the apparition in the mirror of his room. And, according to his mother, after this experience the young man started to get into all kinds of trouble and to be aggressive. She thought that one should better avoid speaking to or having contact with deceased people, not only for the sake of one's own well-being but also for that of the deceased, as their way to the after-world would be blocked by living people who try to communicate with them.

Several younger people told me of having seen apparitions of friends who committed suicide. The dead would be looking for company and trying to persuade friends and family members to join them. Some interpreted these apparitions as delusions by Satan, who would use the shapes of the deceased to persuade others to kill themselves as well. Others experienced that every year around the time a friend or family member had killed him-/herself, pictures of suicide victims forcefully come back to memory. One way of avoiding unwanted contact with spirits of the deceased was not to despair in the face of death, but to control one's grief.

Only a few people told me about positive experiences with the apparition of a deceased. One woman saw her grandfather who informed her that her afterlife would be good and that there was nothing she should worry about.

Various pre-Christian beliefs of life after death are taught at school during traditional knowledge classes. Children listen to old stories, for example about the Northern Lights who were said to be deceased Inuit playing a game of ball (see also, for example, Boas 1888: 590); or about people who were, according to their wish, reincarnated as animals, for example as seagulls. Most people I asked about these beliefs expressed that they were not sure what they thought about them, but that they could very well imagine that this or that relative would reincarnate as a seagull or polar bear.

Not only the spirits of deceased were believed by many Inuit to be (occasionally) present in the settlement, but also other beings populate houses, the nearby vicinity of the settlement, as well as specific places out on the land. I am not going deeper into the matter of Inuit beliefs in spirits. However, in order to indicate that the spirit world consists of a variety of beings and not only demons, I want to give a short overview of the spirit inhabitants of the community and the land used by the people of Qikiqtarjuaq. This overview is not intended to be conclusive.

Besides demons, spirits, such as *taraituq, anirniluk* and *anirniqtitauvut,* and *tungaq* ('monsters') share the island and the coast with the Inuit. *Taraituq* are transparent persons without a *taaq* ('shadow'). They had been real people before, live in long big houses and go hunting. Between the community and the garbage dump, some people believed that a camp of *taraituq*-spirits would live a life between the community and the garbage dump, just like the Inuit of former days – with dog team, *qammaq*, and skin clothing. There are places inhabited by *anirniluk* where many Inuit would not set up their camp, whereas others do not believe in the ghost stories and would go there as well as anywhere else. There is, for example, a particular stone at the shore close to the airport that is said to be inhibited by a spirit. *Anirniluk* are evil spirits, who have no shadow. Satanasi and demons are believed to focus on the spiritual, physical, and mental destruction of human beings. They can occupy houses[117] but also human beings. Many people consider that demons may be identical with the former helping spirits of shamans or with the evil spirits these shamans had to deal with. These beings evoke an eerie feeling. These spirits can also be associated with people who committed suicide. It is not clear to me if these are considered to be evil spirits or *tagaisu* ('smoke, ghost of a person who recently died') or if that concept refers to spirits of (some of) the dead in a more general sense. *Anirniqtitauvut* ('good spirits') are not often talked about. Pauloosie Kunilusie told one story of a woman who had resided in Atamie Nookiruaqs camp before people moved to Qikiqtarjuaq. She had visited in difficult times a spirit community close by and successfully asked the spirits for food. A*ingili* ('angels') are thought to be around people to protect them and may even reside in humans. Angel brooches, figurines, and illustrations are very popular and found in most households.

Funeral

Most Inuit believe that the soul of deceased people should leave human society to move into the realm of God. The funeral service I observed of the highly respected elder Atamie Nookiruaq that I will discuss below is representative of the way in which the funeral services were celebrated. Atamie Nookiruaq died in January, 2000. He was active as a volunteer in the Anglican Church, the community radio, a variety of committees, at school, and in the relation between R.C.M.P., community and offenders. Close relatives from outside Qikiqtarjuaq fly in with special airfares and the number of mourners grew to such an extent that the service had to be held in the school gym. His corpse was laid in a coffin that was stored in a little shack at the Anglican church building.[118] Before the service in the gym, the coffin was placed in the center aisle dividing the right and left rows of chairs in front of the altar. Loasie Kunilusie, a lay-reader in charge of the funeral, opened the service:

> We ask you, Lord, to be with us during this difficult time. Death is not the end, it is a whole new beginning.[119] A beginning of new life, where there is no pain, sorrow, hardship, worries, and destruction. Where there is a lot of love, understanding, happiness, worship, and harmony. Those, who believe in God, Holy Spirit, and Jesus Christ will have an everlasting life with the Lord. Our brother Atamie will welcome us and meet us when we are done with what God had planned for us.

Then, the congregation was invited to come forward to speak. Close family members, old friends, and representatives of committees to which the deceased had contributed pointed out their relationship with him and expressed their emotions and their esteem of the work and life

---

117   *Taitulik* ('haunted house').

118   I have not come across any specific beliefs related to the handling of the corpse.

119   Note the similarity with the vocabulary employed for the Spirit baptism at the Full Gospel Church.

of the deceased. His daughter, Geela Kunilusie, spoke on behalf of the family. She put her grief into perspective by honoring the deceased for his ideal social conduct in supporting others – because after his death people will follow his teachings – and by referring to the better life he has now. Loasie Kunilusie, her husband, continued her line of thought acknowledging the deceased's relevance to the community and his capability to deal with difficulties with the help of Jesus and God. He presented the deceased as a model of proper life in every possible respect and he advised everyone to follow his example in order, like the deceased, to reach heaven.

After the service, the coffin was taken outside by four men who regularly volunteered for these occasions. This was a moment of high emotional intensity. Close family members, mostly women, and close friends hugged each other crying; others remained on their chairs sobbing loudly. Meanwhile the truck transported the coffin to the graveyard up the hill outside the community. At the graveyard, each grave is marked by a cross and the name of the deceased. Artificial flower bouquets covered the grave's surface. Many crosses, in particular those of graves of people who died at a young age and often due to suicide, were decorated with little tokens of affection, such as tiny teddy bears, a plush-heart, a little carving, a coin, a necklace, or a picture, left there by family members or friends. The coffin of the elder was placed on a wooden platform that would later be covered with a wooden lid. The coffin would be buried when the soil thawed sufficiently in early summer. When the mourners had arrived at the wooden platform, the lay-reader read Bible verses and closed the ceremony with a prayer. Many people placed artificial flowers on the coffin before helpers covered it with a wooden lid. People went home and only the closest family had some refreshments together. Shops, which were closed during the ceremony, opened again and life recommenced. Later on in January, the postponed Christmas caribou feast was dedicated to Atamie Nookiruaq to honor him for always sharing whatever food he had when people came to visit. And soon after, two newborn babies received his name.

Discussion of the funeral
The various beliefs about after-life and spirits of the dead, the speeches held at the funeral, the decoration of the graves, and the naming practices all deal with the relationships between the living and the dead.

The most visible form in which the deceased are remembered in the community is by becoming ancestors through the naming practices. These practices perpetuate Inuit society through the continuation of names. Names are not objectified, but are linked to their bearers and connect them with each other. The dead are, thus, part of the community formation.

While Inuit wish the soul of the deceased to stay in God's realm in their after-life, there are numerous stories of encounters between the dead and the living. Particularly people who committed suicide, but also people who, for instance, were kept from moving to heaven by people wanting to talk with them, appeared to the living. These encounters were perceived in various ways, but in most cases, they were seen to present substantial danger to the well-being and even the life of community members contacting them.[120] These dead try to hold onto their

---

120 The belief in spirits of the dead who remain within the realm of the community and the harm caused by them is not new. Boas described beliefs about the threatening presence of the dead during camp times. Having, after death, stayed for three days with its dead body, the soul of a deceased person then "descends to Sedna's house. During its stay in Adlivun the soul is called tupilaq." The tupilaq did not stay in Sedna's house but tried to enter the houses of the living again and is feared as a malevolent spirit. One was safe inside a house as "the tupilaq is not allowed to enter the houses, and if the angakoq perceives and announce his presence no one

appearance and social identities, which is an endeavor to continue their old relationships. It is interesting in this context that especially the graves of young people – most, but not all, of whom died by suicide – were decorated with little tokens of affection. It may be significant that many of them are placed on the cross. Although I lack adequate data, I would like to suggest that they are meant to reassure the dead that relations towards him/her are positive and that s/he is not disregarded. I base this interpretation on gift giving practices[121] and on past funerals. People are free to choose to whom they want to give gifts. Having received a gift, there is no obligation to reciprocate. A gift expresses the perception of a relationship as valuable for the giver. Bringing a special little gift to the graveyard could thus express appreciation of the deceased person.

Besides being a token of affection, the token may in cases of suicide also be associated with feelings of having failed to prevent the person from dying. I know from many young people that they try their best to keep friends from committing suicide, when, for instance, the person will go to prison or has relationship problems.[122] Particularly since those who committed suicide tend to appear to friends to persuade them to follow them so as not to feel lonely, such gifts may be seen to comfort these dead. Especially placing items on the cross, itself, indicates that these items refer to the receiver as a person who is wished to reside with God in the after-world.

If my interpretation is adequate, it would indicate that people try to transform the potentially dangerous relationship with the troubled deceased into amiable relations wherein the deceased does not enter the settlement, but moves on to the realm of the dead. The assurance of the dead that they continue to be appreciated is not a new feature in Inuit culture. Boas, for example, reported that people frequently visited the grave of a recently deceased person. They engaged in an ordinary conversation, emphasized the goodness of the deceased person and how much s/he was liked, or they talk about the transfer of his/her name to a newborn baby. A deceased person was thought to become burdened by improper behavior of the living during the mourning period and would roam the camp trying to detach him/herself of it (Boas 1901: 144f.).

In the context of amiable relationships, such as expressed during the funeral of the elder Atamie Nookiruaq, the elder becomes an ancestor whose past life can guide the community and who can be remembered without danger. We encountered the transformation of spirits of the dead threatening the community into ancestors and namesakes with whom one could play the game of the dead in the Sedna festival described before.[123] There, the establishment of good relations with troubled dead were part of the rituals performed to ensure good hunting. Like troubled spirits of the dead in the past, today they are considered a danger to the individual, to social life, and thereby also to hunting success that is thought to be based on a functioning community in which all of the dead become ancestors.

---

would dare to leave the houses. His touch kills men at once, the sight of him causes sickness and mischief." Whereas deceased persons who led a proper life would move on to other realms of the dead, "murderers and offenders against human laws, after they have entered Sedna's house, will never leave it" (Boas 1888: 590f.).

121   See for a more detailed discussion the chapter on Christmas gifts.

122   Suicide among Inuit is a complex and not at all recent phenomenon (see Boas 1888: 589, 609 and Rasmussen 1929: 74, 95f.) and I am not going to deal with it in this study. What I am presenting here is based on statements made by Inuit in conversations.

123   See chapter *Life in Qikiqtarjuaq.*

3.4 Discussion of Christianity in Qikiqtarjuaq

In past camp times, cosmological relations were relevant to the formation of social relationships in Inuit camp communities. In previous chapters (see: *Theoretical background and methodology* and *Life in Qikiqtarjuaq*), the continuation of naming practices indicated that the cosmological and the social domains continue to be connected. Furthermore, Laugrand & Oosten (2002) argued that aspects of the Sedna festival that constituted community were incorporated into the Christmas celebrations in Inuit Christian camps of the past. With the movement to modern settlements, modes of social life changed. Discourses on proper social life and values often refer to a Christian framework. But Christianity itself is an issue of a dynamic discourse in Qikiqtarjuaq which during the last twenty years received a strong impetus from the adoption of Pentecostal beliefs and practices.

How, then, do cosmological relations articulated in a Christian framework continue to be of relevance for the formation of the modern community? To find an answer to this question, I first described and discussed the institutions of the Anglican and the Full Gospel Churches and church leadership in part one of this chapter. In respect to our question, we saw that Inuit are more concerned about questions of the proper practice of Christianity than about the corporate identities of the Churches. Part two of this chapter, then focussed on Christian beliefs and practices. A feature common to almost all practices discussed was that they were issues of ongoing discourses about proper ways of practicing faith. The relevance of propriety is based on Inuit perceptions that improper conduct, social or spiritual, has an immediate effect on the well-being of a person, his/her family, and the community. Social and spiritual difficulties were dealt with within a Christian framework, for instance by confessions or prayer sessions for a person and his/her house.

One measure taken was articulated in terms of Christian conversion. In most conversion stories, this transformation was described as replacing the 'old person' by a 'new person'. In particular the disturbed social and spiritual relationships of the proselyte were substituted by fresh relations – those of a 'child' unaffected by previous improper behavior. By changing the relational identity of a person, the person was 'healed' from the harmful effects of relations disturbed by his/her misdemeanors. This conversion could be manifested in a Pentecostal baptism in the Holy Spirit.

The central focus of these processes of transformation were the concepts of household and close kin relations, in particular the relation between parents and children. Even religious relations were described in terms of family relations. The house was perceived as a focal location of family life as well as a focal location of social life, and a place for religious practices. As indicated by Sami Qappik's expression of 'the house follows the person', the house, the focal point of family relations, was thought to be affected by the quality of the social and spiritual relationships of its inhabitants. It represents its inhabitants. It was not enough to 'heal' a member of the household's relationship, but also the house, representing the household, had to be treated. Only then could the individual again be functional in a larger social context. Comparing these perceptions and practices with those described by Boas, we find continuity in terms of the centrality of the household for the formation of the community.

Relationships with the dead also had to be properly established. If things went well, then the name of a deceased was given to a newborn baby and the soul of the deceased entered some location of after-life. Beliefs regarding the after-life varied among Inuit. Souls that remained or frequently returned to the settlement, for instance in form of apparitions, were in most cases perceived to be dangerous to the living. Which way a soul would go was thought to be linked to the deceased's way of life, but also to the proper conduct of the mourners. Focusing on one's grief or trying to get into contact with the deceased, for example, might keep the soul from leaving. The focus on affectionate and positive relations, as, for instance, expressed in the funeral ceremony as well as through the items of affection placed on the grave, showed that the dead are perceived to be remote but present.

Proper relationships were not only of relevance for social and Christian relations, but also to the wider framework of Inuit as hunters. Game animals were believed to require that all relationships of a hunter are functional, if and when they accept to be killed. Hunting is central to Inuit cultural self-perception.[124] In this chapter, I showed that in their social and spiritual efforts to constitute themselves as a hunting society, two feature were particularly marked: Firstly, the relevance of the Christian framework in renewing social as well as spiritual relations. And, secondly, the household and close family relations that were perceived to be, and were dealt with as, the central relationships. Only if they were functional could other social relations could be functional.

---

124 See chapters *Theoretical background and methodology* and *Life in Qikiqtarjuaq*. See also the chapter the *Christmas feast*.

Chapter 4
The seasonal cycle of Qikiqtarjuaq

4.1 Introduction

When I went to the mayor, Lootie Toomasie, to ask him for permission to extend my stay in Qikiqtarjuaq from seven months to more than a year, he welcomed my request, saying:

> It will be very good for you to stay the whole year round, because we have four seasons, spring, summer, fall, and winter. Each different season we deal with differently. So it is very good for you to learn from each season. Like in spring time, we go out on the land camping and seal hunting and all that. In summer time, we go boating and berry picking and so on. And in fall, people start to stay in the community, because it is starting to get too cold, but the hunters are still hunting a lot on the water. [...] As soon as the ice freezes up, it is winter.

The contrasts between the seasons are marked and appreciated. Activities, movements to and from the settlement, and locations of residence vary with the time of the year; thus, temporality, locality and sociality are linked. Preferences concerning the advantage of each season will vary from one person to the other. Billy Arnaquq, a man in his forties, explained:

> Elders have a passion for spring, because the winter is so long and so cold. People always have a passion for when the spring is coming, the birds are coming, the animals are more plentiful. It's a time to go out and be part of, what you may say, the celebration. That is also a time that many people get together. [Hunting in that season] is something that is just so much part of you that you just go try to do it. [...] It is like that season comes for you to enjoy it. It is inside the people. Some men even have a passion for early fall, when the harvest is plentiful and the animals are migrating through. Some have a passion to go out seal hunting in the winter. Some of them cannot wait until it is frozen. [...] Once you are part of that, it just becomes part of you.

Lootie Toomasie and Billy Arnaquq refer to the seasons as combinations of the conditions of climate, of ice and ocean, and of animal migrations. While participating in the seasonal cycles from winter 1999 till spring 2001, I observed that the contrasts between the seasons determine the day to day practices. People moved to different localities according to the season, formed distinct social configurations, and participated in seasonal tasks. How do the seasonal patterns of dispersal and concentration operate in the formation of Inuit community?

4.2 The ritual cycle

In the pre-Christian past, the annual cycle of the nomadic society was organized by ritual injunctions and seasonal celebrations.[125] Ritual injunctions marked the transition of seasonal hunting practices. Boas, for instance, reported that deerskins obtained in summer might not be worked on until the sea-ice formed and the first seal was caught. And "later, as soon as the first walrus is caught, the work must stop again until the next fall. [...] All families are eager to finish the work on deerskins as quickly as possible, as the walrusing season is not commenced until that is done" (Boas 1888: 595).

Seasonal celebrations took place either on an annual basis or incidentally. For instance, when a whale was caught, the people present came to feast together (Boas 1888: 603). The only annual celebration Boas referred to is the Sedna festival. "At this season the great religious feasts of the natives are celebrated, which announce, as it were, the commencement of winter" (Boas 1888: 578). Apparently, the transition from the open sea to the frozen sea season was especially marked, whereas the transition from winter to the open sea season was not, except by ritual injunctions pertaining to the work with game. The Sedna festival linked the Inuit community to their game animals, to Sedna the sea-woman, and to the dead.[126] It organized the nomadic society in connection to the cosmos. Before the introduction of Christianity, calendars, and clocks, Inuit did not have a fixed or formalized measurement of time. Franz Boas wrote in 1888:

> The Eskimo have a sort of calendar. They divide the year into thirteen months, the names of which vary a great deal, according to the tribes and according to the latitude of the place. The surplus is balanced by leaving out a month every few years, to wit, the month *siringlang* (without sun), which is of indefinite duration, the name covering the whole time of the year when the sun does not rise and there is scarcely any dawn. [...] The days of the month are very exactly designated by the age of the moon. Years are not reckoned for a longer space than two, backward and forward (Boas 1888: 644 continued at 648; italics by A.N.St.).

Thus, Inuit notions of temporality were based on the situational reference to moon-months, the seasons, and astral correlations. Significant personal experiences, such as the first kill by a boy, and ritual periods, such as the Sedna festival, shaped Inuit notions of temporality of the yearly cycle. By examining the weather, the seasons, the animals, and the world of the spirits, the elders of a camp decided when to perform a seasonal ritual to ensure successful hunting and a prosperous camp.

With the introduction of Christianity, new forms of temporality were implemented.[127] Inuit made considerable efforts to observe the western temporal structures of day and week units in

---

125   See for a discussion of Inuit periodicity as expressed in Inuit mythology van Londen (1994).

126   See Franz Boas' description of the festival in the introduction chapter.

127   Holidays are ordered in an annual ritual cycle which organizes the society's temporality. Individual holidays may or may not carry a temporal component. For example, Christmas is scheduled to take place at the winter solstice – a time which was recognized in many pre-Christian western cultures by festivals and was adopted into the Christian ritual cycle. In many Christian Churches at Christmas time, the priest interprets Jesus Christ's birth in analogy to the solstice referring to the return of the light. Other temporal associations of Christian holidays are often lost sight of. For example, it is little known and not particularly valued that Easter is scheduled at the day of the first full moon after beginning of spring. Other celebrations, for instance Mother's Day, do not carry a temporal component.

order to be sure not to miss the Sabbath to which special rules pertain. Noah Piugaattuk from Igloolik recalled in interviews with John MacDonald in 1991:

> The concept of keeping one day a week to observe Sundays was passed from person to person. [...] The people knew in advance that there would be a number of days without restrictions or taboos followed by one day that should be observed (MacDonald 1998: 204).

He further explained how they kept track of the Sunday without having calendars:

> The women of the camp would consult each other [to determine Sunday] and, after that, they made sure to keep track of the days, making a mark on [a piece of wood] for each day that passed. Whoever was recording the days would make sure not to lose their record (MacDonald 1998: 204f.).

> Certainly there were times when two people, from different camps, met on the trail and exchanged stories and so forth, and wondered which day it was. During periods of intense hunting no attention was paid to days (or nights). [The hunters] would not keep track of time. This responsibility usually fell to the ones who were not engaged in doing other things ... One must realize that, at times, the hunters would not sleep for days on end when hunting conditions were favorable. Under these circumstances they would, no doubt, lose count of the days. But there were always elders that kept the track of time for the rest of the camp (MacDonald 1998: 205).

After their conversion to Christianity, Inuit have observed the Sabbath and have celebrated Christmas for about a hundred years. Christmas was celebrated by Inuit as well as by resident Qallunaat and had been an occasion of Inuit-Qallunaat interaction. Later on, other liturgical holidays such as Good Friday and Easter were integrated into the Christian ritual cycle. With the establishment of modern communities, new holidays, such as Canada Day or Hamlet Day, were introduced.

The communities of Nunavut started to follow the holiday cycle of civic and Christian holidays familiar to the Western World.[128] Presently, hardly three or four weeks pass by without a celebration in Qikiqtarjuaq. The following list gives an overview of the annual civic and liturgical holidays celebrated in Qikiqtarjuaq in the year 2000:[129]

Date	Holiday[130]
January 1st	New Year's Day
February 14th	Valentine's Day
April 21st	Good Friday

---

128 Although Western states are secular organizations, with a separation between State and Church as a fundamental organizing principle, Christian holidays are included in the list of holidays in a secular fashion, indicating a day free of work but without comment on the relevance of the holiday in religious terms.

129 Holidays such as Pentecost or Epiphany are not part of the list as they are not especially observed in the community.

130 In addition, the school regularly holds graduation ceremonies to which the community is invited. The municipality organizes local or regional sport tournaments and provides occasional community celebrations

April 23th/24th	Easter
May 14th	Mother's Day
May 22nd	Victoria Day, annual Fishing Derby (20th -22nd)
July 1st	Canada Day
July 9th	Nunavut Day
August 7th	Civic Holiday
August 31st	QIA celebration
September 4th	Labor Day
September 17th	Terry Fox Run
October 1st	(moved to October 9th
because of narwal hunt)	Hamlet Day
October 9th	Thanks Giving
October 26th	Annual community feast provided by the Hunters and Trappers Organization
October 31st	Halloween
November 11th	Remembrance Day
November 12th	Alcohol Awareness Day
December 24th-26th	Christmas Eve, Christmas Day, Boxing Day; Christmas was celebrated from about the third week of December (for example staff Christmas dinners) till the first week of January.

This holiday cycle provides Qikiqtarjuaq, formally, with a fixed formal temporality in reference to the yearly cycle. But, not all holidays are valued in the same way. The more recently implemented holidays usually have a different value for Inuit than the Christian holidays, in particular Christmas, that have been long integrated. Inuit perceive that Christmas is an indispensable community event at which the community is renewed while celebrating the birth of Jesus Christ. In this way, the Christmas festival shapes the temporality of Qikiqtarjuaq. The more recently introduced holidays often mark social or political occasions that are perceived by Inuit to be of relatively little relevance to community life. Furthermore, several of the holidays take place during times of community dispersion in spring and summer. People do not return to the settlement for these occasions nor do they celebrate any holiday in the camps. Still, most holidays are celebrated in the settlement, translated into feasts and games and financed by government institutions. The efforts to provide festivities irrespective of the local Inuit seasonal cycle of concentration and dispersion reflects the value governmental institutions attach to sedentary community life.

4.3 The seasons

Lootie Toomasie informed me: "The season is already winter [...] as soon as the ice freezes". Inuit divide the seasons in connection to the breaking up and formation of sea-ice. The condition

---

for visiting government committees, passing expeditions, or other special events. In 2000, the new Co-op store organized an opening celebration for the entire community. Others festivities which involve the community are life-cycle events such as baptisms, funerals, and weddings. First kill celebrations are often held in hunting camps. The boy who killed his first game shares it with the entire camp (or community), without eating from it himself.

of the ice determines game migrations, the travel possibilities, and hunting methods. Between periods of open and solid frozen sea are a number of transitional phases, all of which require specific hunting techniques and modes of transport. Inuit distinguish between these periods in discourses on hunting, traveling, and other outdoor occupations. The year is divided into four principal periods:[131]

1. 'Spring' *upirnaaq* starts in mid April when the sea is still frozen and the sun above the horizon. It ends when, about the mid of June, the advancing break-up of the sea-ice obstructs further travel by snowmobile.
2. 'Summer' *aujaq* extends from about July till the end of September. Summer is marked by an open sea and by snow-free land.
3. 'Autumn' *ukiaq*, starts in October and lasts until the end of November. It becomes much colder and around early November the sea begins to freeze up.
4. 'Winter' *ukiuq* is marked by a frozen sea.

Beside dividing the year into periods that focus on changes in the weather, ice conditions, plant growth, and animal migrations, and related hunting and gathering techniques, Inuit also talked about the seasonal cycle in terms of movement between the settlement and camps. There are periods of concentration in the settlement during periods of freeze-up and break-up of the sea-ice as well as during mid-winter, and periods of camping, in spring and summer. As each season has its own activities, besides variations in location and social formations, I decided to structure this chapter according to the sequence of the four seasons described above rather than according to the sequence of the practices of community concentration and dispersal to camps.

4.3.1 Upirnaaq – Spring

The sun rises above the horizon after the long and dark winter months, and it becomes warmer.[132] In early spring, the snowy surface of the sea-ice melts during the day and freezes over at night, forming a hard crust. This process provides optimal travel conditions on the sea as well as on the land during the night and early morning hours. The sun is up a bit longer each day, and the melting of the ice and snow accelerates. In late May the sea-ice starts to break up. Due to the increased humidity, fog forms almost daily in June. Inuit will keep on traveling by snowmobile until the water puddles on the ice become too deep, the ice too thin and the cracks too broad, which occurs around July.

After a more or less sedentary winter, early and especially mid spring are the main periods of the year to start camping. By mid May, most families of Qikiqtarjuaq are out on the land in their camps. This can be for a few days, but is often for several weeks. Families with school-age children either confine their trips to weekends and school holidays, or they arrange babysitters for the time of their absence.

People of all age-groups participate in camping. Older teenagers, however, frequently decide to stay in the community. They told me about feeling bored or homesick when camping.

---

131   These categories were used in conversations with me and among Inuit when referring to the basic outline of the year into its major periods. For detailed subdivisions see MacDonald (1998).

132   In 2000, the mean temperature in March was -27.2 °C, in April it was -13.2 °C (Environment Canada Monthly Data Report for 2000, url: http://www.climate.weatheroffice.ec.gc.ca/climateData/monthlydata_ e.html).

Picture 19 *Geela Kunilusie, Alice Keyooktak, and the author cleaning goose-down in a spring camp on Pilaktuak Island (courtesy of Taiviti Nuqingak).*

Husband and wife usually prepare together for camping. They pack the sled, and together with their children and other members of the household and relatives they travel to the camp site.

Often two or three snowmobile-sled teams will travel jointly to assist each other, for the eventuality that a sled become stuck or a machine should break down. The teams stop for a hot drink and a snack every hour or two. The tea breaks are welcome occasions to socialize with fellow travelers and passers-by. Married children with their families frequently join their parents' camp, but have separate tents or shacks. Other relatives or close friends may also join. There are camps from one to about four or five tents or shacks, ranging from about four to 15 persons. As soon as the camp is set up for the night or for the coming weeks, people use radio telephones to inform each other of the latest news, the ice and weather-conditions or missing persons. Others send friends a personal message or share an amusing experience.

The camps are located in areas that provide good sealing and/or fishing opportunities. These sites are often used for several years and by several generations.[133] Families which are associated with the former camp-settlements of Padloping, to the south, and Kivitoo, to the north, have their camping sites in those areas. People associated with the Cumberland Sound region select camp sites to the north[134] as well as to the south of Qikiqtarjuaq. Beautiful landscapes, and

---

133 Jassie Kunilusie, a man in his fifties, for example, told me that he was going to camp at a place where he knows the land and ice very well, since he went there every year with his parents.

134 To the north, camp sites were situated up to the vicinity of Home Bay. Even though a number of relatives of Qikiqtarjuaq families were living close by to Clyde River, various people told me that they consider the ways of life and language as practiced in Clyde River to belong more to northern Baffin than to the south, to which Qikiqtarjuaq belongs. Hall Beach was considered as a region of overlap.

the presence of friends or other members of the family in the vicinity, are also appreciated in the choice of a camp location. Older people often decide to establish their camp closer to the community than in previous years, because provisions can be replenished more easily and health care is closer.[135]

Some camps are situated in isolation while others are set up in a cluster of three or four adjacent sites. More distant camps do not socialize much with each other, but passers-by shake hands and enjoy a cup of tea or an overnight stay. People said that nobody would be a 'visitor' (*pulaiaqti* 'somebody visiting from another community') because everybody would know each other. Guests are invited to sit along the sidewalls or close to the door in a tent. If more closely acquainted, he/she is asked to sit on the sleeping platform with the family. Tea and bannock (pan-baked bread) stand ready and people serve themselves. When a hunter brings game to the camp, his wife prepares the seal, goose, fish, or caribou for everyone to eat.

People frequently told me that it is a tradition on these occasions to share a meal with the entire camp. Seal meat was prepared in a big pot from which everyone served him/herself. Part of the catch is cached for fermentation or brought to the community for storage in the freezer for later use. Particularly in June, some households and Inuit businesses, such as the pool-hall, in the community invite people via the local radio to pick up some game and fish. Sharing country

Picture 20 *While three men (to the left Loasie Kunilusie, to the right Pauloosie Keyooktak, in the middle Jaypootie Alikatuqtuq) butcher caribou, Gideon Keyooktak (to the left) gives his little brother, carried by its mother Alice in the amauti, a kunik (inhaling hard through the nose that touches the other person's skin).*

---

135   Most data concerning camp location and patterns of camp use were collected in a camp survey through interviews and a field-trip. Taiviti Nuqingak did most of the interviews and was my guide during the trip.

Picture 21 *The floe-edge, rich with animals (courtesy of Taiviti Nuqingak).*

Picture 22 *Checking the engine before the snowmobile race during the Easter festival.*

food is highly valued and is considered to be an obligation of the hunter and his family in respect to the game.

From early to late spring, various hunting techniques are applied. In April, baby seals are caught in their dens. The hunter jumps on the den, breaking through the ceiling and hooks the baby seal. A few weeks later, the older and the young seals, now called silver jars because of their pelt that turned from white to shiny grey, are basking in the sun. Hunters pursue them, camouflaged by white clothing and snowmobile covers. It is usually not difficult to find, approach, and shoot young seals at this time of the year as they are curious rather than alert. If they are wounded or otherwise hunted without skill, they are believed to remember the experience and will not show themselves to a hunter anymore. The fur of the silver jar is of high quality and considered to be particularly beautiful.

As freshwater lakes and rivers become ice-free, jigging and netting Arctic char is another productive activity. If caribou herds are sighted, hunters team up in small groups to hunt them. Geese are also welcome game. The down used by the geese to build their nests is collected from their breeding area, cleaned, and used for winter parkas or pants. Women process the game and the collected materials as much as possible in the camp.

In June, teams of hunters go to the floe-edge, which is rich with animals. They hardly ever take women with them. I was eager to go along with some hunters but, as a woman, I did not get an opportunity to do so. The hunters' wives, who had to work and stay in the community, assured me that it would be very comfortable, relaxed, and enjoyable in the community as the men's absence was an opportunity for a 'girls day out'. And indeed, women visited each other frequently and organized outdoor tea parties.

On Sundays, most of the hunters refrain from working and the women from processing the catch. People congregate in the morning in the biggest tent/shack for a short service. It is usually an elder or a lay-reader who leads the ceremony. Inuit take their Bible, prayer book, and song book to the camp. It is quite common to regularly read their Bible. The appropriate Bible texts for a particular day are chosen according to the itinerary of the Anglican Diocese's *Daily Bread*. Some people will bring a cassette player and a few tapes of (Inuit) Christian pop music.

Religious life is usually active in this period, before most people leave for the more extended camping expeditions in late May and early June. Just before Easter in 2000, a group of leaders and members of the Bible Study group from the Anglican church went to Clyde River for a Bible Conference. Billy Arnaquq, the pastor of the Full Gospel church, went to Chesterfield Inlet in early spring. In late April, he went with a group of followers, to a Bible conference in Akulivik. In May, a Youth Bible Study Conference was organized by the Anglican Church in Qikiqtarjuaq. A team of instructors from Northern Quebec was invited to lead the large and enthusiastic congregation in charismatic prayer, services, and teaching sessions. Shortly afterwards, the annual suicide prevention walk was organized by the Youth Committee. A group of about 15 teenagers and two leaders walked from Kivitoo to Qikiqtarjuaq. The walk was intended to build self-confidence.

The community and camp settings differ in respect to celebrations. Celebrations of the ritual cycle took place in the community rather than in the camps. People staying in camps do not celebrate the holidays, nor do they travel back to the community for the celebrations. Good Friday and Easter, at April 21st – 24th in 2000, were the first holidays in spring and many families were still in the community, as the school vacation had not yet started. On the Thursday before the holidays, the school organized an Easter festival for students, their parents, and the community elders, which was well-attended and moderately cheerful. The atmosphere changed considerably the next day – Good Friday. This day is perceived as the day that Jesus died on

Picture 23 *Preparing for a tug-of-war game during the Easter festival.*

the cross and it is a day of mourning. It was as if a member of the community had died. Stores were closed, people did not work, there was no laughter to be heard, and only a few people were to be seen outside. Saturday passed by somewhat gloomily. On Sunday, most adults and elders attended the Easter service at the Anglican church, which was held in a happy atmosphere. Outdoor games, such as snowmobile races, rope pulling, obstacle races, and harpoon throwing were attended by all age-groups with much merriment. The pool-hall was open for refreshments and people went there for coffee and to chat, and men played some rounds of checkers. A dance with modern pop music concluded the day. On Easter Monday, people were again working outside of their houses and repairing things, but the school and stores were closed.

Mother's Day, at the14th of May, 2000, was hardly celebrated. Children presented their mothers with drawings that they had prepared at school. On Victoria Day, at the 22nd of May, a Fishing Derby, introduced by the Nunavut agency *Papiruq Fisheries Enterprise* in 1997, is usually held. The Fishing Derby is the only occasion that the entire community goes out on the land to camp together. In 2000, it took place at Nalusiaq Lake, about a day's journey from Qikiqtarjuaq. People pitched their tents close to family members and friends and soon made visits. The fishing competition was held for two days. It was opened with a Church service and a meal of game and fish, which took place on a small plateau surrounded by high and steep mountains.[136]

Some people remained at the camp after the derby ended, but most others returned to their community, as children had to attend school. Also, considerable prizes, among them a snowmobile, were to be awarded in the community the following day. There were also people who did not participate in the derby, and had remained in the community. Some did not find an opportunity to travel; others were against fishing in the context of a competition, explaining

---

136 The Fishing Derby in 2001 was not opened with a service or a shared meal.

that killing animals as part of a game is disrespectful towards the animals causing animals to withdraw from the hunter/fisherman. Still other Qikiqtarjuaq wanted to enjoy the quietness in the community or did not like to be out on the land with so many people.

Around mid June the sea-ice was breaking up, and traveling by snow scooter became perilous. Families moved from the camps to Qikiqtarjuaq in time and stayed in the community until summer.

Inuit perceptions of spring

Inuit men and women anticipated the approaching spring camping season already after Christmas. As soon as the sun is above the horizon, people smile at each other walking on the street, laugh and admire the dark-white raccoon faces of the hunters who have already gone out hunting with sunglasses on.

In conversations on spring camping, Inuit usually referred to practices which are perceived to be truly Inuit and which are highly valued. Ipeelee Naujavik, an elderly man, opened a conversation on camping[137] making the continuity with the past explicit: "We always go camping

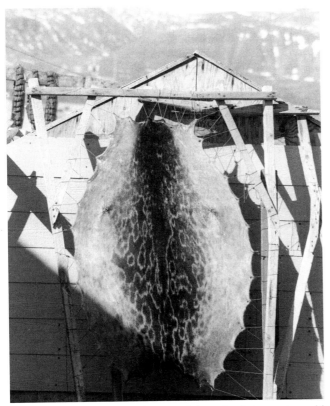

Picture 24 *Products of spring hunting: fish cut for drying and a sealskin stretched on a frame (courtesy Taiviti Nuqingak).*

---

137 The interview was done by Taiviti Nuqingak as part of a camp survey which we undertook.

when spring starts." Simo Alookie, another elderly man, valued the continuity in referring to his experiences of spring activities: "June is very short when you go around [doing things]. June is very short. It has always been like that."

There are many agreeable aspects of camping. And elderly woman, Aka Keyooktak, expressed her delight that "it is more beautiful in Ukialivik and in the different camps near Ukialivik." Sharing, eating country food, and socializing were the favorite elements for other women. As Aka Keyooktak stated enthusiastically, "I always like it when spring comes. Yes, I like it a lot when spring comes. We eat more healthy food when we are out camping." Leetia Kokseak added a social dimension to eating, "It is very good when you eat with your friends and family, when we are out on the land. When we eat with others, it is even more delicious."

The appreciation of spring camping is often expressed by contrasting it with living in the community. Younger and middle-aged people especially noted the contrast between community and camp-life.[138] According to Yukipa Audlakiak, a woman in her fifties, "camping is for resting, to have a good time. And for hunting. It is not possible like this in the community." Taiviti Nuqingak, a man in his thirties, added: "Camping is like holiday, getting out of the community, spending more time with the family and the kids. No TV, no toys, no stores." No TV, no toys, no stores – these are exactly the issues many teenagers addressed when they complained about feeling *iqianuq* ('bored') and *angiagasiq* ('homesick') in camp. Whereas most adults and elders take spring (and summer) camping as the 'normal' thing to do, many youths have a different perception. A former teacher of Qikiqtarjuaq, Bert Rose, recalled how in the 1980s this phenomenon of resistance against camping emerged among Inuit teenagers:

> In 1984, men and women got ready to go out camping by boat. They were helped by people of the age of 20 to 25 to bring the stuff to the boat. The teenagers were standing on the beach road watching, not participating at all.

In Rose's view, the reluctance of Inuit youth to go out camping at that time was motivated by the *Greenpeace* anti-sealing media documentation, which presented sealing as repulsive. In his experience, teenagers had difficulties dealing with this criticism of their way of life.

In conversations with me, teenagers often stated that they feel the community – the place they grew up – to be their home. During longer stays in camp they miss their friends, the community, a shower, and TV. In camp, they are often isolated from their peers. Moreover, discipline in camp is much stricter than in the community, and teenagers have to assist their parents and older people with all kinds of tasks and are often responsible for unpopular tasks, such as emptying the urine cans of elders in the morning. A young man whose parents were deceased told me that he does things according to his own counsel in the community, but would strictly follow all orders of the leader when in camp. He was not against camping, but would always choose very carefully with whom to attend camp, as he wanted to avoid older men who are too pushy, not very capable, or otherwise unpleasant to work with. One could not escape them when being out on the land.

Young people change their ways when they acquire a more autonomous position. When young women become mothers and young men get their own equipment to go out on the land, they soon establish their own camps or gain more influence in the decision making processes of the camp they

---

138 The reference to 'holiday' in respect to being out on the land is not opposed by elders. They expressed that they experience camping as relaxing, but did not formulate it in terms of 'holiday' – as a time apart.

stay in. The link between ownership and agency in land-related activities is not new. Boas pointed out that "Property [was] necessary for establishing a family," in particular, "the hunting gear of the man and the knife, scraper, lamp, and cooking pot of the women" (Boas 1888: 579; see also Stevenson 1997: 129, 218, 234).[139] Boas further reported that men who lost sledges and dogs (means of transportation) were sometimes integrated into a household and "fulfill minor occupations, mend the hunting implements, fit out sledges, feed the dogs, etc. Sometimes, however, they join the hunters. [...] This position, however, is a voluntary one, and therefore these men are not less esteemed than the self dependent providers"(Boas 1888: 581). At least in the past, these men did not seem to loose prestige. Whereas these hunters who had lost their equipment were still recognized as hunters, modern young people often still have to start their hunting careers.

The complaining of teenagers about long-term camping does not imply that they do not actually value the skills learned by being out on the land and related activities. Taiviti Nuqingak told me that when he was a teenager and sometimes unwilling to go out hunting, his stepfather Atamie Nookiruaq had said: "Never complain that you are bored when you are out on the land. If you do not hunt, you will not help anybody." He recognized that his stepfather's advice that hunting to support others was, and continues to be, relevant and it benefitted him in orienting his life and activities.

Being out on the land was perceived to be beneficial for the community also in other ways. Youth camps lasting several days were organized for troubled boys and girls. Most of them had dropped out of school, engaged in criminal activities, and abused drugs. Staying in a camp for a few days, is thought to support the young people in dealing with their troubles. Most of them very much enjoyed these trips. If they feel bored or homesick, their parents considered the program to be badly conducted by the leaders.

Middle-aged people said they enjoy a shower when they are back in the community, but that the camp life feels better than living in the community – at least in spring and summer. During the camping period, the community appears to be mainly useful for replenishing provisions, washing clothes, taking a shower, resting for a few days, and watching some TV before leaving again. When I asked the middle-aged hunter Loasie Kunilusie, if he has ever felt homesick out on the land, replied: "everywhere is my home, everywhere is my living room."

All age groups agree that living out on the land facilitates a more 'truly Inuit' way of life than living in the community. Inuit are convinced that their ancestors, who lived out on the land permanently and had to face many hardships, were much stronger and more knowledgeable than they themselves. The present camping practices are thought to be as close as possible to these 'truly' Inuit ways of life and they are valued for this proximity.

Also the value of the changes which have taken place in the practices of camping are acknowledged. For example, the implementation of new technologies is perceived by many Inuit to be practical, as they make life (out on the land) easier and facilitate hunting. They argue that the present Inuit ways are indeed sometimes different from the old ways, but that the integration of new things is 'truly' Inuit. Therefore the modern Inuit ways are seen by some as just as authentically Inuit as were the ways of the past. A few other hunters think that easiness and comfort disqualifies the use of modern technology from being 'truly' Inuit. An elderly woman, Leetia Kuksiak, for example, did not perceive any significant change in the practices of camping throughout her life: "I do not know if it has changed ever, since I remember. It looks never

---

139 Though s/he had established their own family, a groom was expected to work for some time for his parents-in-law. And "it is not until his parents-in-law are dead that he is entirely master of his own actions" (Boas 1888: 579f.).

changed, except that we went by dog team with our father when he was still alive and we were kids at that time." Leah Nuqingak, an elder woman, stated:

> Nowadays, we just go to get silver seals. Before we moved to Qikiqtarjuaq, we lived down in Padloping. When we went camping there, we did not only think of silver seals. We liked the place where we camped, and our parents had camped there before. We used to camp to get peaceful and waited to clear the snow in our camping area. We used to do that. Nowadays, they only go for silver seal skins. Yes, that has changed. In the past they used the skin to make the tent and clothing. I remember my mother telling me a story like that. [...] Nowadays we usually still camp with my own tent. But there are many cabins nowadays. That is another thing that has changed.

Simo Alookie, an elder man, stated:

> Things have changed. I hardly go [to my camp] now. I just drive around there, down at Padloping. [...] I just go where I want to go in spring. We go fishing and goose hunting. [...] We people lived there before. I think we will always go down there. [...] In the south, it is fun there. I grew up there. There were lots of fish.

In their views, camping and hunting – in respect to range and quantity of their products – decreased in relevance and became optional. One could live from what the community offers and be very selective as to which products to take from the land. The community provides a number of conveniences which are welcome in old age.

In spring, when most of the community population resides in camps, community institutions, such as the municipality and the churches, continue to operate. Lay readers of the Anglican Church alternate their performance of Sunday services so that all of them can go out camping. Communal activities and celebrations are continued for all who remain in Qikiqtarjuaq. Participants enjoy these activities, but they do not have a high priority in conversations nor do they play an important role in perceptions of the spring season.

Discussion of the spring season
Spring marks the onset of community dispersal, which continues far into summer. Household and family groups often travel to campsites once occupied by their ancestors. The practices of camp life represent and re-establish to a certain extent pre-community regional social patterns. The artificial establishment of the community is not forgotten or rendered irrelevant. Nomadic ways of life are further pursued in the spring and summer, and are highly valued.

Camps consist of about five to fifteen people. They form a small scale cooperative community with frequent direct contacts. Inuit perceptions and practices of camp life include close interactions with the extended family and occasionally with good friends, hunting and related occupations, sharing and consuming country food in the camp, hard work, and the enjoyment of relaxed conditions.

Teenagers form the exception here. Several of them prefer to stay in the community as they soon feel 'bored' and 'homesick' in the camps.[140] Whereas social ties that go beyond close family

---

140 Parents told me that they also feel linked to the community when their children remain there as they always worry about them.

and friendship relations are less frequent in spring for adults and elders, it appears that teenagers maintain social relations with their peers in the community rather than with their families in the camp. On closer scrutiny, it appears that youths do not appreciate to be subjected to strict camp discipline and to the less favorable work expected of them in the camp. When camping with a youth camp, however, most of them express that they like camping and enjoy hunting. Once more independent of the authority of their parents through the ownership of equipment and parenthood, most will continue the camping practices of their parents.

Spring holidays are observed in the community. They are celebrated by the people present, whose number continually decreases after Easter. People in camps, on the other hand, do not observe the holidays and usually do not move back to the community to participate in the festivities there. Camping is of higher value to them than the communal festivities in the community at this time of the year. Festivities are apparently linked to the community rather than to the dispersed camps.

The Sabbath (Sunday) is observed, both in the camps and in the community. Sunday services are held in both locations, but from mid spring onward services are shorter and less elaborate than during the autumn and winter seasons. Regular religious practices, such as a Sunday Service, are observed in short and comparatively basic performances during the camping season. Many Inuit experience being out on the land as beneficial for their well-being, and in addition it was perceived by a number of people as beneficial to their relationship with God. Not being distracted by the bustle of community life and being in touch with the land and the animals, they said they felt closer to God. Closeness with the land and animals is also addressed in hunting and camping practices. In contrast to residing in the community where there are supermarkets and one frequently receives game through third parties, such as at feasts, through the Hunters and Trappers Organization or through one's extended family, the relation to the game and the land becomes more direct when camping and hunting.

4.3.2 Aujaq – Summer

The snow-free, ice-free, season of *aujaq* ('summer') lasts from July till about September. It gets notably colder around mid September, and some people talk about September and October in terms of falling into the season of early autumn. For others September is simply the month of late summer. In early summer, the muddy soil quickly dries due to increased evaporation. The landscape turns from shades of white and grey to tints of brown and green. Various community agencies organize clean-ups to remove pieces of candy wraps and plastic sacs, which were covered by snow, and soon the community, lakes and rivers are undefiled. Patches of Arctic flowers decorate hills and meadows and the sound of rushing rivers breaks the silence of the Arctic winter and early spring. The last ice-floes drifting on the water melt rapidly. Boats are transported to the shore and prepared for use. Boating in early summer is not without peril, as collisions with the drifting ice easily damage the propellers. It requires skill and experience as well as the cooperation of at least two persons to maneuver a boat through the ice floes.

After a short interruption of camping due to the final break-up of the sea-ice, more and more families get ready to go camping and hunting by boat. People choose their summer camps according to the possibilities for net-fishing and, later in the season, of berry-picking. Most frequently the same sites are occupied for many years and often their parents have stayed at this site before them. For a few days to several weeks at a time Inuit net seal[141] and fish and, later

---

141 If the weather is calm, seal is also hunted with the rifle from a boat.

in the season, women pick berries. Collecting plants is another anticipated practice of summer camp life. Around mid-August, women collect bucketfuls of Arctic Blueberries (*Vaccinium uliginosum*), Black Bearberries (*Arctostaphylos alpina*), and Mountain Cranberries (*Vaccinium vitis-idaea*). Their husbands and sons continue to fish and hunt, as well as to monitor the berry-collection area for polar bears.

Arctic White Heather (*Cassiope tetragona*) covers the meadows. It is used to smoke tea. One needs about a large garbage sack of heather for a camp fire above which the *igaaq* tea is prepared.[142] It is served with bannock (bread baked in a pan) and jam – a seasonal delicacy much looked forward to. Edible sea-weed, such as Devil's Apron (species of *laminaria*), is washed ashore before the freeze-up sets in. Women walk along the shoreline of Qikiqtarjuaq on windy days to collect what they need for the daily consumption of their families.

Similar to mid and late spring, Qikiqtarjuaq is almost deserted during summer. Only employees, a number of teenagers, people with health problems, and a few other people remain in the community. Many of them organize outdoor activities in or near the settlement and thereby create some kind of camp life. For example, acquaintances and friends visit each other as much as possible; women organize many tea parties and picnics and prepare *igaaq*; people from the camps bring in country food and berries, so that small groups will get together for a meal; and women, and less often men, frequently take a stroll with friends in the vicinity of the settlement.

As community life has slowed down, the hamlet council usually reduces the frequency of its meetings by half. For the councillors and the mayor, this is an opportunity to leave the

Picture 25 *The annual sea-lift.*

---

142 *Igaaq* was a much appreciated black tea that received a smoked aroma by boiling the water above a fire of heather.

Picture 26 *A healing and berry picking camp for women at Maktak Fjord south of Qikiqtarjuaq.*

community for periods longer than just a weekend. The hamlet organizes a berry-picking trip for its female employees as part of their policy to support 'traditional' occupations. While middle-aged and older people are busy during the day and the evening, adolescents and a few children are up during the sunlit night and the early morning hours. They usually gather for talks, strolls, to play street-hockey or other games and sports, or to 'hang around'. This conduct is not particularly appreciated by the elders and the parents, but practically no measures are taken to keep youth at home and in bed at night.

The annual sea delivery arrives late in August. One ship brings gasoline and oil and another transports house construction sets, cars, snow scooters, bulk ware, private food orders, and so on. In 2000, only a handful of people watched the unloading of the ship from the beach and helped to transport the items to the correct addresses.

Each year, one or two healing camps are organized for people with social and family problems. In 2000, for example, the *Community Wellness Councillor*, Leetia Kuksiak, organized the annual healing and berry-picking camp for those adult and elderly women who also participated in her weekly counseling group. Loasie Kunilusie, a lay-reader of the Anglican church, organized a trip for troubled youth to Pamiujak camp, close to Kivitoo.[143] During the day, boys learn and practice hunting and land skills, whereas the girls are taught to take care of the camp. The day's activities are reviewed with the camp leaders in the evening. Loasie Kunilusie also counseled the young people from a religious perspective to make them change their life and go back to school.

---

143 He also organizes winter camps. Both initiatives, as well as similar projects of other people, are financed through funds of the Nunavut government, such as the Brighter Futures Program.

Picture 27 *Searching for narwhal during the hunt in late summer.*

The first snow falls on the mountains in early September, and mist hovers over the sea. A number of people consider this time of the year to be the begin of the autumn season. The sky is cloudy and it is windy. Some men go caribou hunting in a region about a two days' journey to the north. By the end of September, most families are back in the community. Sealskins dry on frames leaning against the houses, and women start to prepare winter garments. Evening dances, which were attended by only a handful of people earlier in summer, are now well-attended. Church services take place more regularly and, except for the period of the narwhal hunt, are also attended by an increasing number of people.

The coming narwhal hunt is a topic of conversation in late summer. Shortly before the narwhals are expected to pass Qikiqtarjuaq, people move from their camps to the community. As soon as the whales are sighted on their way through Davies Strait, the hunt begins. Their exact position is communicated by hunters with CB radios. The boats are equipped with ropes, harpoons, rifles, and a floater. At least two men work together on a boat. One of them steers, the other one shoots the whale in the head or front flippers as soon as it comes up. About ten other boats join the hunt to tire the whale out; moving as quickly as possible they frequently overtake each other. Any hunter with a good chance will shoot. When the whale is lethally injured, a harpoon is fastened to draw the whale to the boat. Ideally, the hunter who gave the lethal shot also harpoons and obtains the whale. It is considered his kill.

However, Larry Poisey explained to me that the hunter whose harpoon sticks in the whale owns the whale, even though the harpooner might not have seen it or shot at it first, or even dealt the final shot. Everyone else can and should try to harpoon the whale to prevent it from sinking. The successful harpooner is expected to share the whale with the hunter who killed it. It is not appreciated if the harpooner keeps it, unless it is not known who killed the whale. According to hunters and women in the community, serious conflicts arise almost every year concerning the actual hunting practices considered to have been improper by one of the parties. The hunt of the year 2000 was no exception. In a few cases, apparently another person than the killer and harpooner took the whale when the harpoon line broke, even though the hunter was still close to the whale trying to retrieve it. These incidents led to considerable arguments and acts of revenge among hunters and their families. More than one hunter found ice or water in the engines of his boat or four-wheeler on the morning after the hunt.

After the whale is killed and fastened to the boat, it can be transported to the shore and butchered. *Maktak*, the skin of a narwhal with blubber attached to it, and the tusk are taken to the community. The skin is distributed among the family and given to people in need. The meat is given to dog teams, and some carcasses are left to the Greenland sharks in the harbor. In the year 2000, the HTO[144] repeatedly admonished hunters to use the entire carcass instead of only retrieving the tusk and the epidermis and letting the carcass sink. The hunters met in the evenings for a coffee in the Co-op hotel to discuss the events of the day and to make plans for the next hunt. The coffee bar was kept open later than usual to facilitate the meeting. Elders spread information about the weather conditions on the community radio.

In previous years, the hunt was supervised by the government. The year 2000 was the first year of narwhal hunting controlled by the community through the *Hunters and Trappers Organization* (HTO). On October 17th, 2000, the narwhal hunt ended by decision of the HTO. In the following months, Qikiqtarjuaq faced severe criticisms in the press for exceeding recommended quotas.

A number of holidays are scheduled during the summer months, such as the Canada and Nunavut Days. Similar to spring, only those who stay in the community participate in the celebrations which are organized by community institutions. The camps do not observe these holidays. At Canada Day and Nunavut Day, July 1st and 9th, the municipality organized a feast, games, and dances. In 2000, the feast of country food was held outside in fine summer weather. Some employees used the holiday as an opportunity to go out on the land, instead of participating in the celebration.

The Civic Holiday in August was not celebrated but was a day free. Employees used the holiday for trips to the countryside. The celebration of the *Qikiqtaaniq Inuit Association* (QIA)[145] festivity began with outdoor games in the morning of August 31st and continued in the gym of the hamlet building. A feast and a Qallunaat dance completed the evening. Labor Day, like the Civic Holiday, was not celebrated in the community, but used for a trip to the countryside by many employees.

The next festivity of the annual cycle is the *Terry Fox Run* on September 17th. This fund-raising event for cancer research has been organized in Canada since 1981. Qikiqtarjuaq has participated in this event for a few years, collecting donations for the *Terry Fox* organization. As cancer is a significant health problem in Qikiqtarjuaq, many community residents wanted to participate in the run. In 2000, younger children and people who did not want to run the longer distance that covered all community roads, went for a walk around the community. Everybody met again in the community hall and coffee, tea and cookies were served as refreshments.

---

144 *Hunters and Trappers Organization*

145 The QIA is an Inuit organization operating from Iqaluit. It was established in 1996, replacing the Baffin Region Inuit Association registered as a society in 1975, as a community non-profit organization. Its mission is to promote Inuit benefits and to establish Inuit rights. In this context, the Nunavut land claim was signed on July 9th, 1993.

It was planned in 2000 to celebrate Hamlet Day on the 1st of October with a feast and games. However, many men were busy with the narwhal hunt – among them members of the organizing Community Service Committee – and the festivity was postponed to October 9th, Thanksgiving Day. The Sunday before Thanksgiving Day, a Thanksgiving church service was held. About thirty people attended the service and brought objects of special value as a donation. These items were sold for fund-raising a few weeks later by the Women's Auxiliary group. During the afternoon, people went on the radio – which provided extra hours on the air – to express their gratitude towards God and specific persons or institutions. Most of them thanked their parents or siblings for support and the hamlet and other organizations for their contributions to community life. Also the Qallunaat teachers were thanked for their work. Most people having returned from camping were in Qikiqtarjuaq and the games were well attended. The feast, postponed from Hamlet Day to Thanksgiving Day, had to be cancelled, because the weather had made seal hunting difficult and most hunters were engaged with the narwhal hunt, there was a lack of seal meat.

The ice-free season ends as the temperature drops and heavy snowstorms rage about the middle of October. Impressive icebergs come floating by from Greenland at this time of the year. As the sea-ice thickens in late autumn, the icebergs freeze and shape the seascape for the coming winter.

Inuit perceptions of summer
Early and mid summer continue the camping season of spring. Lootie Toomasie comments:

> During the summer, we are more scattered on the land, because the weather is warm compared to [winter]. We had 24 hours daylight, sunshine in June and July, for us to enjoy to be away from the community during that time. Being away from the community is really good for us who keep continuing the traditional ways of life. [...] If they have to go there, nobody can stop them [he laughs].

Most adults and elders expressed the view that the summer season, like spring, is a time for both relaxation and work out on the land.

Berry picking, preparing *igaaq* 'smoked tea' in camp or in the vicinity of the community, as well as narwhal hunting are marked practices of mid and late summer. Berries were appreciated food in mid summer. In late summer, *maktak*, the skin of the narwhal with a layer of blubber attached to it, was anticipated and enjoyed. Family and friends are always invited to take a share of the *maktak* that a hunter has brought home. The narwhal hunt is the sole occasion where a large number of hunters work together to procure the game. A mixture of cooperation and competition is indispensable for a successful hunt, but it is also the context in which conflicts arise.

One hunter, for example, disapproved of the fact that some people are only interested in catching a narwhal with a tusk[146] and not a whale without one. People also complained that some hunters would only go hunting when there was a large number of whales. The middle-aged wife of a hunter told me that she wished the whales would quickly move on, because their presence caused so much anger and stress in the community.

---

146 Tusks are sold carved or plain. One foot of tusk costs about $100.

Discussion of summer

In early and mid summer the highly valued and widely practiced camping of the spring season is continued, and in contrast, community life and activities is of little significance to those camping. The celebration of holidays takes place exclusively in the community and those present participate. People who remain in Qikiqtarjuaq do their best to create a bit of camp life in the settlement. Summer, as the spring before, is marked by specific kinds of food, especially berries, seaweed, and *maktak*.

Found also in spring, healing camps are organized during the summer for groups, especially for women. The leaders and participants find winter to be too cold for girls adn women.

As summer draws toward its end and autumn comes and the narwhal hunt is in full swing, a transition toward a different social setting and perceptions of community life sets in. Families successively come back to stay in the community. Men immediately prepare for and then engage in the narwhal hunt. Several teams cooperate and compete with each other to catch the whales. People are happy to meet friends and family members whom they have not seen for some time. However, both the narwhal hunt and the renewed concentration in the community appear to revive long-lasting resentments as well as to create new tensions.

Hunting and countryside activities continue to be highly valued and practiced throughout the summer (and into early autumn). With the move back to the community, the social setting of the hunting activities changes. People return in a similar way to their departure: on their own terms, in their own time, and without observing a ceremony that would structure these social dynamics. Inuit do not express a specific value associated with the concentration in the community – except for being once again together with friends and family members they have missed during the camping season. In this setting, conflicts about the proper ways of cooperation, competition, and of sharing the kill emerge, which have no equivalent in the hunting practices during spring, early and mid summer.

4.3.3 Ukiaq – Autumn

In late October, heavy snowstorms swept the open sea. The community breakwater started to freeze up and boulders on the beach were covered by layers of ice. The last leaves of seaweed were washed ashore, but hardly anybody picked them up anymore. The boats were taken out of the water and set on dry land. For some six to eight weeks, traveling by sea or land would be impossible or at least difficult. Most Qikiqtarjuarmiut remained in the community during this period.

After the long spring and summer months, the community was once again staying together. The tense atmosphere which had developed during the narwhale hunt got heavier as more incidents of domestic and external violence occurred. People's stories often dealt with feeling threatened, pressured, or angry about someone else. Corporal Jeff Johnston from the RCMP station of Qikiqtarjuaq told me[147] that he sees a pattern of increase in domestic violence and, to a lesser degree, of property offences[148] during the period of freeze-up of the sea-ice.[149] Offenders

---

147 Telephone conversation August 7th, 2003.

148 Most property offences (breaking and entering) are committed by Inuit offenders to Qallunaat homes or businesses. According to Johnston's observation, Inuit rarely break into a house of other Inuit.

149 He found a similar, but less accentuated, pattern pertaining to the break-up period. I made no corresponding observations during late spring and early summer in my fieldwork period.

frequently explained to the police officers that being confined to the community and the emerging tensions were conducive to their violent outbreaks.

People focussed their attention, visits, and activities as far as possible on family members with whom they had good relations and on their circle of best friends. Elders and church leaders were often asked for their advice and help to handle these difficulties. Prayer sessions were organized several times a week in private homes and there was increased attendance in church services. Primarily the victims of violent acts or of distressing apparitions approached their leaders or attended prayer services. People who had committed wrongful acts often found it difficult to do either. One woman, for example, told me that she avoided going to church for the last weeks, even though she felt the urge to do so. She thought herself to be too guilty of haughty-sinful thoughts to participate in a service and to face God and members of the community of whom she had been critical.

Increasing tensions were, however, just one side of community life in this season. People also came together for festivities. The highschool graduation ceremony for Lucy Anaviapik and Ruth Kunilusie was the first celebration of the freeze-up period, on October 20th, 2000. A week later, the *Women's Auxiliary Group* (WA) held a fair. They offered for sale their own craft works as well as donations from Thanksgiving. Next, on October 26th, the *Hunters and Trappers Organization* HTO organized a community caribou meal. Members of the board had gone to Iqaluit[150] for a hunting expedition for this annual feast. Arctic char and bowhead *maktak*, distributed throughout Nunavut from the last bowhead whale hunt, were served as well. Many people participated and expressed their enjoyment of the feast.

On October 31st, Halloween, masqueraded children and women with small children and babies went from house to house to collect candy. Some were dressed as clowns, some as cats, one or two dressed like devils, others had painted their faces with scary motives, such as scars, drops of blood, and spiders, in black and red. They also teased other people on the street.[151] Later in the evening, a costume competition and a dance were organized by the Youth Committee. The most ugly or beautiful babies and small children, the most scary older child, and the most funny, scary or ugly adult won a prize. About 25 persons were masqueraded, and the school gym was packed with people watching the competitions. Adults were completely disguised and often cross dressed as old and usually fat persons of the opposite sex. Others wore traditional clothing and concealed their faces. Discovering who is who was a favorite pastime. Most people went home after the competition, and only a few returned for the dance.

November the 12th was assigned to be Alcohol Awareness Day. The Fire Brigade decorated their truck and paraded through the community to remind people of the dangers of liquor. Many people of Qikiqtarjuaq joined the parade walking behind the truck. During the rest of the week, games and dances were organized in the evening. Ideas and materials for the games were provided by a social worker and the community wellness institution, which is associated with the Nunavut government. The underlying idea was that people should go to the games, such as word puzzles, instead of smoking or drinking alcohol in the evenings. The game materials themselves also carried educational messages designed to heighten the awareness of the destructive effects of alcohol abuse and to stimulate a person's self-esteem. Additionally, people who managed not to smoke for a week participated in a draw and could win a prize. The effects appear limited

---

150 They went to Iqaluit, because the caribou herds were too far north from Qikiqtarjuaq at that time of the year.

151 Police patrolled to ensure a safe Halloween. In the past, some younger men had robbed children, taking their candy bags.

because only a handful of people participated in the games. A woman told me that they were boring, too complicated, and had an educational tone she did not like. She preferred to smoke instead of participating in the games.

Remembrance Day, November 13th, was commemorated by the community radio station, by playing exclusively country & western and modern spiritual music.[152] In former years, some elders had gone on the radio to talk about their life-histories. These festivities did not change the difficult situation in the community, but they were occasions of communal socializing and sharing.

Inuit perceptions of autumn

Most Inuit experienced autumn, marked by the freeze-up of the sea-ie, as the most difficult time of the year. Social and spiritual difficulties were frequently named. Inuit have various ideas concerning the causes of specific difficulties. Two middle-aged women told me, independently from each other, that the presence of a bad spirit in a house may lead to or may deepen family problems. Alcohol consumption or drug abuse are also thought to cause or deepen problems. One middle-aged man thought that the 'out of tune' moon phase at this time of the year[153] was responsible for the increasing difficulties in the community. Another middle-aged woman told me that brooding over destructive thoughts and acts, activities she felt particularly drawn to in autumn, caused the appearance of deceased relatives and friends.

There was an attempted suicide by a teenager, and a woman in her late twenties felt reminded of the year 1987. During that year, five teenagers committed suicide, two of them in November. She perceived the suicides as an uncanny epidemic at that time, going from person to person and she was worried that a similar wave could hit the community again. Due to the tensions that arose during the narwhal hunt in late summer, she also felt threatened and would not go outside in the dark without taking a short rifle for protection. Being confined to the community was another cause frequently noted for the difficulties of the freeze-up period.

The effect I experienced was that my usual research activities became increasingly difficult. More people than usual preferred not to participate in interviews. The eager curiosity of an outsider to learn about Inuit ways of life, tolerated and occasionally encouraged at other times, was felt to be annoying now.[154] In consequence, I withdrew from actively pursuing research undertakings. I focused my attention and also my casual social activities to a closer circle of friends and acquaintances and I worked with the community and church files.

---

152 This is also common practice on days when funerals take place.

153 Unfortunately, I did not inquire further to elucidate this idea. The influence of the moon was the subject of another conversation, however, in which elder Simo Alookie explained to me that the scar he has from a kidney surgery feels different in correspondence with the moon phases. Sometimes he does not feel it at all; at other times, especially with full moon, it troubles him more. The moon is, thus, thought to have an influence on the physical and social life of Inuit.

154 It may have been that I myself changed. At that time and also after screening my diary and letters of that time, I, however, find no indication of feeling affected by the season or showing a different conduct than during summer time. Initially, I also had expected the freeze-up period to be a season well suited for interviews because people were available in the community. My conduct, at first uninformed about the social dynamics evolved in that period, may have contributed to the occasional feelings of irritation among people I approached for interviews.

The freeze-up period was, however, not only a time marked by difficulties and tensions. It also was a time of well-attended and enjoyed community celebrations. Children, adults, and elders prepared for and enjoyed the Halloween candy collection. They looked forward to and participated in the feasts and in most games of the season.[155] For example, Ina Sanguya commented, when we were sitting together at the HTO feast, that she was enjoying the feast and that there had been too much time between the last feast and the present feast.[156] Jaypootie Alikatuqtuq, sitting with his wife Susie beside us, added that the feast was held every year to make people happy.

Later in autumn, when talking about the social difficulties of the freeze-up period, my conversation partners often expressed their anticipation of Christmas. At Christmas, people said, things would become better. At the end of November, a number of houses were decorated with colorful Christmas ornaments and outdoor lights were out up with the intention to give the streets a cheerful look and to make oneself and others happy.

Discussion of autumn
The community was perceived in ambivalent terms in autumn. After the months of dispersion, Inuit lived concentrated within the community. To be expected at a time when people join again in a large group, old grudges revive, new resentments appear, and social tensions arise; additionally, a number of households and individuals were distressed by spiritual difficulties, which were thought to be encouraged by social tensions and individual troubles. Many people focussed their daily life on their circle of relatives and friends. At the same time, people came together to play games and share a feast at community festivities in a congenial atmosphere.

4.3.4 Ukiuk – Winter

From around mid December, the sea was frozen solid[157] and the wind ceaselessly swept the snow off the ridges, re-arranging the drifts. The mid-winter sun did not rise above the horizon and provided hardly more three hours of twilight to Qikiqtarjuaq. During winter, the average daily temperature was less than -30 ºC. 'Highways' formed on the snow-covered land and sea-ice where people used the same snow scooter tracks to go north or south or just around the community. Few people traveled for long periods at this time of the year. Some Inuit families went for short leisure rides and a few hunters caught seals at their breathing holes. During January, lay reader Loasie Kunilusie took troubled young men out to a hunting camp at Pamiujak, which he did each year. They were trained in outdoor skills and their performances were discussed in the evening. The evening session ended with counseling that was based on Christian beliefs and practices. At the end of February, when the temperature slightly rose and the hours of daylight increased, men left the community for a day, or for weekend trips, to hunt seal with nets at ice cracks or at their breathing holes. Caribou hunting required longer trips, and only a few hunters engaged in it. Around this time, people started talking about the coming

---

155   A few people, among them Peepeelee Nutaralak, an elderly woman, and Norman Koonoo, a middle-aged man, felt uncomfortable about this celebration. Norman Koonoo said that he does not like that day because people have made something evil out of something holy. Also Peepeelee Nutaralak perceived Halloween as a celebration, which is, to a certain degree, frightening.

156   The last one was organized for Hamlet Day at October the 1st.

157   Traveling in December can be still difficult as the ice can be covered with water, or it can be thin or slushy due to sea currents.

Picture 28 *Qikiqtarjuaq and a snowmobile 'highway' leading South.*

spring and about going out camping. As spring was approaching with the return of the sun, all hunters had their equipment ready to hunt basking seals and to go out camping with their families once again.

In winter, the streets and houses were covered with layers of snow and ice. Only a few seal skin frames were leaning against the houses. Women waited for the spring sun to come up again, which would help bleach the skins. Whereas many children were playing on the streets during the rest of the year, only a few could be seen in mid-winter. Whenever I was walking down the street on a windy day, somebody would stop his/her car to offer me a ride. Gray and green Northern Lights swept over the sky in the evening, and people often asked me if I was aware that Inuit used to believe that these were their ancestors playing ball. Many houses were already decorated with Christmas lights in early December and this colorfully lit up the streets during the evening and night hours.

It appeared that the unrest witin the community evident during the freeze-up period subsided as Christmas approached. Invitations were extended by community institutions to attend their yearly open meetings, the reading of their annual reports and discussions of past and future projects. People prepared for the Christmas celebration and used the local radio station to express their wish for safe and happy celebrations. Year after year, the hamlet council unanimously decided to ban alcohol during the days of celebration. Only a few incidents of alcohol abuse and other criminal acts precipitated the intervention of by-law officers or of the RCMP. People who tended to feel irritated by my research activities during autumn, now asked me to stay 'for good' in Qikiqtarjuaq explaining that they had gotten used to my presence. Other visitors were welcomed to the community as well. For example, a regional hockey tournament was scheduled after Christmas. Teams from all over Nunavut were welcomed by families and lodged in the community guesthouse for several days.

Winter, as in autumn, brought an intensification of religious life. On December 8th, 1999, the Anglican Church, in cooperation with the Full Gospel congregation, hosted a Bible Conference. The little church was packed with about 100 people of all age groups. Elders left early, but younger people often stayed through the whole program, which took about three or four hours. Reading from the Bible, singing hymns, soft-rock Christian songs, public confession, as well as Pentecostal practices – Holy Spirit inspired prayer sessions with glossolalia, healing by prayer, and exorcizing demons – were practiced during the meeting.[158] Also regular services were well attended and the Bible Study group met two or three times a week. Members of the Anglican Church and of the youth group *Northern Lights* went to Inukjuaq for another conference in March. In April, Pauloosee Kunilusie held a prayer service to deal with problems within his family. Several members of *Northern Lights* left to attend a Bible conference in Clyde River around the same time.

The winter holidays were all celebrated elaborately and in a happy atmosphere. Preparations for Christmas were in full swing from early December onward. The post-office was packed with catalogue orders. Women were busy sewing winter garments, which were often worn for the first time at Christmas. Community institutions, businesses, and groups as well as the Qallunaat residents held feasts and games for their members, clients or acquaintances. A few days before Christmas, most Qallunaat left Qikiqtarjuaq to travel home.

From shortly before Christmas until New Year, the local radio stations sent greetings from relatives and friends within and outside the community almost 24 hours a day. The community Christmas celebration started around the 22nd of December. It lasted until the celebration of the New Year. Every day, with the exception of Sunday, morning and evening games were played and dances were held. Two feasts were organized, for which more food was provided than for other feasts of the yearly cycle. Two community church services were celebrated, one at Christmas, the other at New Year. They were held at the community gym and almost the entire community participated – including the middle-aged woman who had felt too sinful to participate in the services of autumn and early winter.

In early January, people took about a week to rest from the festivities, if their employment permitted, Valentine's Day, February 14th, was the first community event of the year after Christmas and New Year. At Valentine's Day, a dance for teenagers and adults, a costume competition for children, and an artwork competition for adults were organized by the municipality. For the competitions, the girls were dressed in cute costumes decorated with hearts. Handcrafted objects dealt with the topic of love, embroidering heart-shaped pillows and arranging flowers in the shape of a heart. In the evening, all age-groups participated in the dance. It was one of the rare occasion of the year that people danced in pairs in addition to group jig-dances (introduced by the Scottish whalers)[159] and dancing alone. The dancers frolicked until late at night.

Inuit perceptions of winter

Difficulties in the community emerged in autumn and continued in early winter. Concern for the well-being of the community became an increasingly relevant and pressing issue in Inuit conversations. Christmas was perceived to be the occasion when social life would improve. During the celebration of Christmas and New Year, Inuit attributed a high value to the

---

158   See for further details on religious beliefs and practices the chapter on *Christian ways of life in Qikiqtarjuaq*.

159   Jig-dances are called Inuktitut dances. They are accompanied by Scottish accordion music.

community. To be together with everybody, to share feasts, to compete in games, and to dance together were anticipated. After Christmas, the topic turns to the anticipation of the spring camping season and replaces Christmas.

Many Qallunaat residents emphasized in their conversations the challenge of dealing with the darkness of winter. They contemplated psychological and medical theories about its negative effects on the well-being of people. In this context, Christmas was often perceived as the celebration of light. Interviewing Lootie Toomasie, mayor of the community, on his recollections of Christmas in the past and his perceptions of present celebrations, I asked him if he sees a connection between the darkness of the season and the Christmas celebration. He commented:

> We have four seasons up here, but we cannot run away from it, you know. We can not avoid it. This Christmas celebration came and it had to be done. [...] Because it has been going on right from the beginning at this time of the year, during the dark season, nowadays it seems to be the good time. During the dark season is a better time for us, because we are so used to it. [...] We don't really bother about the dark season. It is not really affecting us, because it is there and we live with it. We cannot run away from it. Even if we would run away from it, down South to Florida or so, it would be a different celebration. [...] If I would go down there, I would miss my people who are celebrating.

The darkness of winter is rarely an issue of significance in Inuit conversations on the well-being of people. Only a few, especially those who once lived further north where there is not even twilight in December, said that darkness would make some people act strange. The cold of the winter season, however, was an issue of comment in conversations on hunting practices and other outdoor activities. Jaypetee Nookiruaq and Loasie Kunilusie were among the few hunters who went out sealing during the coldest period of the annual cycle, December and January. Both stated that the cold could not hinder them going out on the land. Their bodies would be trained to brave the low temperatures and their clothing would be adjusted to the climate. Other hunters, mainly elders and young men, frankly admitted that it would be too cold for them to be out on the land. Having a choice, they preferred to stay in the community. Women expressed a similar opinion. They looked forward to hunting and camping in late winter and early spring.

Discussion of winter
Around Christmas, the transformation of the sea-ice to a solid layer was completed and extensive traveling on the sea-ice became possible again. Whoever did not mind the cold could leave the settlement by snow scooter or dog sled. Most people perceived this possibility to benefit their well-being, but only few actually made such trips. The social atmosphere improved considerably with the celebration of Christmas. The community, otherwise often referred to as a source of difficulties, is addressed and highly valued in the celebration as well as in daily conversations. Difficulties were perceived to be removed from the community by celebrating Jesus Christ's birthday together. People were ready to cooperate with each other once again. The focus of the community on itself was of relatively short duration. As Christmas passed, people anticipated the spring camping season, the value attributed to the community was relegated to the background. The potentials for cooperative relationships created at Christmas, however, could be implemented in hunting and traveling.

4.4 Discussion of the seasonal cycle

In the introduction to this chapter I asked: In what way are the present seasonal movements of community dispersal and concentration relevant mechanisms in Inuit community formation? Analyzing my data, I was struck by the analogy of my results and the central argument in Mauss & Beuchat's study (1979 [1904]) *Essay sur les variations saisonnières des sociétés Eskimos: Étude de morphologie sociale*. They proposed a seasonal pattern of two contrasting social formations of the *-miut* group[160] generated by the population concentrating in 'winter' and dispersing in 'summer'.[161] They concluded that these social formations were accompanied by variations in social, religious and juridical life. Mauss & Beuchat delineated the main features of life in the 'winter' and 'summer' camps: Animal migrations and travel conditions of the winter season facilitated larger agglomerations of households than was possible in summer. The population of a region moved to a winter camp engaging in an intensified social and religious life. Several families shared a camp and often also a house (Mauss & Beuchat 1979 [1904]: 38).[162] Mauss & Beuchat emphasized that:

> The settlement is more than a simple accumulation of houses or an exclusively political and territorial entity; it is also a domestic unit. All its members are united by strong bonds of affection. [...] The rules of the settlement are not just the sum of the rules of each household; the settlement has its own rules which are reminiscent of large family gatherings. [...] Most observers have been struck by the gentleness, intimacy, and general gaiety that reigns in an Eskimo settlement (Mauss & Beuchat 1979 [1904]: 66, 67).

The community itself became a focus of Inuit practices: "Their social interactions become frequent, more continuous and more coherent; ideas are exchanged; feelings are mutually revived and reinforced. By its existence and constant activity, the group becomes more aware of itself and assumes a more prominent place in the consciousness of individuals" (Mauss & Beuchat 1979 [1904]: 76f). In the juridical domain, property became more collective, food was shared more widely and collective consumption was more marked than in summer. Leaders of the camp emerged on the basis of their age, gender and capability. Their influence in the community was limited basically to decisions on logistic and social issues (Mauss & Beuchat 1979 [1904]: 72f., 66).

Summer life was marked by smaller and dispersed social groups and a slackening of social and religious life. A summer camp was constructed of a nuclear family and occasionally other relatives, widows and their families, and guests (Mauss & Beuchat 1979 [1904]: 37). In the small camps, the father, as the provider, was the head of the family. He decided on the whereabouts and activities

---

160 They thought the *-miut* group, forming the winter camp, to be the most cohesive unit of Inuit society, not only in territorial and social, but also in religious terms (Mauss & Beuchat 1979 [1904]). Their model was challenged, for instance, by Stevenson (1997) and Dorais (1997), who emphasized the flexibility of camp membership. See the chapter *Theoretical background and methodology* for a critical discussion of the *-miut* concept as a designator for the most cohesive social unit.

161 They were aware that "dispersion takes different forms according to local circumstances" but chose to highlight the contrast in their model (Mauss & Beuchat 1979 [1904]: 48).

162 For Cumberland Sound, Stevenson (1997) described that winter camps were formed by a group of core members, usually a leader and his family, and attached individuals or families.

of his group. Property was assigned to individuals and families and food was shared primarily with the inhabitants of the one-family tent (Mauss & Beuchat 1979 [1904]: 63, 70-71).[163]

The ethnographic foundation of Mauss & Beuchat's study, which synthesizes data from Canada, Alaska, Greenland, and Russia, is rather fragmentary.[164] But Mauss & Beuchat's intuition concerning the marked patterns of concentration and dispersal in Inuit social organization is challenging in view of my own initial findings. I will use their model as a heuristic device to discuss the links between temporality, locality, and sociality in present day Qikiqtarjuaq.

Qikiqtarjuaq is formally organized and administrated as a western sedentary community. Notwithstanding, social practices appertaining to the 'old' nomadic model continue to be implemented in settlement life as well as in the spring and summer dispersions to camps (see chapter *Life in Qikiqtarjuaq*). Furthermore, the 'old' model, given shape in the ideal image of the *inummariit* ('real Inuit'), is prevalent in Inuit discourses on dealing with modern community life (see chapter *Theoretical background and methodology*).

The description of the present practices in connection with the seasonal cycle showed that there are still periods of dispersal and times of concentration. Inuit appreciate the seasonal variations of social modes and locality and, as we could see from the implementation of the ritual cycle, each seasonal movement is associated with a different value.

Beside individual preferences, spring and summer, being seasons of community dispersal, are generally most highly appreciated. Often, an extended family, composed of two to four nuclear families, camp together. A minimum of about five and a maximum of about twenty people share a camping site. Camps form a cooperative domestic unit, and members enjoy the close social relations. Cooperation, sharing of food, and relaxed and cheerful socializing involve all camp members. Most activities are related to procurement, mostly hunting, fishing, and berry picking. These activities position people, as well as the camp, within the circuit of social and cosmological relationships to other camp members, animals, and the to the land. Some people also told me that they feel closer to God when being out on the land. It is a time perceived to contribute to everybody's well-being. Camping is perceived by most Inuit to be a more 'real' Inuit way of life compared to living in the settlement. The modern spring/summer camps address not only the ideal of the *inummariit* but include present day Inuit formulations in which they identify themselves as Inuit through their relation to the land.

The past winter camp and the present spring/summer camp share the value of being considered 'ideal' communities. Furthermore, the features of the camp as a domestic unit, the value placed on togetherness,[165] the perceived increased well-being, and the perception that it

---

163 Boas observed that households in Southern Baffin Island did not cook for themselves in summer, but that women provided for the entire settlement in turn. This practice indicates a socially more open setting of the summer camp than suggested by Mauss & Beuchat (Boas 1888: 577). See also Stevenson (1979: 245) for variations in communal and individual food storage and retrieval of different camps.

164 Qikiqtarjuaq is composed of people from former Davies Strait camps, as well as from Cumberland Sound camps. Whereas Boas and Stevenson provided detailed data on seasonal movements for the Cumberland Sound region, both, unfortunately, have not discussed the groups from Davies Strait in their specifics. Boas considered them sufficiently similar to Cumberland Sound practices to omit further details (Boas 1888: 428ff; 440, 461).

165 Billy Arnaquq, for instance, said that for him spring is "a time that many people get together." (See the introduction to this chapter)

is a time of an intensified performance of 'real' Inuit ways, remind one of Mauss & Beuchat's characterization of past winter camps.

Today, the perceptions of and dealing with periods of community concentration are complex. Firstly, living concentrated in the community carries ambivalent values. On the one hand, living concentrated in the settlement is perceived to have the potential of detrimental effects on people's well-being. On the other hand, togetherness with all community members has a positive value, which is expressed especially in the context of festivals, in particular at Christmas. Secondly, and in particular the period of the freeze-up of sea-ice that is also the onset of community concentration, the community more marked by tensed social relationships and by increasing spiritual difficulties. In part, these difficulties are attributed to the effects of being in the settlement, but are also perceived to be related to this particular season. The social and religious difficulties are expected to be solved during the Christmas celebration. I will discuss the ambivalence of living in the modern community first. Then I will turn to the social and religious difficulties perceived to be connected to this time of the year.

In contrast to Mauss & Beuchat's description, the concentration of the largest possible social group is presently not perceived to be the 'ideal' configuration, but to be rather problematic.[166] A significant difference between the past and present winter communities is the number of people constituting it. In South Baffin Island, the population of winter camps did not average more than 50 before the 1850s, when whalers started to overwinter causing locally larger group sizes (Stevenson 1997: 58-63). This size supported social practices, cooperation, and leadership to be based on direct social interactions. Social order was maintained by direct social control. The operation of these features is much more difficult to implement in a modern settlement like Qikiqtarjuaq, which has more than 500 inhabitants. The difficult patchwork composition of the community add further obstacles to the situation.[167] Furthermore, the land became inhabited in a much more concentrated way than before. Compared to earlier camp settlements, it is more difficult in the new setting to move from one community to the next. The next community is not a close neighbor anymore, it takes a day or more by snow scooter, or an expensive flight to get there. The requirements of finding housing and work after having moved to a new location are further obstacles to mobility. And last but not least, experiences and recollections of relocation and enforced unwanted changes, add to the perception that the modern community is not an ideal social configuration.

Coming to the second point of discussion, the social and spiritual difficulties perceived to be connected to this period of the year, it is actually the togetherness of all Qikiqtarjuaq residents that is emphasized during fall and winter community festivals, and in particular at Christmas. In the past, it was the most concentrated social formation, the winter camps, that provided the context for communal festivities of the ritual cycle. Mauss & Beuchat (1979 [1904]) pointed out that the establishment of the winter camp configuration went together with the emergence of cosmological conditions that were dangerous to the physical, cosmological, and

---

166 This does not mean that Inuit do not appreciate the amenities and other features of settlement life (see for a description of settlement life chapter *Life in Qikiqtarjuaq*).

167 Tensions and disagreements between groups are not a new phenomenon. The dynamic composition of the camp of the past and the relative proximity (often less than a day's journey) of other camps distributed along the coast, however, permitted one to move around more easily (see Boas 1888: 424, 462-464, 467 for communications between Davies Strait and Cumberland Sound groups; see Stevenson 1997: 236f., 248f. for conflict management by migration).

social integrity of people.[168] In this context, shamanic rituals and festivals that focussed on the renewal of relationships and the improvement of hunting success took a prominent place in their description:

> The winter settlement lives in a state of continuous religious exaltation. [...] The slightest event requires the more or less solemn intervention of the magicians, the *angekok*. [...] A minor taboo can be lifted only by public ceremonies and by visits to the entire community. At every possible opportunity these events are turned into impressive performances of public shamanism to avert famine that threatens the group, particularly [...] when hunting is unreliable (Mauss & Beuchat 1979 [1904]: 57, 58).

Festivals, such as the Sedna festival (see chapter *Theoretical background and methodology*), were part of the rhythm of social life. They provided the nomadic society with structure and constructed temporal relationships.

The seasonal feature of the combination of large scale sociality and an increased potential for difficulties is, thus, not new and only related to the particular setting of the modern communities. Inuit perceive the modern living conditions to contribute to the situation, but they also linked the potential for crisis to the season. Whereas in the past it was the Sedna festival that dealt with communal and cosmological relationships, at present it is the Christmas celebration that does so (see chapter *Christmas in Qikiqtarjuaq*).

As in the past, community formation takes place in connection to the temporality and locality of the group. Christmas is part of a formal holiday cycle that includes other civic and Christian holidays celebrated with community festivities. Even though holiday celebrations are generally appreciated, not all holidays are equally successful, i.e. celebrated by the entire community. What then, is the capacity of the annual holidays? We can see that celebrations of early spring (Easter), freeze-up (e.g. Halloween), and winter (e.g. Christmas) – all periods of community concentration – are well attended. Festivities of summer (Canada Day),[169] and autumn before freeze-up (Terry Fox Run) – periods of community dispersal – are attended only by people who stay in the community and they are not celebrated in the camps. During times of dispersal, Inuit attach a higher value to being out on the land than to staying in the community and participate in community celebrations. People do not take the opportunity to celebrate in the camps. Apparently the celebrations of communal holidays should take place in the largest possible group and I find the central factor shaping this pattern of participation to be the emphasis placed on the public character of these celebrations. In particular, the feature of the communal sharing of food in a feast, a constituent of all community celebrations, appears to be central in this context. Food should never be used exclusively, but the occasion should be open to all who wish to partake. It can be noted that considerable efforts are required to provide enough food for the entire and ever growing community. It would be comparatively easy to organize a holiday-feast in the confines of the camp, but it would mean confining the feast of a public holiday to a small fraction of the community. One camp alone could not provide food for the entire community, and this option has apparently little attraction for Inuit. My conclusion therefore is that holiday celebrations are associated with the community.

---

168 See also, for example, Rasmussen 1929: 227; Boas 1888: 574; Boas 1900: 630; Balikci 1970: 175; Hawkes 1916: 110.

169 There are no further community festivities in late spring after the well attended fishing derby.

This finding is homologous to Mauss & Beuchat's description of Inuit social and religious life in which rituals addressing social formations are only practiced by the groupduring the period of greatest assemblage – the winter camp. Mauss & Beuchat (1979 [1904]) argue that the seasonal social-demographic concentration is linked to collective festivities by means of which the group constitutes itself and its relation to the cosmological domain: "Festivities are not only collective in the sense that very many individuals assemble to take part; they are the object and the expression of the group" (Mauss & Beuchat 1979: 58). Considering the past and present data, we may say that the movement of concentration continues to require social-religious rituals to establish and maintain community life. From this point of view, the celebration of Christmas is of central relevance to the formation of the community of Qikiqtarjuaq.

In how far and in what ways is the alteration between the dispersal and concentration of the community itself a mechanism of community formation? Today in relation to the social domain, how does the temporal and spatial flexibility work? The strength of Mauss & Beuchat's account is their emphasis on the connection between temporality, locality, and social organization. The production and disintegration of the social cohesion in Inuit social organization is embedded in a cosmological framework in connection to which the movements of falling apart and coming together are structural features of Inuit social organization. The various modes of Inuit social life are, in analogy to Mauss & Beuchat's model, associated with different values. Inuit continue to perceive the contrasting relationship between small and large scale social formations. However, the values attached to the seasonal social formations are reversed. Whereas the winter camp was the ideal social configuration in Mauss & Beuchat's description, it is the spring/summer camp that is perceived by Inuit to be the ideal configuration at present.

Though we have not examined yet the ways in which the modern community is ritually constituted, we can conclude from the examination of the seasonal cycle of Qikiqtarjuaq that the western ideas of community do not work very well for Qikiqtarjuaq. They do not account for the connection between sociality, temporality, and locality that are crucial for Inuit perceptions and practices of community life.

Chapter 5
Quviasuvik – Christmas, 'a Time of Happiness' in Qikiqtarjuaq

5.1 Introduction

Mayor Lootie Toomasie explained to me why he thought that Christmas is important to the community:

> In the old days [Christmas] was just the way it is now. At that time we were much closer to each other, however, because the families usually had their own camps. They were always close to each other, seeing each other. They were really independent that time. But nowadays we have to work somewhere else, in other parts of the territory. And now we always want to gather during Christmas time. Well, we feel good to get together during Christmas time to sort of renew our relationship.

He emphasized that Christmas has been and continuous to be a time of getting together and then focussed on the set-up of the festival:

> During the time of nomadic communities we usually gathered for one day, just that, right on December 25th. But now we celebrate at least a week or two weeks at a time during Christmas. This is very new to the people. It started to be like this back in 1970s.[170] For a one whole week we have games and so on. Every day, every night games. Back then we used to have community feasts. We still practice that to celebrate Christmas, the birth of Jesus.

He elaborated on the relevance of Jesus Christ's birth for the celebration of the Christmas holiday:

> We are very aware that this is not just a holiday season – it is the time to celebrate the birth of Jesus. It is Jesus' birthday. Our parents usually reminded us, in the old days, that it is not just happening because it had to happen. It was really happening because Jesus was born on that day. So it is still continuing for us today. Even though nowadays it seems that the real meaning of Christmas sometimes is getting weak, because so many things are happening besides that we really believe in Christmas, in terms of its religious status. But we also find that it is a good time. We have a good time and start to gather.

For Lootie Toomasie, Christmas continues to be a time of happiness, of intensive socializing, and is to be distinguished from other holidays by its cosmological relevance. He concluded his explanation, saying that:

---

170 This is when Qikiqtarjuaq received its hamlet status.

People get close to each other. Closer and closer to each other, the more they seem to open up to each other. It is the time to credit themselves in terms of forgiving each other. That is one of the good things about Christmas. Some people start to heal from the way they think and act toward other people. We know, we have been told, this is not just a holiday season. It is the time to get healed from our imagination or so, forgiving each other, and getting close to each other. [They come together to] be with others, to feel good like everybody else in the world. Hopefully [laughs]. That's how we've been practicing this from way back, from the time religious ministers were coming to the North in the late 19th century. We've been trying to continue this.

Lootie Toomasie perceived Christmas as an occasion of healing. But the benefits to the community of celebrating Christmas are dependent on celebrating it properly. Lootie Toomasie was not negative about changes, although he was skeptical about some developments. Similar to most other people I talked with on this matter, he referred to Christmas performances in nomadic camps of the past as ideal.

What actually constitutes a proper Christmas celebration is the issue of an ongoing discourse in Qikiqtarjuaq.[171] The Christmas Committee, constituted by the Community Service Committee, plans each year's celebration, particularly the games. Its members took this discourse very serious and discussed and integrated suggestions coming from the community in their planning for the following Qikiqtarjuaq Christmas festival.

Picture 29 *Winning prizes during the Midnight Madness Sale in the Northern Store.*

---

171 Discourses on the proper Christmas celebration are not new, however. Laugrand & Oosten (2002) demonstrated that Inuit and missionaries have thought about the most appropriate way to celebrate since the celebration was first introduced.

5.2 Christmas in Qikiqtarjuaq

After the fall, people were confined to the settlement for as long as there was sea-ice. Most people limited their social interactions to a small circle of friends, family members and their work. At the same time, people gradually started to prepare for Christmas. Women started to sew new garments to be given and worn at Christmas. The Christmas Committee as well as other institutions and businesses arranged special meetings to organize their contributions to the Christmas events.

From early December, an increasing number of houses were decorated with colorful lights and a large illuminated cross had been set up beside the community's *inukshuk* stone cairn on the nearby hill. The post-office was stacked with mail-ordered Christmas gifts. Around mid-December, activities multiplied. Institutions invited their staff for a Christmas feast and games. The Youth Committee cleaned the homes of elders. Organizations, such as the Women's Auxiliary Group and the Youth Committee, raised funds with lotteries, to support people in need with extra food for Christmas. The stores organized special sales. Children of families in need were provided with gifts by the RCMP, Social Services and the Health Center in cooperation with a national gifts-for-children program. Everyone was very busy and especially women expressed feeling exhausted with all the preparation.

The beginning of the school holidays was heralded by a Christmas concert by students and teachers, after which the majority of Qallunaat residents left Qikiqtarjuaq to stay with their families down South. A day or two before Christmas some Inuit family members from other communities arrived by plane. The local radio station continuously broadcast holiday greetings phoned in by Inuit from within and outside the community to their relatives and friends in Qikiqtarjuaq.

Picture 30 *Inuksuit School teachers performing at the Christmas school concert.*

On December the 23rd 1999,[172] the community festival was opened with a prayer and games in the school gym. The next ten days were filled with outdoor competitions in the morning and indoor competitions in the evening, except on Sundays. Dances followed the evening games and lasted into the early morning hours. Another highlight of the festival were two feasts, one organized by the municipality on Christmas Eve, and the other by the Hunters and Trappers Organization on New Year's Day.[173] Christmas Day and New Year's Eve were celebrated with community church services. The New Year service was followed by fireworks and by a not officially planned but each year spontaneously assembled snowmobile parade with torches going through the settlement, over the maintenance roads and onto the sea ice. The celebration was concluded with a last day of games on January 2nd. Besides the community events, people also held private festivities. Many families organized a Christmas dinner on Christmas Eve and exchanged gifts after the church service or the following morning.

5.3 Christmas and New Year services

Introduction
The Christmas and New Year services were organized by the Anglican Church in cooperation with Church groups, the Full Gospel Church, and other volunteers. The services were held on December 24th in the evening and an hour before midnight on December 31st, respectively. About 300 teenagers, adults and elders of the community participated – hardly anyone stayed home. Due to the large number of attendants, the services were held in the school gym.[174]

5.3.1 The Christmas Service of 1999
December the 24th started with morning outdoor games, followed by a few evening games and a competition for the best outdoor Christmas lights decorations. People then went home to get dressed up, while the gym was prepared for the church service. Men set up a stage at the long side of the gym. Benches for the choir were placed at the back of the stage and a lectern from the Anglican Church was installed at the front. Also the church's organ was brought to the gym and installed at the left side of the stage. Elaborate hi-fi equipment was set up. Twelve long rows of chairs were set up for the congregation. A leaflet with the program, produced by the Anglican Church, was placed on each chair. Its front page was decorated with two trombone playing angels, an open Bible and two candles. Underneath a Bible verse related: "Suddenly a great army of heaven's angels appeared with the angels singing praises to God: 'Glory to God in the highest heaven, and peace on earth to those with whom he is pleased." On the last page, the reader was blessed with the words: "May God love you, keep you & give you peace, this season & always."

---

172 As was also done in 2000.

173 In 1999, the feast was moved to a later date, as the caribou meat that the HTO (being the organizer of this second feast) had ordered, did not arrive.

174 John Ayaruaq was the main translator of the video documents of the Christmas and New Year services. His translations cover about 90 % of the verbal data. Gaps in the documentation are due to low quality of the voice recording.

I participated in the services in the years 1999 and 2000. As they were very similar, I am focusing my description on the services of 1999 and will use data from 2000 for comparison when necessary.

All seats were occupied 10 minutes prior to the begin of the service, and in addition people sat down on their jackets in the little space left on the floor along the walls. Couples tended to sit together and preferably in the vicinity of close family members. There were only two formal seating arrangements made. In the first row, chairs were reserved for elders. Coincidentally, other seats in the first row were preferred by middle-aged or older Inuit with an orientation toward Pentecostalism. The benches along a side wall were set up for the members of the Wolf Cubs ranger group, who in 1999 participated in the service in full uniform.[175] An alternative program was organized by the Youth Committee for younger children in a classroom adjacent to the gym.

When the choir,[176] dressed in robes, and the lay readers ascended to the stage, conversations faded away. Preparing for the first hymn, Lootie Toomasie (a member of the Full Gospel band) stretched his fingers to play the organ. After welcoming everyone, Loasie Kunilusie announced the first Christmas hymn, *quviasuvvik nulliutippa* ('Christmas Eve'). Most adults knew the verses by heart and joined in. Loasie Kunilusie and a few members of the congregation held up a hand Pentecostal style. He thanked the Lord for coming back to all of them by the birth of Jesus Christ.[177] While speaking, his voice changed into a more pious modulation and he stressed his words with his gestures. Bible readings[178] by Inuit (in Inuktitut) and Qallunaat (in English) related the Christmas story. Several hymns were sung. The favorite, measured by the enthusiasm with which it was sung, was 'Silent Night, Holy Night'.

Picture 31 *Drama performance by members of the Northern Lights.*

---

175 The initiative to dress in the Wolf Cub uniform and to sit together as a group came from the Qallunaat leaders, who went on the radio with their request.

176 A larger number of choir members participated at the Christmas service than at normal Sunday services.

177 The audio quality of my recording of his speech was inadequate for transcription. In 2000 Loasie Kunilusie opened the service with the following words:

We are celebrating the birth of Jesus. Without him there would be no celebration. We would be nothing, if God our Father did not send his son to save us. This celebration is special to each and every one of us. The birth of our Savior comes each year. Although he was crucified for our sins, he came back to life. For this reason we celebrate his birthday on this date. I am going to give each and every one of you the opportunity to say a few words about Christmas and you can say your testimony before the service is over. Let us sing a hymn.

178 Bible verses: Luke 1:26-38, birth of Christ; Luke 2:8-20, shepherds& angels; Matthew 2:1-12, wise men visit.

Then followed a highlight of the service. Twenty members of the *Northern Lights* youth group, dressed in blue or white long robes, performed a song by emphasizing its word through gestures, a so-called drama, evoking the performance of a gospel-choir. The young people were especially trained by a group of Pentecostal church leaders from Iqaluit, who had visited Qikiqtarjuaq in early December for a Bible conference. Mary Killiktee told me that the dance was supposed to have an uplifting effect on the singers and the audience as the words would become more powerful. She and Loasie Kunilusie were singing to a melody from a tape recorder. Two of its members, Leo Audlakiak and Danny Audlakiak, waved a blue flag and a golden flag. Blue was meant to symbolize the water and yellow the sun that feature in the following song:

There is brightness in my heart
and the waters are flowing into my body
we are holding on to our loves
and the sun is shining upon us
and the water is pouring into my body.

The second drama performed was the song 'My God is an awesome God!'. When the youth choir bowed at the end of their performance, the audience stood up, cheered, and applauded. People were so excited that the Northern Lights gave an encore after the conclusion of the service. Then, Loasie Kunilusie invited people to share their testimonies. Only Mealeah Audlakiak, the eldest person of the community, climbed the platform. She said:

As one of the eldest persons in our community, I want to thank God that I am able to celebrate with you the birth of Jesus. I have been helped and blessed, because of our prayers. Although I do not often go to church on Sundays, I pray. When I pray it seems that I am in church with you, because I have a good feeling being part of you, as though I am with you in church. I have many grandchildren and great grandchildren. I am so very grateful for them. I am fed with country food from all the hunters and I am so happy that you people think of me to feed me. Without your generosity, I would be helpless. With your help I am able to be part of our community. Once again, I would like to thank each and everyone here for your help. Let us celebrate the birth of our Christ with pride and prayers to our God. Thank you.

Mealeah Audlakiak presented herself as an elder and spoke on behalf of the community's elders expressing gratefulness for participating in the community's Christmas celebration. She emphasized that, on the one side, prayer and, on the other side, sharing of food by hunters gave expression to her social relatedness with the community.

The congregation applauded, heartily. Loasie Kunilusie concluded the testimony session reminding the congregation that:

God has not created us for fun, but to believe in God. If we take advantage of the world, we would be nothing. That's why Jesus came to help. [data loss due to poor audio quality] Be happy at Christmas for Jesus' sake, because he is born. Jesus has arrived. [Audience is applauding and cheering.] Let us ask ourselves: Are we blessed? Are we faithful now that Jesus has arrived? Now, let us ask ourselves again: Do I believe in Jesus?

The service was concluded with a prayer, a benediction and a hymn. All participants got up, shook hands with each other and hugged their friends and family members wishing them "Merry Christmas!"[179] A few people who cried, missing deceased loved ones, were comforted by relatives or friends. After about twenty minutes, the first people started to leave while the *Northern Lights* assembled on the stage for their extra performance. Afterwards, about 30 people, most of them in their twenties and some being older, gathered around the organ, played by Stevie Kakka, and sang modern church songs known to all from Pentecostal-style services and Bible conferences. Sami Qappik, the lead singer, used the microphone. The inner circle was formed by young people; older men and women gathered around them. Singers clapped and danced to the rhythm of the songs, and Loasie Kunilusie joined them with a raised hand. Gamailee Nookiruaq took over the microphone, shouting: "Merry Christmas!" This spontaneous performance was not appreciated by all community members. Someone told me: "I think some people get over-reacted by praying and singing."

Meanwhile, people started the annual Christmas snowmobile-parade through the settlement, the street to the garbage dump, and the sea-ice. Lizzy Anaviapik told me later that they wanted to express their happiness. A few men enjoyed themselves with traditional wrestling on the sea-ice. After the parade, everyone went home, and many households did not want to wait until the next morning to exchange their presents.

Some 30 people met the next morning for the Christmas Day service at the Anglican church, officiated by Jacopie Koksiak. Among the congregation were Billy Arnaquq and his father Silasie Angnako, both prominent members of the Full Gospel Church. The service was traditionally Anglican until close to the end, when popular modern Christian songs were sung.

A young woman went to the altar and kneeled down. Six other Inuit, five women and one man, followed. Some of them were crying silently or sobbing loudly. Several members of the congregation had tears in their eyes. The singing continued and some people lifted a hand in the air. Apparently, people were dealing with personal troubles or feelings of loss. Participants seemed to feel better after the prayers and blessings. At the conclusion of the service, Jacopie Koksiak invited everybody to say "Merry Christmas!" loudly and cheerfully.

Inuit perceptions
Inuit always emphasized that Christmas is about the birth of Jesus and that it is important to celebrate the service with the entire community. Lootie Toomasie, the mayor at that time and a leading member of the Full Gospel Church, stated:

> Well, during the Christmas service the minister is always reminding us and always reading the Bible verses to make sure that we are really focussed on Christmas' real meaning. From that point, I think that peace was there by that time. Nobody seemed to be against each other. They loved each other as they loved themselves. I don't know what else to say about this. I just know that there is so much peace there.

He emphasized the absence of conflict at Christmas. When I asked him how differences in Christian beliefs and practices were dealt with at that occasion, he replied:

---

179 At the Christmas service of the year 2000, Loasie Kunilusie introduced this practice by saying: "Our last hymn. During this time, during singing the hymn, you may embrace or shake hands to whomever you want to. Hug for the sake of our Savior's birthday."

We did not want to separate. This is one community in terms of – we decided not to separate, because we all are one, united in God. [...] We never want to do that. We never want to have two services really, especially during Christmas, and New Year as well. [...] It is better for the whole community, it really is better for the whole people that everybody was with each other. We feel that way. Everybody feels more comfortable, not pointing at somebody. I don't know, they start to open to everybody.

Apparently, a traditional Anglican-style service was most adequate to bring all people together. Care was taken not to introduce any spiritual obstacles to participation. People were expected to participate properly and therefore children were discouraged from attending the service. Ina Sanguya, at that time head of the Youth Committee, explained:

[Children] do not stay at church during Christmas Eve and New Year's Eve. There are lots of kids here, right? They can run around. Because we do not want the kids to run around, disturbing the service [...] one of the members of the Church [committee] asked for volunteers. He went on the radio and asked for volunteers. I went over to his house and told him that the Youth Committee can look after the kids during the service. So, when we looked after the kids I was singing with them [...] Christmas songs and hymns and whatever the kids liked to sing, what they usually sing at school. [...] And there were two Youth Committee door keepers. So kids would not go in and out. And for those who stayed with their parents, two Youth Committee members were in the gym looking after the kids.

Christmas is organized and perceived as an adult business by many Inuit. Although the presence of children was appreciated and care was taken that they would have a good time, they were thought to lack the *isuma* ('understanding') required to participate properly.

Discussion
The traditional Anglican service format was thought best to accommodate all community members. The format's special Christmas repertoire was well-known to all participants. For example, elders recalled having already learned the hymn 'Silent Night, Holy Night' as children, and that it had always been part of the Christmas celebrations in camp. Why were new features that were already integrated and valued in Anglican services and accepted by many Inuit, such as ecstasy, repetition of songs, or speaking in tongues, not part of the service? I suggest that the traditional Anglican format and features, such as the well-known Christmas hymns, were perceived to connect the congregation to the Christian ways of the *inummariit* ('real Inuit').[180] Most elders preferred the traditional Anglican ways, and they were considered to be the closest representatives of the *inummariit*. The orientation towards a traditional framework, however, does not imply that new features could not be integrated. The performance of the *Northern Lights*, for example, was considered acceptable in the service and very much welcomed.

Mialia Audlakiak expressed in her testimony that she attached great importance to being part of the community in daily life and during the Christmas festival. She particularly emphasized the traditional values of sharing and cooperation. The value placed on being together with the whole community was, according to Lootie Toomasie, a central focus of the services. It was important

---

180 See the chapter *Theoretical background and methodology* for this concept.

that the community should not be divided by daily conflicts. To some extend, this community also included the Qallunaat who participated in the service.

Lootie Toomasie perceived that the set-up of communally celebrating the service was: "really better for the whole people [because] everybody was with each other. [...] Everybody feels more comfortable not pointing at somebody." To him, reading Bible verses and being reminded of the meaning of Christmas helped to create a conflict free service. By connecting to God, conflicts could be removed.

5.3.2 The New Year's Service of 1999

On December the 31st, people went home after an evening of games to dress up for the New Year service. Because no separate service was provided for the children, many of them came along with their parents. The Anglican sexton Jacopie Newkingak supervised the children during the service. When the church choir, this time not dressed in robes but in fine ordinary clothing, had taken their seats on the stage, the service was opened by Loasie Kunilusie:

> While we are in the world, not one person is just playing, fooling around, because we believe in God. God created everything. There are misunderstandings as we travel on different paths in the world. But God has made it easy for us, because he is our guide. We are thankful, Father, that we are here to celebrate together and we are also here for Your forgiveness. [...][181] Your happiness will have room in our hearts and we open our hearts for Your happiness. Hallelujah, thank you Jesus, Hallelujah.

By stating that proper conduct is relevant for a person's relation with God and also a product of this relationship, Loasie emphasized the communal aspect of the service. The members of the congregation (should) undergo a spiritual transformation by pursuing forgiveness and seeking a relationship with God. The issue of transformation was recurrent in this service.

The congregation joined in the song 'I am a Christian Soldier'. Loasie had closed his eyes and stretched out his arms. He repeated the hymn, interspersed by shouts of: 'Hallelujah!'. The intonation of the song by the congregation increased in volume and expression, and some people raised their arms. But, I also saw a number of people who appeared not affected, and I detected some people who seemed annoyed. After the singing, and apparently still excited, Loasie gave a long sermon emphasizing that, in the 'last days', God would intensify his work among humans through the Holy Spirit. He encouraged the congregation to share their testimonies:

> If anybody wants to say anything, they can come up. [...] There are a lot of people on earth, who are not talking or saying anything. Although they have a feeling of God's work. But God says that we have to convey our feelings to the people. Our Lord has said that we don't have to be embarrassed to talk about it. If we are ashamed of God, when we die we will see shame.

This warning connected to the traditional Inuit believe that remaining silent over spiritual experiences and wrongdoings – even if already salvaged by God – would cause misery.[182] He,

---

181   These brackets indicate that I left out repetitions in his speech.
182   See chapter *Christianity in Qikiqtarjuaq* on the issues of testimonies and confession.

therefore, invited people to share their testimonies and, leading the congregation, he paved the way by starting with his own story:

> We are all looking for a better life as well as to be healed. For this reason we have to celebrate the birth of Christ. He came to the world to heal us, to help us. There are lot of invisible things in the world, like Satan and the bad spirits. In the name of Jesus Christ, we don't hear or see them. Jesus' name is the winner. Jesus Christ's name is the kingdom of God. And bad spirits don't want to hear the word of Jesus Christ. Hallelujah! For this reason we all have lots of things to say in respect to God. And we have testimonies to tell. Jesus Christ is the only person, who can actually heal us. The only person. I can talk about him easily, because I have found him. I have been in Qikiqtarjuaq as a drunkard, women chaser. I used to use bad languages. You know me very well, especially these grown-ups. They know exactly what I have committed. They are wondering, I am sure, when I will come back to my old way of life. Hallelujah! I am happy! That is how Jesus can heal us. He can gradually fix our way of life. [...] Anybody is welcome to say a few words. So you can come up. Telling your testimony is not a competition between two people. It is not to say 'he is better than me or he is worse than I am'. Its not competing with each other. But the real meaning is to make God as big as he is. You don't make me big, but you make God big.

The structure of his account – wish of improvement, warning about remaining silent, healing, and the assurance that all was brought to the open – followed, at the same time, a traditional Inuit way of confession (see, for example, Boas 1901: 121, 126-127) as well as a Christian tradition of testimony and a format of Pentecostal stories of conversion.[183] Subsequently, three older women and a middle-aged man testified to the congregation of their experiences.

Peepeelee Nutaralak, a woman in her late fifties, already started telling her story of both spiritual and physical recovery while in the process of ascending the stage. Acknowledging the obligation to testify she explained:

> If you love Jesus, we have to talk about him. Yes, myself, too. And I have found Jesus. And only him, nothing else. And I believe in him. I thought I had forgotten him. But he still returned to me.

Then she related a dream:

> In 1968 I had a dream. I saw a person with a letter, whom I couldn't touch. I couldn't understand then, but today I am able to understand it. We have to find out the word of God, before we can actually start walking. The letter said: 'Now Jesus is living!'. I used to think, the Bible was only used in church. The Bible is a tool that we can use to understand God more. And sometimes we, the unbelievers, think that God cannot do great things. And we can go the wrong way, if we don't read the Bible.

Peepeelee took care to present her spiritual improvements and, at the same time, to not present herself as different from others. The tension between an individual having gained spiritual insights and "we, the unbelievers" was a recurrent feature of her testimony. Just like Loasie

---

183 See chapter *Christianity in Qikiqtarjuaq* on practices of confession, testimony, and conversion.

Kunilusie, she started her personal story with the announcement of the beneficial working of Jesus' presence. Then followed her confession that she had at first forgotten the Christian message. She continued:

> I am telling you about the gift from God for myself and Levy [husband] as well. Levy and I are blessed through our bodies as well. This is a known fact, because I had a cancer and I have been healed. I have to bring this out. And Levy had a heart problem, but he is alive today. During 1999, I had a tremendous movement of understanding, because I believe in Jesus. Jesus said, when he touched and healed a person 'you are healed, because you believe in God'. And to my knowledge now we have to believe and I have found out that God is the only way. I am very thankful.

Thus, having confessed, she and her husband then received what she perceived to be a gift from God – spiritual and physical healing. She continued formulating her spiritual transformation in terms of the traditional Inuit symbolic of 'seeing':[184]

> I expected to be in hell, because I was a very hard person. I was not able to talk freely about my sins.[185] I am very thankful, because it was easy for me to talk about my sins at a later date. Jesus, who is the son of God, has indicated that my sins are washed away. I wanted Jesus to come into my heart, because I am a bad person. Because I am blind, I am not able to see the commandments of God. I thought this could have been hard for me to talk about my sins, but it was very easy to talk about. I wanted to testify for a long time, but I was not ready. Because I am now an easy going person, I thank you for that.

The congregation applauded after Peepeelee's story, and Leah Kuniliusie, an elder woman, took over the microphone. She referred to a case of which John Ayaruaq subsequently gave specifics: Leah Kunilusie had been flying from Iqaluit to Pangnirtung. The breaks froze and when landing, the pilot steered the plane off the runway to use the snow to slow down. This strong experience triggered her vision:

> I am going to talk about how I feel in my body. During the month of December we were traveling from Iqaluit, through Pangnirtung [to Qikiqtarjuaq]. We left Iqaluit 9:00 a.m. As we reached Pangnirtung at that time, there didn't seem to be any problem with the aircraft. As we landed in Pangnirtung the aircraft was moving very fast outside of the runway. And we were moving a lot. To me it didn't seem that we were moving a lot, that was my feeling. I don't know how the other passengers felt. I didn't even think about my children. Because God has given us a good place. I felt the movement of the aircraft. I felt as if I was somewhere else. I only knew that we were moving very fast outside of the runway. I got more understanding from God, how he looks after us. I was very thankful. I forgot to mention that before we left Iqaluit I was told by a person in Iqaluit that s/he had experienced flying when the weather was so bad, the aircraft was moving a lot, there was a lot of turbulence. So

---

184 See, for example, Boas (1888, 594; 1901, 168; 1907, 504). See also Sami Qappik's story of conversion in chapter *Christianity in Qikiqtarjuaq*.

185 See the chapter *Christianity in Qikiqtarjuaq* on the issues of confession and conversions as well as their association with transformations in the social domain.

that person closed his/her eyes very tightly and had a vision of Jesus' hands that were holding on to the aircraft. I was told that before we left, and we almost had the same experience. And the person wasn't scared at all anymore, because in his/her vision with eyes closed Jesus was holding the aircraft, when this person spoke about it s/he was very wet, sweating, hot. That's how good he is to look after us. When we almost had an accident he looked after us so well. The rest of the passengers got out of the plane in Pangnirtung and I was the only person coming up to Qikiqtarjuaq. I was the only passenger to Qikiqtarjuaq, also Jasi [her son] was in the aircraft, his destination was to Pangnirtung. We were brought to this community by a different aircraft. For this I want to be thankful. God looks after people so well. That is what I wanted to share with you.

The congregation applauded and a hymn was sung and then followed two more testimonies. Aitaina Nookiguak, an elder woman, shared a dream with the congregation:

I was with my mother alone and we were outside. We were told by something, because there was nobody else around – I don't know, where the voice came from or from whom it was. It said: 'It is possible that there comes an earthquake.' That's what the voice said. And I was looking for that person, who said these words and I thought the earthquake would be small. In my mind I truly believed the voice that spoke to me and my mother. For this reason I expect something to happen during the week. That was my dream and I still believe it to happen.

The congregation applauded while Aitaina went back to her seat. Just like the two elders before her, Aitaina referred to an intense and impressive emotional experience, which they associated with God. They related their story in a traditional idiom of confession, vision, and dreaming.[186] This was appreciated by the audience that honored each speaker with applause. John Ayaruaq, a man in his late middle-ages, expressed his feelings in the last testimony of the evening. He emphasized that he wished to believe and not to criticize the community's elders who spoke and also those who were seated in the first row:

I'd like to acknowledge and respect these people in front, who are our elders. Without these older people in front of us, none of us would be here today. We have to respect them and have to believe in them, understand their needs. For the respect and our way of saying thank you, let us give them applause. [Congregation applauded and whistled enthusiastically.] These elders have helped us a lot, although we don't see them physically helping us. I know each and every one of you have had a gift and these older people have had a great gift. They lived in a very harsh environment and they lived in a very cold climate and to see them celebrating the New Year with us is a pleasure. And we'd like to see them in the years that are coming, we want in the future for them to be able to celebrate with us again.

Then, he shifted the subject of his speech to himself and his family emphasizing their positive relations with the community in terms of mutual help and prayer:

The Qikiqtarjuaq people understand the need of helping one another. For the people of Qikiqtarjuaq's benefit I am available to help you in any way that you need help. And I would

---

186 See chapter *Christianity in Qikiqtarjuaq*.

Picture 32 *Ragalee Angnako and Rosie Alikatuqtuq lighting their candles at the conclusion of the New Year service.*

like to say thank you, the people of Qikiqtarjuaq, that my family was welcomed back to Qikiqtarjuaq. We are thankful for your support and I'd like you to pray for my wife. Her younger sister died of cancer on the 25th of December. And a few years ago her mother was buried on January the 1st. For this reason, please pray for her.

The congregation applauded, cheered, and whistled. Another hymn was sung and Bible verses were read. It was now just before midnight. After a brief period of silent prayer, concluded with the Lord's Prayer, the lights were switched off and people lit candles they had brought and shared the flame with neighbors. Everybody joined in the song 'Auld Lang Syne'. Several women started to cry, commemorating (recently) deceased loved ones. Close relatives or friends took care of them by hugging them tightly. Also family members and close friends were hugging each other. The lights were switched on again, people applauded and Loasie Kunilusie told the congregation to shout "Happy New Year" – one, two, three times, louder and louder. Everybody shook hands wishing each other "Happy New Year!"

Elaborate fireworks organized by the Fire Brigade started exactly at midnight. Most people rushed outside to watch the spectacle above the *inukshuk* hill. A huge '2000' and a cross were illuminated with bulbs. People praised it with playfully dramatized "Oooh!"and "Aaaah!" Before long, people got on their snowmobiles and drove through the settlement, over the maintenance roads and onto the sea-ice in a parade. The gym became a place to warm up, to have coffee, tea, and to chat. Later on, everyone came together again and the games resumed.

Discussion
The New Year service was, just like the Christmas service, celebrated in the traditional Anglican format. Marking the conclusion of the old year and the beginning of the new year, people took it as an opportunity to express their appreciation of the community and the wish to improve one's life. And, similar to the Christmas service, it was emphasized that social tensions were subordinated to the relationship with God.

The service was marked by the active participation of the congregation that dynamically constituted social formations. The church leader provided people, and in partiuclar the elders, with ample opportunities to speak in the framework of testimonies and thereby to preside over the service. Elders spoke, choosing traditional formats, about strong experiences and their spiritual dimension. The audience listened to their stories, expressed their appreciation and their respect. Though some children were present in the service, they did not feature in any particular way. So that just like the Christmas service, the New Year service was an adult business.

The service brought together the whole community. The congregation, by placing the elders in the position of highest status, was organized along traditional Inuit ways. The church leader facilitated this by providing them with the opportunity to speak, the audience by being attentive listeners, and the children by being passively present. The dead were also connected to the community when several women expressed their affection for (lately) deceased family members in public mourning toward the end of the service.[187] Afterwards, everybody participated in the cheerful exchange of best wishes for the New Year and the enjoyment of the fireworks as the old year had just turned into the new one.

5.3.3 Elders' recollections of Christmas and New Year services

When I interviewed elders on their memories of Christmas in camps, they usually referred only obliquely to the services in camp, whereas they explained most elaborately the gift exchanges and the feast. The elders perceived that things were changing in the practices of gift-giving, however they were content with the continuity in how services were celebrated. Even though some elements of the services were recently introduced, such as the drama performance of the *Northern Lights*, elders were quite satisfied with them. How did they recall the services in the camps? Jacopie Koksiak, who lived in a camp close to Pangnirtung as a young boy before moving to Padloping, recalled:

> We would sing songs. We had Christmas songs. Less than today, but one song is still used today. I never forget it: 'Silent Night' (*unnua upina*). In the evening at 11 p.m., we would gather in the biggest sod house mainly, for prayer services, just like a Christmas service. In the evening we would gather again for a feast. We gathered in a private sod house. Depending on the family. If the family was a well-to-do family, they had the largest sod house. It would be in the living quarters not in a separate sod house for activities. It was in my adoptive parents' sod house.[188]

Martha Nookiruaq, his older adopted sister, added: "We had a service in the sod house and if it was not too cold we had a service outside. [...] Makiktua [did the service]. He was Iqalik's father. They were singing songs which were in the Bible." Martha Kopalie and Peter Paniloo, who came from Kivitoo, had similar recollections of the Christmas service in their camp. Martha related that: "after eating they would get together and start singing and they went to the largest sod house and said their prayers. Everybody would be invited into the largest sod house to pray." She recalled: "My father [Naujavik] was the leader of the congregation. They would say prayers. But everybody was sort of involved, in coming there to pray. The prayers were done by everybody who would come." Peter Paniloo added: "[It was] my father, Paniloq, as well as Naujavik who read the Bible. We were singing from the hymn book." Children did not participate in the service. Martha explained: "As a child they did not sing it. When they were old enough they

---

187 The dead are always close by. See chapter *Christianity in Qikiqtarjuaq* on the issues of death, funeral, and naming practices.

188 His adoptive father's name was Kuksiak.

did." Aka Keyooktak who grew up in a camp close to Pangnirtung, vividly recalled how she felt about the service as a child. She laughed when she related: "After shaking hands, we waited until after praying together. We could hardly wait for the church service to be over, because of the gifts. The service seemed to be so long. I couldn't wait for the church service to be over, because I wanted my gift."

New Year's services were also celebrated in the past. Jacopie Koksiak recalled: "We were told that we had arrived in the new year or that the new year is arriving. For New Year Eve we held a church service, prayer service. Afterwards we would greet each other, hug each other and give more presents. They gave presents at that time."

5.3.4 Discussion of Christmas and New Year services

Continuity with the past was emphasized in the ways services were celebrated now, even though new elements were integrated. Martha Kopalie said that she had greatly enjoyed the presentation of the *Northern Lights*. She did not think that the modern service was different from that of her childhood:

> [Back then] they sang carols, Christmas hymns, the real traditional Christmas carols. And the Bible they use today was already been used then, in the early days. They would read the Gospels, very much the same as today, because there was no change in the Bible.

Martha Kopalie, like other elders, emphasized continuity in the Church services. The elders based their view on their perception that the Bible was unchangeable. Newly introduced elements had been integrated into the traditional Anglican framework in such a way that they did not foster a sense of change – with the possible exception of the Pentecostal singing style, disapproved of by some members of the congregation. In this way, the services constituted a proper community because connected to the ways of the inummariit.

5.4 Christmas presents

Introduction

Gift exchanges were a much anticipated part of the Christmas festival. In late November 1999, the post office was packed with mail orders that would be picked-up as soon as the pay-checks were handed out. Gifts could also be purchased at the Northern store, which also organized special sale-nights for women, men, children, and elders. Some Inuit prepared handmade presents, such as *kamiit* ('seal skin boots') or an *ulu* (fan-shaped women's knife). Gifts were hidden away until a few days before Christmas, and then, nicely wrapped, displayed underneath the Christmas tree or on a shelf in the living room.

Christmas presents were not only exchanged within a circle of friends and relatives but also at Christmas celebrations of local organizations and of the community. There, the gift exchanges were organized as a game, such as the 'Secret Santa' or as a bingo.[189] The specific features of the

---

189 In these contexts, presents were in various degrees also used as prizes. In comparing these occasions with the exchange of presents within families and a circle of friends, the relationship between the notions of present and prize will be explored.

various kinds of gift exchanges will be studied to explore the capacities of gifts in the formation of relationships.[190]

5.4.1 Christmas presents for relatives and friends

During the first weeks of my fieldwork, I stayed in Lizzy Anaviapik's house and was welcome to participate in the gift exchanges. Until some years ago, Lizzy, her siblings and their families all met at their parents', Silasie and Ragalee Angnako's, house for the gift giving. As the family grew, they decided that it had become too crowded in the home of their parents. From then on, each household conducted its own giving of gifts, and then people visited each other to exchange gifts with the extended family, namesakes, and a number of friends.

Lizzy had initially planned the giving of gifts for December the 25th, but spontaneously decided not to wait that long after coming home from the Christmas service on the evening of December 24th, 1999. In the presence of her family, she lit the Christmas tree in the living room. Her family had already placed some presents underneath it a week earlier. I asked if I might put my gifts for the family under the tree as well, and they readily agreed. I had the impression that my gifts were not expected, but were welcome, if that was what I wanted to do. Gifts for me were purchased at the last minute.

Lizzy told me that she used to give gifts to many people in the community. Since the number of people she wanted to give something to was growing, she decided to give cakes to persons and families she cared for the most. That evening, Lizzy exchanged gifts with her children, and the siblings had prepared gifts for each other. Underneath the tree, there was also a gift for Simon, Lizzy's son, from his friends, Conner and Megan Ross-Ejangiaq.[191] And there were gifts, all of them referring to name-relations, that would be distributed later on. One was from "Sakiasi for his parents." Simon was named after the deceased son, Sakiasi, of Loasie and Geela Kunilusie. In his capacity as Sakiasi's namesake, he gave the gift to Loasie and Geela the next day. Others were from "a girl for her beloved spouse" and from a "spouse for her husband." And Jacopie, an adopted son of Lizzy, who was named after the deceased first child of Ragalee and Silasie Angnako, gave a gift to them.

Each of us were handed gifts by Lizzy or one of her daughters, after reading aloud the name of the giver and name or kin term of address of the receiver that was written on the gift tags. A few tags carried a message such as: "I love you!" We all opened the gift right away and expressed our appreciation. Then we thanked each other for what we had received, took some refreshments and chatted.

Most of the presents given to Lizzy were household gear, such as a pot and a baking set, because her household was still incomplete after her recent move from Pond Inlet to Qikiqtarjuaq. Her daughters received, among other things, bath oil, socks, a telephone card, and some items to furnish their room. Simon received mostly toys. Jacopie got some clothing and a hockey stick. I received a basket with bath oil and lotion from Tapisa and Lucy, and a pair of socks from Lizzy. She and her sisters expressed that they wished that had more time for sewing

---

190 Also the RCMP contributed to institutional gift exchanges. They cooperated in a program called *Gifts for Kids* that was organized by southern companies focusing on distributing Christmas presents to children of poor families. As Inuit were not active in the management of the program or in providing or distributing the gifts, I will not discuss this initiative in the framework of this study.

191 Their mothers engaged in mutual babysitting services and gave gifts to each other.

prior to Christmas in order to produce handmade presents. However, all of them were fully employed and therefore had little time to do so.

Lizzy's parents, one of her sisters, Geela Angnako-Kunilusie, as well as an adoptive brother of Ragalee's, Salamonie Kanajuq from Pangnirtung came to visit. They had left their gifts for the family at home and would distribute them when Lizzy and her family would come for a visit. Only Salamonie Kanajuq[192] brought gifts and gave a picture of the Holy Mary to Lizzy; he gave some matchbox cars to Simon.

People went for visits to distribute gifts to relatives, name-relations, and close friends or gave them during the evening games in the school gym on December 25th. I visited some households of acquaintances to bring small gifts. I gave a decorative Delft porcelain and some chocolate to a friend of mine, Monica Nuqingaq, a woman in her late twenties and mother of four children. She was out for the dance, but her brother was at home. He asked me to wait and brought a gift for me from upstairs. He said that he wrapped it himself. It was a scarf, a rather unexpected surprise. This was the only return gift I received during these visits.

Discussion

A few days prior to Christmas, nicely wrapped boxes were placed under the decorated Christmas tree or on a shelf. It was easy to determine who the giver was and who the receiver would be. Monica Nuqingak told me that she felt happy to look at the gifts. Under Lizzy's tree, gift-tags referred to mother-child and sibling relations, to relations of adoption, to friends, and to close name-relations. Through the living namesake, relationships to the dead were also recognized.

Gifts were chosen on the basis of the wishes of the receiver, gender and age, the practical use and the status as a luxury good. Most objects were purchased, but handmade presents were thought to be gifts closer to Inuit tradition and to express the maker's skill and care for the family. But also the value of the gift as such was appreciated and generosity valued. At Christmas, households were willing to spend more money and most households had to reduce their daily expenses in the following weeks to compensate. Members of households with a very low income wished they could give more gifts.

Gifts marked relations in terms of closeness. Quite often, the most money or time was spent on gifts for one's children and grandchildren. Then came spouses, parents and siblings, and finally others. In relatively well-to-do households, like Lizzy's, usually one or two gifts were given per giver and receiver relationship but more may actually be exchanged. By modest display, a household not only showed a proper social conduct, but also avoided marking social inequality.

5.4.2 Elders' recollections of Christmas gifts

The elders Jacopie Kuksiak, Martha Nookiruaq, Mealeah Audlakiak, Mary Oonga Audlakiak, Aka Keyooktak, and Martha Kopalie talked about gift practices in camps. Aka Keyooktak vividly recalled their excitement as children. The morning started with shaking hands and a church service and "I couldn't wait for the service to be over, because I wanted my gift." Whatever they received, "as soon as you got your gift it was very uplifting." Jacopie Koksiak, from Padloping, recalled:

When I first learned about Christmas, my adopted parents told me to go to sleep early so that we can get up in time for Christmas morning. [As kids] we knew that we were going

---

192 He had, to my knowledge, received a gift from Ragalee earlier in the evening.

to receive new clothing in the morning. Sometimes we couldn't fall asleep, because we could not wait to put on our new clothing. It is different today. Back then, we did not have too many material things. We just knew that in the morning we could put on new garments, new *kamiit*. Nowadays, we have these presents. Kids today, they can't wait. Like, when they do not know what they will receive, they can't wait. Back then, we knew what we would be receiving.[193] We did not have that sort of looking forward, that type of thing. We were always all the same happy receiving new clothes.

He emphasized that it was exchanging gifts that had made him excited, rather than the objects received as gifts. Gifts were taken from daily life:

As we didn't have many material things, we would give our personal belongings and also receive what was practical, like ropes. Homemade ropes made out of harp seal skin. Men would give ropes to other men. Women would receive something like seal skins. As a child, you received, for example, a small *qamutik* ('wooden sled') for towing and the small *qamutik* would have a box, harpoons, spears. If we were to give presents to other kids of our age, we would give them something from the *qamutik* or the whole *qamutik* itself. If children were to give to adults, parents would give something to their children to give to other adults. [...] Women would make something like mittens [to give to a man]. And a man would give to a woman what a woman usually used. And if a woman didn't have anything to give, she may get it from her father and give it to another person. [...] For New Year, they held a church service, a prayer service. Afterwards, they greeted each other, hugged each other, and gave more gifts. They gave gifts at that time.

He in particular recalled the gift he received from his future father-in-law:

I can never forget the first time when I received a gift, it was from a man. He gave me a rope made out of harp seal skin and the man told me that this would be a whip [for a dog team] when I would be grown up. My father gave me a snow-knife to give back to the man who gave me the rope. In return, I gave a snow-knife to this man. [...] As it turned out, who gave me this rope was eventually to become my father-in-law.

Martha Nookiruaq, Jacopie's step-sister 23 years his senior, recalled: "They gave each other presents, like their old things and maybe a dog." The objects did not have to be new but could be taken from a person's belongings and from the gifts s/he had just received. Also Mary Oonga Audlakiak, from the Cumberland Sound area stressed that gifts were small:

When we celebrated Christmas, because we lived in a very small camp, we didn't have a lot of things to give. They are so rich right now. They have everything in their house right now. We lived in a very small community with a very small population, we celebrated the birth of Jesus Christ. And it was only that day that they celebrated the birth of Christ. We didn't wear anything fancy because we were so poor. And because we were so poor, we would give whatever we had in the *qammaq* (house made of grass sods). We all lived in a *qammaq*. [...] They were very simple gifts, nothing fancy like store bought items. Nothing was wrapped. If

---

193 Some elders thought that the practice of wrapping would contribute to making children inquisitive.

I was going to give this [took a piece of chocolate] to you, I would have gone to your house. I would hide it first [laughing].

And Jesus Christ was born in a manger, and he was born very poor – we did not try to copy him, but they had no other choice but to celebrate with whatever they have. We were very poor and we did not have anything [big] to give as a gift to a person, but it might be a very small thing. And if she gave a person something that she had made and they were very happy with it. And the men would exchange their gifts, maybe a rope made out of the skin or a harness or a little puppy.

By associating the camp state of having little material possessions with that of Jesus birth, Mary Oonga Audlakiak suggested that the camp was actually in a 'divine' state. Connected to this ideal condition was the high value attributed to the smallness of the gift. Today, the majority of gifts are produced down South and are purchased. Jacopie Koksiak thought that finding gifts required much more time today, was less relaxed and less fun than in the past, where objects were taken from daily life.

Not only Inuit, but also Qallunaat occasionally gave presents. Among the many gifts received and given, these objects became memorable for some elders. Aka Keyooktak particularly recalled a gift that she had received from a missionary:

My most memorable present was a present from the missionary, the Anglican minister. It was a doll, a little Negro doll with a little crib. And I had it for a long time. It was very special to me. It might have been a little ugly but it was a precious thing, a little black person, a little Negro, with a little crib. And that was my most memorable gift, that from the Anglican minister.

Also Martha Kopalie had received a gift from a Qallunaat that became special to her:

To this date, I still remember a Scotsman who gave me a little box. I put all my bone toys in it. Maybe the box was too small then. I couldn't put all my bones inside. I still remember the Scotsman giving me that box that he himself had made.

Martha Nookiruaq stressed that, in contrast to today's practices, the gift exchange in the camp: "was not just for relatives and friends. It was for everybody – everybody knew everybody." Mealeah Audlakiak emphasized that in considering what to give: "my friends came first and I thought about giving a gift to cousins and best friends," and not primarily about giving to her closer relatives. Whereas today, as Aka Keyooktak thought:

It seems that they were only worried about which Christmas gifts to give to our relatives now. It used to be for everybody, but now it is only for the sons and the daughters, their grandchildren are going to think that Christmas, the presents are only for relatives, but before it used to be for everybody in the whole camp, the community.

Elders contrasted the practices of gift giving of the past with those of the present and suggested that the choice to whom one gave was different. However, people sharing a camp were usually relatives of each other. Thus, gifts were exchanged among relatives back than as they are today.

What, in the perceptions of elders, has changed is that the feature of a generalized gift exchange has been replaced by a selectiveness that tends to mark social distinctions.

Mary Oonga Audlakiak talked about changes in gift giving in terms of changes she perceived in the way people deal with country food:

> They were very happy with what they were given, and sharing was very important to the camp at that time. We feel sorrow in the sense that we get so much stuff now – if a person catches a seal now, they eat just a little bit of it and everything is thrown away. It was not like that years ago.

Mary Oonga Audlakiak suggested a connection between the distribution of gifts and the distribution of game. Both belong to different circuits of distribution. Country food could not be given as a gift. Game and gift objects are not interchangeable. Inuit believe that animals decide to be hunted. If the hunter was successful, he is obliged to share the food with others. By providing people with food, the hunter gains social prestige and maintains social relationships. Country food has to be shared and, in contrast to objects, cannot be part of the gift exchanges. In Inuit society, the hunting circuit and social relations are closely connected. Both have to function properly and improper conduct in one affects the other. By pointing out that, from her perspective, the practices of distributing game and of distributing gifts are deteriorating, Mary Oonga Audlakiak made a strong statement on the condition of the community.

Picture 33 *Silasie Angnako unwraps a gift he received during a gift-exchange game called Yankee Swap. (To his left his wife Ragalee Angnako, Peepeelee Nutaralak, her grandson Charlie, and her husband Levi Nutaralak. To his right an elder woman, probably Mialia Audlakiak.)*

5.4.3 Gift giving in the context of games

Local organizations as well as the municipality organized ludic gift exchanges as part for their Christmas celebrations.

The 'Secret Santa' at the Arctic College Christmas party

The Arctic College offered courses to adults and teenagers in various subjects, such as carpentry, sewing sealskin boots, and Inuktitut language instructions for Qallunaat. All students and instructors of these courses were invited to a Christmas celebration that included a potluck meal, games, and a Secret Santa gift giving event. Students and teachers had to pick a name and to purchase a gift for that person worth around $10. The giver's identity had to remain a secret. As requested, all participants gave their wrapped gifts to the coordinator, Lizzy Anaviapik, for distribution. Qallunaat participants complied with the rule of secrecy. Some Inuit participants preferred to make themselves known as the giver of the gift by adding their name to the gift-tag.

Lizzy Anaviapik gave a short speech explaining how students in different courses participated separately in the Secret Santa. Thus, the sewing course, the Inuktitut language and the carpentry courses drew names among themselves for the Secret Santa. I had just started to attend the sewing and the Inuktitut classes. Louise Vuillermin, a nurse who attended the Inuktitut class, explained to me that the Inuit students did not know the Qallunaat students who attended the

Picture 34 *Simon Anaviapik is waiting to deliver the gifts of the Secret Santa.*

Inuktitut class and that it therefore would be 'unfair' to mix the groups. I was assigned to the sewing course by Lizzy.

Lizzy asked her son to assist her in distributing the gifts. She read the names of the receivers on tags, and when the tag also named the giver, she read that as well. Otherwise she said that it was a gift from Secret Santa. The presenter got up and everybody applauded. Sometimes, she requested the audience to applaud harder. When receiving the gifts, people usually thanked Lizzy, the 'Secret Santa', or the person who identified him/herself as the giver, often shaking hands. Everybody opened the gift immediately and some were holding it up for all to see. Appreciative comments and some applause were the response. Sometimes, things went wrong. Two men who were added to the list at the last minute were listed as female. They received ladies' gifts: scented candles to the great amusement of all participants.

After everybody had received a gift, some people went around to shake hands to say thank you to their 'Secret Santa'. I received a huge stuffed toy polar bear from Elisapee Kopalie. She approached me and told me that she was my Secret Santa. She asked me if I liked the gift and I thanked her a lot. She smiled and her young daughter asked me if she might play with the bear for while. She put it into her play-*amauti* ('women's hooded jacket for carrying babies').

Discussion of the 'Secret Santa'
The idea of the anonymous gift was incorporated as a ludic element into the performance of the game – though not totally. Some participants did not comply to the rule of the anonymity of the giver from the start.[194] Others complied with the rules at first, but identified themselves later on. This transgression of the rule was accepted by the other players. The players who identified themselves introduced the feature of a personal relation between giver and receiver to the game. Lizzy, the game leader, supported their decision by reading their names aloud when handing out the gifts. By associating the giver with the gift, the anonymous connection was transformed into a relation in which people could shake hands and express their appreciation for the gift. In this way, the players could invest into relationships.

There is another aspect to the importance of identifying the giver, which has to do with Inuit perceptions of and ways of dealing with objects. Objects can be given as gifts, but are also distributed in various other ways. For instance, Inuit borrow and claim objects from each other. In particular among close relatives, it is expected that one has access to, for example, the hunting gear of others. And it is considered very inappropriate to refuse such a claim. Borrowed items should be given back in time. In case the item is damaged or in any way altered, the owner cannot expect the loaner to repair it. Sometimes things are taken without permission of the owner. Even when the person who took something is known, seldom is an effort made to retrieve the object. Even though taking things in this way is definitely not appreciated, emphasizing one's status as owner would be detrimental to the relationship through confronting and embarrassing that person. The relationship between an object and its owner is relatively weak.

This does not imply, however, that the relationship between an object and its owner is irrelevant, as expressed in the practices of identifying oneself in the *Secret Santa* game and in the general use of gift tags. Not only does the identification of the giver provide an opportunity to acknowledge a relationship, it is actually the giver that makes an object manageable. When Inuit, for example, find a knife when out on the land, they usually leave it, that is, when they

---

194   This conduct stands in contrast to Inuit ways of playing other Christmas games, where rules were strictly followed. See chapter *Games*.

do not know to whom it belongs. The avoidance of taking the object suggests a sense of danger associated with it. Though further research needs to be done on this issue in modern Inuit communities, I would like to suggest that, as in the past, there is a sense of danger attached to objects, in particular to objects one does not know from whom they originate. The danger lays in the fact that an object can be treated in such a way that they have the capacity to exert power over the person who receives it.[195] The burning of Heavy Metal paraphernalia that were believed to have harmed young people is a case in point. Anointed oil that is used in a house to keep away evil powers is an example of an object that has been given beneficial powers.[196] Objects whose origin is not known are, therefore, potentially dangerous. The gift-object becomes manageable by its connection to an identified giver.

The 'Community Gift Bingo'

The *Community Service Committee* (CSC) organized a community gift bingo on December 30th, 1999. One male and one female winner would receive all the gifts contributed by the male and female players, respectively. Everybody above the age of 18 could participate and had to bring a little wrapped present. The present was dropped in one of the two sacks, one for men and one for women, and the player received a bingo board.

The majority of the adult population, about 130 people, participated. I had asked Monica Nuqingak what kind of objects would be adequate at this occasion. She answered: "It is up to

Picture 35 *Rosie Kudlualik is enjoying the many gifts she received as the female winner of the Community Gift Bingo.*

---

195 In the shamanic past, objects were used for witchcraft, but also to protect oneself (for example by using amulets).

196 See chapter *Christianity in Qikiqtarjuaq*.

you. Whatever you like to give, it will be appreciated." We will come back to people's choices of gifts a bit later in this description. When everyone was settled and Rosemary Kunilusie, staff member of the *Community Service Committee*, announced the first number, it turned deadly silent. Attention was fixed on the boards, and only when a son or daughter helped the elderly to catch up with the rapid announcements, a quick low murmur was to be heard here and there. Sometimes, when the announcements were shortly interrupted for some technical reason, players took the opportunity to chat or to look at the boards of a neighbor to evaluate their own chances of winning.

Towards the end of the game, the atmosphere reached fever pitch. The only sound to be heard was a muttered "Irk!" if the situation on a person's board did not improve. When Joshua Alookie and then Rosie Kudlualik completed their boards, everyone appeared to take a deep breath and relax while their claims were checked. When the winners were announced, people applauded and moved together to see them unwrap their presents. Two bags were brought to the center of the gym. The winners sat down on the floor and started to unpack the gifts one by one. They were assisted by relatives who put away the wrappings. They raised each gift above their head so everybody could see. When people could not catch a glimpse they would loudly ask "*qannu?*" ('what is it?'). A practical joke, played twice that evening and well known to everybody, was to hide a gift inside a package of a product that would be a rather disappointing gift, for example instant rice. Anticipating the joke, the winner would show the gift around with exaggerated happiness. The winner then opened the package and the real gift item emerged.

After about half an hour, people were still watching, especially the children kept on cheering. They had moved closer and closer to the piles of gifts. The elder Leah Qumuatuq Kunilusie repeatedly told them to move back a bit, as others could hardly see what was given to the winners and could not see how they reacted to each gift. When Joshua finished his bag, some people applauded. Others were walking in and out and some had already gone home, it was late at night. Rosie continued to unpack consistently and to display the gifts she received. People applauded when she had unwrapped all her gifts. Then the winners and their helpers took all the gifts home.

Rosie's many gifts, included a porcelain figurines to be displayed in a cupboard, a bingo dapper, bath oil, decorative wall ornaments, perfume, a small carpet, wool, yarn, a used children's winter jacket, lotion, a new t-shirt, a scented potpourri, and such household articles as plastic food containers. Joshua received such gifts, as a Canadian flag (often used in Qikiqtarjuaq as a curtain), working-gloves, lighters, a fox-trap, music CDs, a video, a screwdriver, a watch, used as well as new trousers and shirts, a blank tape, a chocolate bar, and a small container with engine oil.

Discussion of the Community Gift Bingo

The game involved the whole community in gift giving and, thereby, created a highly valued gift exchange situation.[197] Unlike the regular bingo games for which people had to buy a ticket in the municipal office, the various Christmas bingo games were provided by individuals or organizations. In the community gift bingo, all players became providers by contributing a gift as part of the prize. The feature of the gifts was perceived to be the special attraction of the game.

Though the choice of what to give was free and the giver remained anonymous, most gifts gave the impression that people invested some money and effort to provide attractive presents.

---

197 See also the recollections of gift exchanges in camps by elders.

The display of the large amount of attractive objects by the winners, created the image of a generous community. Furthermore, it was important that everyone could watch the one by one display of gifts.[198] The esteem of each gift expressed by the winners as well as by the audience[199] approved the generosity of each giver, though he remained anonymous. By the performance of the generalized gift exchanges of the bingo game, the relation of each participant to the community was acknowledged and appreciated and a highly valued exchange situation was created.

5.4.4 Discussion of Christmas presents

The gift giving practices of the elder's past emphasized gender and age in what was given. Gifts were exchanged between persons who may live together only seasonally. Furthermore, elders emphasized the high value associated with the practice of a general exchange that generated the image of a socially integrated community. Today, as purchasing gifts requires a considerable financial effort, gifts tend not to circulate in the community at large, but within the close family.[200] The value of a generalized exchange, however, continues to be recognized and supported by the elders. Though Inuit appreciate the value of an object as such, the value of the object lays particularly in it being a 'gift' that is in the relation of the gift. The circulation of objects explicates social relations. As there are no further obligations attached to a gift, the social relations materialized in a gift are temporary.

5.5 The Christmas feast

Introduction

Hardly a month passed in Qikiqtarjuaq without a feast. The dinner at Christmas Day, organized by the municipality, was the most elaborate and anticipated of these events. Youth, adults, and elders were invited to attend the community feast.[201] People assembled in the school gym where a meal was arranged. The first part of this chapter deals with the meal and the food. Part two deals with the organization of the feast and part three with the elders' recollections of the Christmas feasts in camps.

5.5.1 Celebrating the Christmas feast

During the day with members of Lizzy Anaviapik's family, we engaged in lively conversations on pipe smoking and the annual community Christmas feast, which was greatly anticipated. Lizzy advised us not to eat too much during the day, in order to have a good appetite at the feast. While we were talking, the TV or a video tape was running and we listened to the community radio announcements of greetings from in- and outside the community. I left early to attend the preparations for the communal meal.

The preparations, however, had been completed long before. Staff of the municipality and a few other volunteers had prepared the meal, placed the chairs along the walls, and set up the

---

198 In all other games played at Christmas, little attention was paid to the handing over of the prize.

199 Nevertheless, many people gradually got tired of watching, as it took a long time to display all the gifts.

200 As said before, this was not altogether different in the camps as they were often constituted by relatives.

201 Children between eight and thirteen years of age had their own feast at school before the Christmas holidays started.

Picture 36 *Country food served at the Christmas feast.*

hi-fi and synthesizer equipments ready for the musical entertainment during and after the feast. The organizers were inspecting and adjusting the arrangement of food on two rows of chipboard laying on the floor and covered with plastic sheets, each about eight meters in length, and approachable from all sides. There was nicely-cut *maktak* ('narwhale skin'), *igunaq* ('fermented walrus meat'), thick slices of frozen Arctic Char, 80 or more plastic cups with boiled shrimps, and plastic plates with fresh clams, caught by the local clam divers.[202] Two large cooking pots of boiled clams, still steaming and exuding a delicious fragrance, stood between the lines. Boxes containing apples, oranges, mandarins, grapes, bananas, and two platters with turkey were placed on tables at the back wall. As more and more people entered the gym, three staff members of the CSC sat down in front of the tables, probably to keep some all too enterprising children from nabbing the fruit. In the corner, next to the fruit, tea, coffee, an assortment of cookies and a bannock (bread baked in a pan) – the latter contributed by Martha Nookiruaq, an elder – stood ready to round off the meal. Also, plenty of ice cream as dessert was stored in the equipment room.

Aitaina Nukiruaq, a female elder, had announced on the radio that she was going to contribute a huge 'birthday cake'. It was made of three single cakes laying adjacent to each other and was decorated with the following words: "Happy Birthday Jesus – Jesusi Atanivut ('Jesus, our Father')" and a large heart underneath the writing. The elder, assisted by two women, carried the cake to the stage. There they arranged above the cake two little standing crosses and flowers taken from the altar of the Anglican Church. The cake was not touched during the meal and the coffee,

---

202 Caribou meat was ordered, but it did not arrive in time. Seal meat could not be provided due to bad hunting conditions. Lootie Toomasie: "This year [the ice conditions] were a little bit bad. [...] Some years have a good season. It is never the same. I don't blame it – its just the way it is."

although it stood there, already cut. It was finally distributed during the award ceremonies.[203] Attending the community Christmas feast for the first time, I was impressed by the abundance of food served and its lavish and neat arrangement.

Just before the opening of the feast, the first attendants arrived – older teenagers, adults and elders. Most of them were dressed in newly bought or handmade jackets, pretty shirts, pullovers, skirts or trousers. All of the elders and some of the middle-aged women were wearing *kamiit* ('seal-skin boots'). Some brought plates; others used plates cut from the cardboard boxes used for transporting the provisions. Everybody brought a knife or an *ulu* (fan shaped woman's knife).[204] Many women were equipped with a plastic bag to take food home or to give to close relatives who did not attend the feast. People were looking for a suitable place to sit, but several took their time, inspecting the food first. Elders were usually provided with a chair. Their children, some of them having traveled to Qikiqtarjuaq for Christmas, assembled around them, most sitting on the floor. Some people sat together as couples and very few sat alone. The few Qallunaat present at this occasion settled themselves together along the short wall,[205] but surrounded by many children.

About half an hour before the feast started, Daisy Arnaquq asked permission from interim-mayor Jacopie Koksiak to collect food for her mother, Kilabuk Kunilusie, who stayed at home because she did not feel well. Jacopie Koksiak agreed. Everyone sat silently or engaged in quiet conversation, waiting for the feast to begin. A few people started to follow Daisy Arnaquq's example to collect some food to take home. Jacopie Koksiak took the microphone and expressed his appreciation of how the feast was set up: "Adam [Smith][206] is a good man." Several minutes later, he took up the microphone again to finally open the feast:

> I don't think we have to wait for anybody else. If anybody does not understand me, let me know. Thank you for coming. I am sorry that there is no caribou meat. They could not come on the plane. Whenever the meat arrives, we shall have another feast. Its almost seven o'clock. We are a little bit late. So, if people don't start collecting food for taking home, it is easier for us to wait. So everybody gets the chance to eat. I don't think we have to wait any longer. Loasie Kunilusie[207] come up and say the grace, bless the food.

Conversations stopped and silence fell. People stood up for prayer and gathered in three or four lines around the food and men took off their caps and all bent their heads. Loasie Kunilusie closed his eyes and spoke into the microphone:

> Thanks to the chairman. Lets all stand up. Thank you Lord for providing good food for our body! Bless the food we are going to eat! We are going to eat with pleasure. We shall not forget that it is the birth of Jesus Christ. You have given us your only son and we thank you for that. Bless us all in the name of Jesus Christ! Amen. The country food looks good! Amen!

---

203   I did not come to know why people hesitated at first.

204   A knife was used by a man, an *ulu* by a woman.

205   Adam Smith was an exception, as he actively coordinated the feast and worked together with his staff.

206   Recreation Director.

207   Loasie Kunilusie is lay minister of the local Anglican Church.

Picture 37 *People scrambling for country food.*

As soon as the 'Amen' was spoken, people scrambled to help themselves to the country food. People usually took pieces of all kinds of meat, but mostly of their favorite. Guests modestly waited for the first rush to subside and then helped themselves to whatever they liked. Some people settled down at the food arrangement and ate there. Others took a selection of dishes to their seats. Women often attended to their family. Children helped themselves only to fruits. People did not talk much during the meal, but frequently expressed their appreciation of the food: "It is tasty!", "I love clams!", etc. I myself was busy documenting the feast with my video camera and joined various people that I had gotten to know. Most of my companions inquired if I liked country food. I enjoyed eating it, but I often did not know how to eat it properly. People supported my efforts to learn. They taught me about tasty combinations and about specific cutting techniques.

The main course of the meal ended when everyone have had enough. The organizers had anticipated that people would provision themselves for the Christmas holidays and provided enough food to ensure that everybody could take some food home. People packed food into their plastic bags. This done, Jacopie Koksiak informed the dog owners: "There is lots of meat left for dog teams. We are going to start cleaning up." Three or four men took the meat in garbage bags to their dog teams.

Before coffee and dessert were served, everybody went to the bathrooms and cleaned their hands and knifes of the blood and fat; women also cleaned the eating spaces of their family. Qallunaat music played in the background while the CSC crew removed the large boards, swept the floor and collected the last pieces of garbage. People engaged in conversations and wished a 'Merry Christmas' to those they had not seen at the service the day before. Children ran and played around, and some people gave gifts to others. Those who had brought food home did so quickly. When everything was in order, the CSC crew began to serve substantial portions of ice-cream in plastic cups and Jaycopie Koksiak announced: "There is lots of ice-cream. You are going to have lots of ice-cream!" While people enjoyed their dessert, Jaycopie Koksiak closed the feast and announced the coming events:

> Thank you for your good participation in the feast. We are going to give awards to former hamlet councillors, who are no longer working as such. Next, awards will be given to

Picture 38 *Families are sitting together to consume their Christmas meal.*

employees of the hamlet. Settle down kids, settle down kids. To begin, the RCMP is here on the stage with their interpreter [John Ayaruaq].

The birthday cake for Jesus, the crosses and flowers were moved to the tables at the back wall to provide space on the stage. The cake was distributed during the award ceremony. Most people took a piece, but there were also some who declined.

Inuit perceptions of the feast
Geela Angnako-Kunilusie, a middle-aged woman, who as a municipal financial administrator participated in the organization of the Christmas community feast, answered when I asked her, if she could imagine Christmas without a feast: "It sounds sad." Then she explained:

> We use it for the celebration of the birth of Jesus. It is so special. Christmas time is special. It is a time to get together. When it comes, in the beginning of the month of December, people go on the radio looking forward to Christmas and getting together for the games and the feast.

A Christmas dinner is, to my knowledge, part of the Christmas festivals of all Nunavut communities. However, many of them, such as Pangnirtung and Pond Inlet, did not share a meal with the whole community but only with the extended family. Mary Killiktee, who lived with her family in Pond Inlet as a teenager, compared both ways of feasting:

> In Pond, every family member – like my parents, us the kids, my aunts, their husbands, their kids – we would get together in one house and celebrate and have the Christmas dinner in a home, not like we have it now [in Qikiqtarjuaq]. In 1980 [when we moved to Qikiqtarjuaq], it was my first time experiencing that it is more like a big big family, in a big hall. [...] Everybody is welcome to go to the gym, to attend the service. Then, the next day on the 25th, everybody gets involved again when they have the community feast for everyone. That is how they do it here. I like it.

Lootie Toomasie emphasized that the feast was non-exclusive and the participation of everyone present in the community was highly appreciated:

> Late in the afternoon adult people start to have a community feast and right there, they wanted to give to their relatives [who came from other communities]. The feast was completely open. It is an annual feast and it is a very special day here.

In Inuit perceptions of the feast, food was an important issue. Martha Nuqingak-Kunilusie, secretary of the *Hunters and Trappers Organization* (HTO) elaborated:

> Food is the main thing that puts people together the best, because – we give thanks for it, leaving us all kinds of food nowadays.[208] [...] It is a way to say thank you to whoever provides, God, whoever provides us with these foods. [...] Maybe because, in the old days, there was so much hunger that people were concerned [about food]. We have lots of it now. To bring people together is the main idea of the feast. It brings people closer together, like in times of sadness, like it is right now [when Atamie Nookiruaq died in the first week of January, 2000]. That is what they [HTO] are planning to do, have a feast, [to dedicate the feast planned for New Year to the deceased elder]. Atamie always shared his food with the people and helped people in his lifetime.

She thought that food was a means to constitute community. She suggested that country food in particular was of special value to Inuit because of their way of life in the past. The elder female, Aka Keyooktak, perceived this aspect of the feast as well:

> The last feast [the one in 1999] was very memorable, because there was hardly any store-bought food, all traditional food. Because traditionally, a long time ago, they only had traditional food, country food, nothing store bought. This was very memorable. It brought a lot of memories back. It was all country food.

The feast, and in particular the country food served there, was perceived to have the capacity to create togetherness. It also created a sense of continuity between the past – as experienced by elders and imaged in the ideal of the *inummariit* – and the present.

However, not only country food was served, but also large quantities of Qallunaat food were consumed. And though country food had a particular value to Inuit, everybody also appreciated the turkey, fruits, and ice-cream. A few people told me that they indeed wished that there would have been more and a larger variety of Qallunaat food and that tables would have been laid out nicely as in previous years instead of eating Inuit style on the ground. It would have been more festive that way. I will address Inuit ways of dealing with the different kinds of food in the following discussion.

Discussion

Inuit emphasized that the feast was a communal activity – "a feast of the whole community," as Ina Sanguya, a woman in her early thirties and representative of the *Youth Committee*, said in an

---

208 In another context, she said that it is important for HTO to provide the community regularly with country food as it benefits people.

interview. But how was community constituted on this occasion? Participation in the feast was non-exclusive and it actually was highly valued that non-resident guests and Qallunaat residents also participated. Those who could not come to the gym participated, too, because food was brought to their homes. The participation of the largest number of people possible was perceived to be crucial. It was illustrative for this aim that the opening of the feast was delayed for about an hour in order to wait for more people to arrive. At the opening of the feast, all participants assembled as a congregation for prayer. Then, having picked-up food in the first scramble, people organized themselves in smaller groups, mostly household and close kin formations, to consume their meal.[209]

The community was also organized in terms of gender, age, and social position, through variations in the conduct of the people. For example, to prepare the feast, men went hunting; the municipality performed as collective providers of an abundance of food; women prepared the food; people scrambled for country food and lined up for the buffet; elders were served by their children; and guests conducted themselves with modesty. Proper conduct not only appertained to the social domain, but also, directly or indirectly, to relations to animals[210] in that the consumption of country food linked the participants of the feast to the hunting circuit. The ways in which community formation took place at the feast refer to an ideal of Inuit society as addressed in the image of the *inummariit*, though the number of people constituting the largest social formation clearly exceeded that of the past.[211] The opening prayer and the occasion of the Christmas festival explicitly position the relationships established by the performance of the feast in the dominant cosmological framework of the Christian religion today.

Food was perceived to be, as Martha Nuqingak-Kunilusie stated: "the main thing that puts people together the best." And food was the main issue in Inuit conversations at the feast. Two kinds of food were served – Qallunaat food and country food. Though Qallunaat food had, to some extent, replaced country food in the daily diet, the contrast between them was marked by the specific ways in which the food was dealt with and how it was perceived. The distinctions were marked by production, Qallunaat food is not part of the social and cosmological relationships associated with hunting and with other strategies of procurement like fishing and berry picking. Qallunaat food was, however, a much appreciated part of the Christmas celebration. A feast of Qallunaat food on Christmas has a long tradition. It was introduced by whalers and especially missionaries who invited the camp to a Qallunaat meal at Christmas (see for example Harper 1983a; Laugrand & Oosten 2002).

The food's Qallunaat origin was not marked in today's feast, however. Opinions about the reduction of Qallunaat food were mixed. Those in favor of the changes referred to the value of country food as 'true' Inuit.[212] Nobody, however, suggested that only Qallunaat or country food be served at the feast – the mixture was actually appreciated by all.

---

209 Children were in principle eligible to participate in the community feast. Considering the perceived crowdedness in the gym, people preferred to provide the children with a separate dinner organized by the *District Education Council* and the school earlier in December.

210 See the chapters *Life in Qikiqtarjuaq* and *Christianity in Qikiqtarjuaq* on the relevance of proper social conduct for hunting.

211 See the chapters *Theoretical background and methodology* and *Life in Qikiqtarjuaq*.

212 In difference to Qallunaat food, country food was thought to benefit the well-being, strength, and endurance of Inuit people.

5.5.2 Organization of the feast

The communal Christmas feast had a long history in Qikiqtarjuaq. It always took place on December 25th, except when that day coincided with a Sunday, in which case it was postponed to the following day. Several local institutions were involved in its organization. In 1999, the municipality was responsible for purchasing food, the HTO took care of the preparation of the country food,[213] the Co-op prepared other dishes, the *Community Service Committee* (CSC) together with the *Youth Committee* furnished the gym, and CSC staff also maintained the gym during and after the feast. Even though volunteers were welcome to help, it was mostly staff that actually did most of the work, while other organizations provided the major quantity of food.

To facilitate and coordinate cooperation, the municipality, as the main provider, asked other organizations for assistance. Mary Killiktee, the Co-op manager, explained:

> The Recreation Committee prepared ahead of time. In October or November, they gave all the organizations a letter, asking which of them would want to volunteer for Christmas dinner, and the games. We received the letter and responded to it after a meeting. We decided what we were going to spend. Like this year, I ordered 15 or 20 turkeys, I ordered them back in September. Through Arctic Cooperative. I have an account with them so the turkeys were already paid.

Agencies valued being involved as partners and presenting themselves as providers in the organization of the Christmas celebration. They mobilized money resources and worked hard to contribute to the celebration. Geela Arnaquq-Kunilusie was responsible for the municipality's food orders for the Christmas feast. She explained that the municipality had a special budget for community festivities. In 1999, for example, the municipality received 8500 $CAN from the Nunavut Government to finance the Christmas games and feast. Fruits and frozen goods were ordered from *Sasloves' Meat Market* in Ottawa. Caribous, without head and fur, were ordered from Pond Inlet. Shrimps were ordered from Pangnirtung Fisheries. All of these items need to be flown in to Qikiqtarjuaq; the airline *First Air* provided the community with special discounts on the freight costs. Other food items were purchased locally. Turkeys came from the Northern Store. Clams were bought from the local divers via the HTO. Fish, *maktak* and *igunak* were bought from the local HTO.[214] And mayor Lootie Toomasie went on the radio to ask hunters to go sealing for the feast. The first volunteers were chosen and received 40$ to cover gas and oil expenses. As the ice-conditions were not favorable for hunting, they had little success and no seal was served at the feast.

Martha Nuqingaq-Kunilusie, secretary of the HTO, explained that the contributions of the HTO to Christmas would focus on game. Besides selling food to the municipality for the feast,[215] the HTO also ordered from other HTOs food which in Qikiqtarjuaq was unavailable or

---

213 Through the municipal office, the HTO had hired two women to cut the meat.

214 The HTO told hunters ahead of time to store various kinds of meat, such as Arctic Char, *igunak*, and *maktak*, in the community freezer for the Christmas feast.

215 The selling of country food is discouraged in general (see the chapter *Life in Qikiqtarjuaq*). The purchase of food by the municipality from the HTO, however, is more acceptable. I would like to suggest, based on an exchange of ideas in an e-mail communication with Nicole Gombay (December 24, 2004), that the difference is that it is not a transaction leading to profit and that it is an interaction that supports an organization supporting hunters and hunting. The money spent by the municipality on country food became part of the hunting cycle.

of lower quality. They also exchanged food with other HTOs. They, for example, traded *maktak* for shrimp, and they traded *maktak* and clams for fermented walrus meat in 1999. The HTO, the municipality, and the Co-op, thus, made an effort to provide the community free of charge with country and Qallunaat food, particularly at Christmas, but also throughout the rest of the year.

Inuit perceptions of the organization of the feast

The feast was organized by the municipality in cooperation with other organizations and businesses. Representatives of participating organizations all emphasized their high motivation to contribute to the community celebration. For example, Martha Nuqingaq-Kunilusie of HTO stated that: "HTO really believes in providing these kinds of food. [...] They want to do this, because no one else really does it for the whole community." Lootie Toomasie elaborated on the priorities of the municipality: "Important for us is that the people have a good place to gather and it is important to be sure that there are enough supplies for a community feast and that we are the main providers for the whole community to celebrate Christmas." People expected these services and contributions from the municipality and acknowledged that the providers had tried their best. The feast should be organized as skillfully as possible. With this in mind, some people approached the municipality later on to suggest improvements, for example that the planning of the feast should start earlier to ensure that all kinds of meat would be present; that more Qallunaat food should be served and that tables should be decorated and laid as before.

But what was so important about the Qallunaat food and style of serving it? In my diary of the first weeks of my fieldwork, I found the following entry from December 26th, 1999:

> The Christmas feast was celebrated in a way one may call traditional. Most of us were eating sitting on the floor – meat on cardboard and *ulu* in hand – just as one would eat country food in the houses or out camping.

Until I started conducting interviews on the Christmas celebration in January 2000, it did not occur to me that this feast and the feast of 1998 that I was told about were actually exceptional in comparison with earlier, more Qallunaat style, Christmas dinners. Lootie Toomasie (mayor), Geela Angnako-Kunilusie (municipal staff), and Martha Nuqingaq-Kunilusie (HTO secretary) explained that, due to the growth of the community as well as financial and logistic limitations, the use of tables and chairs and dishes of turkey, ham, pork, etc. gradually disappeared from the scene in 1997. According to Lootie Toomasie, the old style of serving people and cooking all the food for the feast was no longer feasible:

> We [the hamlet] needed help to provide [cooked Qallunaat style food] for the whole community. [...] The hamlet used to order 20 turkeys. They gave them to local households to cook them for the feast. [...] We had a hard time finding the volunteers to cook them in the last years. They were all doing their own things during the holiday season and so on. [...] It seemed to be too much work during the holiday season, to feed the whole community. So for the last two years, we were providing country food, some of it cooked, some of it frozen or raw. People are accustomed to eat that way, because it is the way we live up here.[216]

---

216   Part of the cooking, e.g. of the turkeys, is still done by the Co-Op hotel kitchen staff. In an interview, Mary Killiktee, the Co-Op manager at that time, perceived this service to be a positive contribution to the community's celebration.

The elaborate preparation of Qallunaat food, arranged on a voluntary basis, became an inconvenience – an attitude I never encountered in respect to the money, time, logistics, and efforts to provide country food. People require money and time to go out hunting; food items have to be purchased or exchanged with other Inuit communities; the items have to be transported by plane; and country food requires more preparation.[217] Geela Arnaquq-Kunilusie emphasized the financial constraints that contributed to the change: "Two years ago we decided to save money and have a traditional feast." Even though Qallunaat food was appreciated for its taste as well as the exclusiveness of items such as turkey, the financial costs as well as work pressure apparently exceeded these values from the point of view of the organizers.

Discussion of the organization

The Christmas feast was perceived to be an important occasion for organizations to provide the community with food and services. As providers, they positioned themselves in a socially accepted leadership position. The central provider of the feast was the municipality.

    The municipality initiated changes in the proportions in which country food and Qallunaat food were served. This led, as described above, to dynamic discourses on how the feast should be held. The organizations emphasized that the change was mainly motivated by pragmatic reasons based on the perception that the efforts to purchase and prepare a large variety and amount of Qallunaat food would exceed its value for the feast. Although the hamlet decided on the menu, it was important to them to provide the community with a proper feast, and they were open to suggestions. In turn, the municipality's decision was accepted by the people – nobody stayed away from the feast – and it was assumed that the municipality and its cooperating partners had done their best. In this way, despite some disagreements, the municipality and the other participating organizations were acknowledged as providers, confirming their positions of leadership within the community.

5.5.3 Elders' recollections of the feast in camps

A feast was part of the Christmas celebrations in all camps of the Davies Strait and Cumberland Sound regions in which Qikiqtarjuaq's elders grew up. Jacopie Kuksiak explained to me that the winter season often was a difficult time for hunting and he recalled that in times of need the larger winter camps had to disperse. Against the odds of poor weather or ice conditions, food and special treats were saved for the Christmas celebration. Extra efforts had to be made to have a feast together with several families.[218] From the recollections of elders it appeared that providing for and participating in the feast was very much enjoyed. Martha Kopalie, raised in Kivitoo, recalled:

> A person would make a big pot of seal for the feast. They would cut up the seal into small pieces and cook it in a big pot. And they would put bannock [(pan-baked bread)] into the pot so it would be a bit more food. And they would make more bannock for the feast. [...] Everybody in the camp provided food: caribou and whatever a person could bring. But the

---

217 The skin has to be carefully removed and processed. The carcass has to be butchered and the meat, depending on the sort, further portioned, stored, and prepared. In case that fermented meat is desired, it has to be placed under stones for several weeks.

218 And they still have to be taken, as the unsuccessful seal hunting expeditions as well as the food orders to other communities illustrated.

best treat was when a person made a big pot of seal meat with bannock in it. That was a real treat.

Aka Keyooktak was born in Sanikiluaq. Before she got married, she lived in Aurataqtuq. Also she remembered vividly the food and particularly the special treats:

> Caribou meat was very rare. Some people looked as if they did not have any caribou, but when it was feast time they brought out their caribou meat. It was a real treat. Everybody would be involved, from *qammaq* [('sod-house')] to *qammaq*. [...] Martha [Kopalie] said that after eating they would get together and start singing and, I guess, that [with us] after the feast, they would go into the biggest *qammaq* and say their prayers.

Mary Oonga Audlakiak, raised in Pangnirtung, also emphasized the extra efforts made to prepare the feast: "It was the celebration of the birth of Jesus Christ and they had to save [pieces of meat] –they had to feast with everyone." And Jacopie Koksiak recalled the special preparations for the feast in a camp close to Pangnirtung where he grew up:

> On Christmas Day they would hold feasts that took all the people in the camp together. They would eat country food like seals, caribou fat, fresh char. Sometimes they would save the meat of scarce animals[219] which they did not routinely catch. They would save it for Christmas. There may have been some tea.

While country food was very important for the Christmas celebration, and even though the Christmas feast was part of a religious event, people had to observe the Sabbath with respect to hunting. Mary Oonga Audlakiak recalled that: "if you accidentally or purposefully killed a seal on Sunday, you would have to finish it, the whole carcass. Right to the bones, right away."[220] Not only hunting, but also the feast was not to take place on a Sunday. "If," as Mialia Audlakiak recollected, "Christmas crossed with a Sunday, they would have the gift exchanges, but they would have to wait until the next day with the feast and the dances." Also on Christmas itself, hunting was avoided. In some camps, the Christmas period stretched from Christmas to New Year. Peter Anilik Paniloo recollected from the Kivitoo camp that: "They saved food for the period of Christmas till New Year. They did not go out hunting at that time." The length of the Christmas celebration varied. As long as it lasted, however, people had to observe the rule not to go out hunting unless absolutely necessary.

---

219 Big game such as caribou and walrus.

220 Peter Anilik Paniloo explained that hunting on Sunday is possible if the food is really needed. In case that an animal is killed it should be eaten entirely at once. People nowadays accept this rule, but transgress it. David Nuqingaq told the following story: When he was a teenager, he was hanging around with some friends on Sunday. When they went outside, they saw a seal across the sea strait basking on a rock. They had a rifle with them. Even though they were aware of the fact that hunting was not acceptable on Sunday, they expected that they would not hit the seal anyway if they would shoot at it. David aimed at it and hit it. His stepfather, Atamie Nookiruaq, saw the incident and got angry about it. He explained to the boys that they had acted wrongly. He immediately organized a boat and crossed over the strait to get the seal. During the morning church service he told that the seal was shot by David and that everybody was invited to his house to share the seal.

Food had been a focus of the elders' memories of the feast. The elders quoted above indicated that everybody contributed something to the meal. There was, however, some variation in the ways of provision. Mary Oonga Audlakiak recalled that: "the eldest person[221] in camp went out hunting caribou and seal for the feast. There were no stores anywhere nearby, there was nothing store-bought, so we celebrated Christmas with one feast consisting of caribou meat and seal meat." Also Martha Nookiruaq, who lived in the Pangnirtung area, recalled that the bulk of food was provided by a successful hunter: "People did not bring food as my adoptive father, Iqalik, was a good hunter and provided caribou, seal, and fish. Iqalik was not the camp leader, but Makiktua, his father, was." However, game was not the only food served in some of the camps when the elders were still young, as Martha Nookiruaq pointed out: "They saved the store-bought food until Christmas, but we ate native food most of the time." And also Martha Kopalie's still-present taste for seal stew with bannock suggested that game was mixed with Qallunaat food.[222]

Not only was Qallunaat food used in at least some camps for the Christmas meal, Qallunaat organizations were also present in the Christmas festivals recollected particularly by those elders who grew up in camps close to Pangnirtung or in the early settlement of Pangnirtung itself. When Qallunaat were present, the Christmas festival was an occasion of Inuit-Qallunaat interaction. And Qallunaat usually provided a separate feast to Inuit associated with their organizations, such as the Royal Canadian Mounted Police (RCMP), the Hudson Bay Company (HBC), or the Anglican mission. Qallunaat prepared dishes from Qallunaat food or mixed Qallunat and Inuit food with the idea to give their Inuit guests a special treat. Mialia Audlakiak, born in Umanarjuaq and living close to Pangnirtung as a girl, recalled:

> The people that worked for the *Hudson Bay Company* would get together at the HBC at staff housing, and the RCMP would have their own separate little feast for those people who worked for those organizations. When I was a child they would also have a feast at the Anglican mission with games and so on.[223]

This tradition was continued by the DEW Line crew who started their work on the island of Qikiqtarjuaq in 1956/1957, when there was no settlement yet, but an Inuit camp at a place called Qikiqtarjuaruluk and the houses of a few families who had moved to the island to find work at the station.[224] Martha Nookiruaq recalled:

> Employees of the DEW Line lived close to their work and members of the Audlakiak family lived in Qikiqtarjuaruluk [a camp on the island]. During these years, they did not celebrate

---

221 Presumably, a man and still able to go out hunting.

222 Bannock (a bread baked in a pan) is perceived to be traditional Inuit food today. I wonder if it was perceived in the same way in the elders' past camps.

223 Local institutions of contemporary Inuit community life, such as the schools, Arctic College, the businesses, the hamlet, or the fire fighter brigade still continue to have staff or student dinners.

224 The celebrations in the early years of community were a difficult topic in interviews especially with female elders. The answers tended to be very short and general in many cases. Once, an elder started to cry as the memories and emotions connected to that time were still overwhelming. As not all elders experienced the forced relocation, the memories of the early Christmas in the community might vary, but I decided to leave this issue aside in most interviews.

together. The games did not start until this place became a community and after they had built a community hall, the old community hall, the old garage. [...] They really started the Christmas feast when there was a municipality.[225] We went there when we wanted to have a feast. After they had a municipality and the crown came, elders were brought there and interacted with the community. We also had prayer services. I enjoyed the feast. There was food. The games were humorous. Dances and going crazy. It [probably was the idea] of the Recreation Director.

Martha addressed the issue of changes in the social conditions and the developments in the organization of the Christmas festival of which the feast remained a part. She explained that whereas each camp celebrated apart before, everybody celebrated together in the settlement of Qikiqtarjuaq, once the modern administrative and political structure of the community was set up. The inhabitants of Qikiqtarjuaq accepted the position of the municipality as the provider of the festival feast for the whole community.[226] Elders, like Martha Nookiruaq, perceived, despite the drastic changes in the social conditions of daily life as well as of the Christmas festival, that Christmas remained basically unchanged. Martha Kopalie formulated this impression of her first Christmas in Qikiqtarjuaq very vividly:

It was really hard, it was a normal Christmas. But we were told that we would go back to Kivitoo and later on found out they were not going back to Kivitoo. They had left everything in Kivitoo. They had left their *qammait*. All their belongings were in there. They were burnt, demolished, and buried. It really hurts me to talk about that.

In the following paragraph, I will discuss the elder's perceptions of the feast as well as the notions of continuity and change associated with it.

Discussion of the elders' recollections
The Christmas feasts in the camps of their youth were a favorite subject of elders in interviews on Christmas festivals of the past. Both the food and the commonality featured prominently in their recollections. People not only contributed food to feed the camp. They marked the importance of the event by making efforts to provide specialties and often added a playful element to their contribution, for instance by hiding delicacies to later surprise people with a special treat.

The feast in those days, just like today, was part of the Christmas celebration – a Christian festival. Still, the general rules concerning the Sabbath had to be observed also during the preparation and performance of the feast. Social and cosmological relations addressed in the feast were established in reference to the general Christian framework within which the rule of keeping the Sabbath had to be observed.

Most of the food served in the camp days was country food. If available, it could be mixed with Qallunaat food – for instance to make the seal stew that Aka Keyooktak recollected so vividly. It enhanced the meal. Inuit who had their winter camps close to places with resident

---

225 Martha Nookiruaq probably referred to the year 1968, when the *Federal Department of Indian Affairs and Northern Development* had relocated residents from Kivitoo and Padloping Island to Qikiqtarjuaq. That year and the year before, the first community hall as well as the first mission station were built. She might also have in mind the year 1979, when Qikiqtarjuaq obtained hamlet status.

226 Probably also because the formal leaders were skillful in organizing the occasion.

Qallunaat organizations, such as the RCMP or the Anglican mission, were also invited to feasts organized by Qallunaat for their associates.[227] In addition to the camp, also these organizations constituted social formations for feasts. The latter provided a context for Qallunaat-Inuit interactions at Christmas. Whereas successful Inuit hunters had provided for the camp feast, it was Qallunaat (organizations) who provided for their dinners.

This held true when Qikiqtarjuaq was still an island with a camp and the DEW Line station. Both, the camp and the Dew Line station held their own feasts for their own people. Most Inuit working for the DEW Line, however, were not members of the camp. Then the government decided to develop Qikiqtarjuaq into a settlement. Initially, the people who had moved there did not hold a feast together. This only changed when a formal leadership structure was implemented in Qikiqtarjuaq and the space for a community gathering was established. The formal leader took over the responsibilities earlier held by the feast providers in camps. Only then did the people living in the settlement start coming together for a feast. People recalled that the organizing community council provided, as did other formal (usually Qallunaat initiated) organizations, not only country food, but also a variety of Qallunaat food. In this sense, the community council (and later the municipality) continued the function of camp leaders and hunters in providing country food. The function of Qallunaat organizations as providers of Qallunaat food to associated Inuit was also maintained. In the community council/hamlet, everyone living in Qikiqtarjuaq (as well as visitors) was welcome to participate. The formerly more exclusive access to a Qallunaat feast was now open to everybody present in the settlement – as it has been practiced in the camps during the youth of Qikiqtarjuaq's elders.

At the feast, the entire settlement was addressed in terms of a temporary social formation that resembled the formation of the Inuit winter camp. The recollections of the elders provided insights into how Inuit integrate new elements into their ways of life referred to in the image of the *inummariit*. A dynamic discourse on how to celebrate properly have always been a part of Christmas.[228]

5.5.4 Discussion of the Christmas feast

The Christmas feast, as part of the Christmas festival, was organized by the municipality in cooperation with other organizations. The feast was open to everybody who wanted to participate – inhabitants of the settlement, guests and Qallunaat. It brought people together, not as members of a corporate unit, but as people who organized themselves mainly as households, close kin groups, and socializing individuals to share a meal with, most importantly, everybody else. The point was to celebrate the feast with the largest possible group. Commonality and sharing were highly valued features of the feast. The hamlet, in cooperation with other institutions, became the provider for all participants.[229]

It was of great importance to Inuit that the feast be celebrated properly. What exactly would be 'proper' was the issue of dynamic discourses within the community. One point of debate was the amount and variety of Qallunaat and country food to be served. Both were considered part of a Christmas feast, but they were valued differently. Whereas country food linked people to the traditional hunting circuit, Qallunaat food had a different tradition. Many elders recalled that Qallunaat food had been available in the camps at Christmas. Inuit living

---

227 Qallunaat also organized Christmas dinners among themselves (see Harper 1983a).

228 See also Laugrand & Oosten 2002.

229 Beside, all organizations also held staff dinners.

in or close to Pangnirtung also had been invited by Qallunaat to Christmas feasts organized by local organizations. Qallunaat food therefore proceeded from another kind of relationship than country food. In addition, sharing a Christmas meal with Qallunaat in the past had been based on another kind of relationship, for example employment or religious conversion, rather than the relationship based on cooperation (and competition) in hunting and camp life.

Though Qallunaat food and country food were produced on the basis of different relationships, Qallunaat food was not particularly marked as 'foreign' and integrated as such in the feast. Also the Qallunaat who attended the feast were not particularly marked nor associated with the Qallunaat food items or style of serving it. The provision and consumption of Qallunaat food did not deal with Inuit relations to the stranger nor did it represent a wish of Inuit to become 'Qallunaat'. It was integrated into the Inuit Christmas feast by being alienated from its origins. Whereas it was possible to reduce the amount of Qallunaat food served at Christmas because of the efforts required to provide it, this was not an argument used in reference to country food. Producing, providing, and communally sharing and consuming country food linked people to each other in cooperative relationships, as well as to the animals hunted. In the Christmas feast, Inuit established themselves as a functioning hunting society, while it was conceived within a Christian framework.

5.6 Games

Introduction
Considering all the different elements of the Christmas festival, games hold a place of distinction in the context of this study, not only because of the long duration of the Christmas festival that is largely due to the increased numbers of games played. Games were already an important element of the Sedna festival and later also of the Christmas festivals in Inuit camps of the past. Laugrand & Oosten (2002: 21) have argued that "in playing games, the community shows its capacity to deal with [...] tensions and to dissolve them in a general atmosphere of friendly competition."[230] The renewal of social and cosmological relationships was highly relevant as, for example, hunting success was directly associated with proper social life. But what is the capacity of competitions in the Christmas festival of the modern community of Qikiqtarjuaq? Relating the games to the Christmas celebration suggests relationships between social interaction and ritual. All games create forms of intensive interactions that are worthy of detailed examination.

Games took up the largest proportion of the Christmas and New Year celebration in Qikiqtarjuaq. The short hours of daylight in the morning were used for competitions on the small plaza outside of the hamlet building or out on the sea-ice. When the community assembled again for the evening program in the *Kativvik School* Gym, games filled most of the agenda. Only on Sundays were no games played. Admission to perform in community games was basically restricted to adults and elders. However, in 1999, one or two games were organized for children in the school gym each evening. In 2000, the municipality decided to organize a few games each evening in the hamlet's gym building to accommodate the children. Although Qallunaat inhabitants of Qikiqtarjuaq were also welcome to participate in the games, only the Recreation Director and his wife participated on a regular basis.

---

230 See also chapter *Theoretical background and methodology.*

Picture 39 *Referee Stevie Audlakiak (in the foreground) and Joanasie Audlakiak in the final round of an exclusion dice game.*

In 1999, some 20 outdoor (morning) and 70 indoor (evening) games had been organized by the municipality, local organizations and businesses, and by three families.[231] Many games focussed on physical skill and endurance, others on chance, humor, or such accomplishments as sewing fur garments. Whatever the focus, everybody could participate. The participants were organized into teams, into a circular formation or as individual competitors. From the multitude of games that I had examined I chose four that cover these various formations. The first game described, a relay race organized by the Fire Brigade, is discussed at length and the discussion of the other games refers to the results of this analysis.

The municipal organizing committee of the games took care to provide also a few traditional competitions, such as *Russian High Kick* and *Airplane*.[232] Since the organization of traditional games was the same as for 'modern' games, I do not discuss them in a specific sub-chapter.

The winners of each competition received a prize. The municipality organized about 40 games and distributed prizes accordingly. They were subsidized by the *Nunavut Government* with about 7500 $CAN in 1999,[233] of which the largest share was used for prize pay-outs. The

---

231 See for a list of games played in 1999 appendix 2.

232 Both competitions require a high degree of physical fitness. To perform the *Russian Kick* one has to kick with one foot a little ball (made out of seal skin) that is hanging at eye level and then land on the same foot after the kick. The competition called *airplane* was, according to elders, older than its present name may suggest. To perform it, one had to lay down on the floor rigidly, with arms stretched out. Three helpers lifted one's hands and feet. The player had to lift his body and stay rigid as long as possible.

233 Specifically, funds were provided by the *Nunavut Tungaavik Inc* (NTI, Nunavut government) and the *Qikiqtaani Inuit Association* (QIA). The QIA represents the interests of Baffin Region, High Arctic, and

rest was spent for equipment, fees and honoraria. In addition, the municipality directed money obtained by a *Raffle Ticket* sale to the games. Higher than average prizes (20-40$) were awarded for competitions that required preparation and (financial) investments, such as hunting, skidoo and dog-team races, the most beautiful Christmas light decoration or Inuit clothing (handmade fur clothing). Relatively high prizes were also distributed for competitions based primarily on skill. Examples of this kind of competition are the snow-sculpture contest, shooting contest, elders speak English/Qallunaat speak Inuktitut contest, appearing as the opposite sex contest, or the Inuktitut dance competition. For example, one could win $20 playing *Musical Chairs* and up to $300 winning the dog team race, in 1999.

The Christmas celebration was opened December the 23rd, 1999 by the interim-mayor Jacopie Kokseak. He said: "I want to start the games. Everybody feel welcome. Please attend the games, if you can." Then, he said an opening prayer, asking for God's help to have safe games.[234]

5.6.1 Evening games

People left their homes when the evening games were about to start in the school gym. Darkness had already fallen around noon, and it was crispy cold. Many houses were decorated with bright and colorful Christmas lights. After arriving in the light and warmth of the school's vestibule, people drubbed their boots to shake off the snow and unzipped their jackets. Women wearing an *amauti*[235] jostled small children out of the hood. Very soon, a relative or friend smiled invitingly at the child, clapped their hands and opened their arms inviting the child to be carried. Soon, the vestibule was crowded with chatting people.

Queues formed in front of the kiosk and various refreshment stands; the latter were operated by organizations such as the Wolf Cubs, or by private people, to raise funds. Treating oneself to refreshments was part of the fun of the evening for Inuit of all age-groups.

The gym was decorated with neatly manufactured ornaments made by younger students. Together with their teachers they had fabricated many meters of garlands, paper images of Santa Claus, of sugar canes, wreaths, bells, and of boots filled with gifts. Two ornamented paper Christmas trees were attached to the wall behind the stage from where the games were coordinated, the other placed at the center of the side-wall. After several days of games, the decorations were a bit tattered, especially where children could reach them. When the games were about to start, people entered the gym and looked for a seat near acquaintances and close relatives. Men and women mixed. Elders and teenagers/young adults tended to socialize within their own age-groups. Whereas genders mixed, people of various age-groups tended to cluster. The gym was soon crowded and all chairs occupied. People showed respect for the elders providing them with a seat at the center of the long wall close to the entry from where they could best follow the program.

Belcher Islands. It formed as a non-profit land claim and community organization in 1996, registered as a society in 1997. Together with two other Inuit organizations it is affiliated with the NTI and constitute the NTI Board of Directors.

234 The celebration was opened in a similar way in 2000.

235 An *amauti* is a traditional coat worn by women with babies or children up to the age of about three or four. The children are carried in the bulky back of the coat. In this way they are in direct contact with the back of their carrier. The large hood allows the children to peep out of their place and to move around a bit. In cold weather the hood covers both child and carrier.

Having no inclination to sit quietly, children strolled around in small groups shouting and laughing. They imitated games, rolled over the floor, performed athletic exercises, enjoyed themselves with wild round dances, and they entertained their younger siblings, steering them from one adult of their liking to the next. When a game was announced, mothers called their children to sit down. As they were usually very excited about the competitions, they shuffled closer and closer to the field where the competition was in full swing. Jona Audlakiak, municipal staff member, inevitably made his well-known 'frightening' appearance walking with wide and fast strides and spread arms. His thunderous voice harshly ushered the children back to their families. None of the children could resist his authority, and many adults could not resist smiling.

The Obstacle relay race

The Fire Brigade organized about eight games, of which people especially enjoyed a relay race. The Fire Brigade had agreed in a meeting to organize the race as an obstacle course to be performed by two competing teams.

On the evening of the 29th of December, fireman David Kunilusie performed as the emcee of the game. He was in constant consultation from the stage with the volunteers who prepared the equipment. Monica Nuqingaq and Gamailee Nookiruaq, together with a few others, measured out the length of the race track from the stage to the opposite wall and about four meters in width. Then they prepared the obstacles for each team. The first one, a swirl, required a hockey stick that was placed a few meters away from the starting line. The swirl was performed by picking up the hockey stick and spinning around its axis five times. Then dropping the stick, they headed off to the next obstacle, an arrangement of fire fighter attire to dress in. This stop was planned to be the climax of the race. Dressing in oversized boots, a bulky jacket and a large helmet was even more complicated when dizzy from spinning. Monica and Gamailee had arranged these items in painstaking order. After readjusting their arrangement several times, Gamailee thought it would be a good occasion for a joke. He walked over to the attire that Monica had just carefully readjusted and placed the boots with their tips together. He pretended to leave it like that, smiling conspiratorially at a colleague. Monica played her part, put her hands on her hips and looked enraged, yet with a smile. Gamailee placed the boots back into their proper position and readjusted his own arrangement in an exact parallel to Monica's arrangement. Having mastered the dressing obstacle, the players had to run to the wall fully dressed, touch it, and run back to discard their clothing. While they sprinted back to their team and sent the next runner off by hitting his/her hand, Fire Brigade volunteers rearranged the obstacles.

The team that completed the race first would win the round. That team would then split up to form the two teams for the following round. The losing team would go back to their seats. This procedure would be applied in all the following rounds, until one male and one female winner were determined. The prize money was taken from the Fire Brigade's bank account in which they had saved their honorariums for this occasion.

When preparation of the game was nearly complete, David announced the game to the audience: "A woman and a man will each win $30. The Fire Fighters are providing the game. You have to put on a pair of fireman's boots, fireman's jacket, and helmet. The game was played before, so you know what to do." A little later he informed the public: "Who wants to participate – we are getting ready. You have to run down, grab the hockey-stick, dress up, run down to the wall and back and take the clothing off again." About 40 people, most of them between their 30s and

50s, left their shoes and jackets and started to form two teams. Teams, as usual, were constructed by each participant looking for a partner of the same sex, often a relative or acquaintance. As the organizer of the game wanted to see if the pairing up had been completed, the partners stood face-to-face, male and female pairs alternating. Then the partners swiftly shook hands. Players without a partner raised an arm to signal the organizer. The emcee announced the vacancies, which then were quickly filled-in from the audience. It never happened that a player had to leave the field because nobody teamed up. Two young men, while waiting for the recruiting to be completed, seized the opportunity for a quick hand-pull competition between themselves. Their performance foreclosed the next step of the team construction. Namely that the pairs split up and partners joined competing teams. The partners became competitors.

All players concentrated on the instructions from the stage. The four referees took their stations at the hockey stick swirl and dressing arrangements. Everybody being ready, David explained the game a last time and then counted down to the start "one, two, three – go!" The first two contestants sprinted to the hockey swirl. They picked up the sticks, bent their bodies, their heads almost touching the end of the stick. Holding the stick in front of them, they swirled around. The referees sharply checked the number of spins. The contestants dropped the sticks and dizzily ran to dress in the fire fighter's garments. The bulkiness and stiffness of the attire made dressing indeed an efficient obstacle in the haste of the race. Especially putting on the large sized and high boots was a comic struggle as the contestants tried, with spread arms, to find a balance to put on the first boot, and hopping on one leg to put on the second one. Players and spectators were splendidly amused. Most contestants started running towards the wall, while they were still fixing the helmet in its proper position, as it tended to glide forward over one's eyes while running. However, if a contestant, a referee, or the members of the audience had the impression that s/he jumped the gun, then the contestant stopped shortly, adjusted the helmet, or even went back to the dressing position, and only then continued the sprint to the wall. When the competition was tight or a mishap occurred, some people, including the presenter, shouted encouragements, such as "*Ati!* Go!". After touching the wall, the contestants hurried back to the dressing position to cast off the bulky garments and sprinted back to their respective teams. The contestant's arrival signaled the start of the next participant. Monica and Elijah re-arranged the garments in their exact initial positions before the next contestants arrived.

At the end of each round, the losing team calmly left the field and joined the audience while the winning team split up and formed two new teams. If they ended up with an unequal number of players, a member of the audience who had not played in an earlier round joined the game to even out the numbers. During one of the intermediate rounds of the game, two of the referees, Gamailee and Elijah, joined the competition as contestants. Their referee tasks were taken over by colleagues. Lining up at the last positions in their almost equally strong teams, they happened to start their race about the same time, though Gamailee had a head start. When he had touched the wall and was undressing, he gained ground and left his competitor behind. But instead of running straight back to his team, he fell into tip-toeing. He teasingly looked back to Elijah, who had already slowed down, expecting to loose. Challenged by the mock opportunity to win, he started to speed up again, without, however, seriously threatening Gamailee's and his team's victory. After reaching the finish, they applauded each other's performance. Their little play added to the entertainment of the game. Both resumed their referee tasks before the next round of competition started.

Susie Alikatuqtuq and Leetia Kuksiak Jr. were the remaining female contestants during one of the last rounds. They started at the last position in their teams. When their predecessors reached the finish almost at the same time, they started their race simultaneously and with vigor. As it became evident that Leetia would win Susie, as did Elijah in a similar situation described above, slowed down and took off the fire fighter's attire without haste, while her competitor reached the finish. Both left the field without showing any sign of triumph about winning or disappointment about losing.

The all-male teams performed a few more rounds until only two contestants remained, Jaypootie Alikatuqtuq and Larry Poisey. Their race was tight from the beginning, but the competition was settled just before the final sprint. Larry lost time when, trying to cast the boots off, he got stuck in one of them. Jaypootie crossed the finish line with such speed that he slid the last meters on his back in order to manage to stop before reaching the stage. Larry, kicking off the last boot, started his sprint but slowed down a little when he saw that his competitor would win. Still, he retained so much speed reaching the finish line that he slid past the stage and bumped into the wall. He picked up his cap where he had left it on the stage before walking over to the winner, still laying on the floor, and gave him a hand standing up.

Right after the last round, the field was cleared of game equipment and the audience resumed their conversations. David asked the winners to come forward one by one to receive the prize money of $30. Jaypootie went to the stage, received his prize in an envelope and shook hands with David. He shortly raised his right hand victoriously and left the stage to some applause from the audience. Then Leetia was called up. She also received her prize and shook hands, and some people applauded for her. She went back to her seat, smiling broadly. David thanked the winners for their participation and he received a brief applause as well. People started to walk around chatting and taking a cigarette break or getting some refreshments. The children returned to their former activities, occupying once again the game field and imitating the hockey spin to get dizzy. The Fire Brigade's game was followed by the distribution of prizes for outdoor games and a imitate-a-prominent-singer contest that closed the evening.

Discussion

Although the race aimed at producing a winner, the process of the competition was the center of the audience's and players' attention – rather than the winners. The following paragraphs will deal with the team construction, how the game was played and the prize, but also the link between the competition and the Christmas festival from the perspective of the organizers:

Picture 40 *Jaypootie Alikatuqtuq and Larry Poisey compete to win the relay race.*

Team construction

The game was organized as a competition between two teams. The teams did not become stable units and they did not develop a corporate identity in the course of the competition. With every round, new teams were constructed in successive steps with every round. First, players formed same-sex pairs. Second, the pairs split up and the partners produced the two competing teams with additional players. With the next round, new partnerships were formed and so on and so forth, until a winner was determined. The temporal dimension of the partnerships – and of the teams generated by this system – connect elements of cooperation and of competition. The partner-competitors provided each other with the opportunity to participate and the opportunity to win. Each team, in relation to the other, was composed on the basis of relationships of competition integrated with cooperation. The structure of the game suggests that individual success was perceived to be only possible through the grace of a social process. And whereas the category of 'the winner' was marked by a prize, the category of 'the loser' did not emerge in the course of the game.

The ways of playing

The integration of competition and cooperation render participation in the game as a complex social practice. The competition was a communal event. Each player had to be willing and capable to cooperate with everybody else in the community, regardless of whether or not relations between the players were strained. The performance of the competition emphasized central moral values – openness, cooperation, eagerness to participate and modesty.

Particularly winning and losing properly required social skill. The winner of a competition should be modest about his/her position and s/he should be gratified to have won the prize. Boasting would be considered rather ridiculous. Players were adequately indifferent to losing. Complaining and the display of anger or disappointment were considered inappropriate and rather childish. After all, as many people told me, "it is just a game", thus not serious. At the same time, games were a serious business in Qikiqtarjuaq and much efforts were made to organize them. The game gave form to highly valued social interactions and the players had the opportunity to present themselves as socially competent.

The performances of Gamailee and Elijah illustrated skilled conduct. As providers and referees of the game, they also expressed their eagerness to perform in the competition and turned into rivals for one round.[236] While Gamailee did compete earnestly, he additionally introduced the extra moment of comic play to the game.[237] By challenging Elijah in this way and by cooperating in Gamailee's sham, both created an opportunity to present themselves as capable social partners. Both showed that they knew how to behave properly as (cooperative) rivals, and both showed that they also were capable of publicly making fools of themselves.[238]

---

236 The flexibility of positions (provider, player, referee) is not an unusual feature in Inuit performances of games, though care was taken not to put one team at a disadvantage with the other.

237 Inserting features of individual play in the context of games is a frequent feature in games played by Inuit. During the Fire Brigade's contribution the hand-pull between two young men when teaming up as well as Jaypootie's and Larry's dramatic performances were further examples of it.

238 See sub-chapter the *Funny Person* contest for an elaboration on the skill of deliberately and publicly making a fool of oneself. Younger people were usually much too embarrassed to do so and it was usually older people and elders who behaved foolishly for the entertainment of others.

Inuit acknowledged the high degree of social competence and self-possession required to publicly play the fool and were very much amused by those who did.

The audience participated in the game by watching and commenting on individual performances, encouraging or reproving players, and they responded to the atmosphere generated by the game. It was important for the Fire Brigade to kindle excitement in the spectators, and especially in the elders. Actually, the presence of elders as spectators affected the Fire Brigade's choice, set-up, and organization of the game.[239] Gamailee explained:

> I always knew that with elders around we would be doing something without being so lazy. Elders are looking at you. That they are happy and you are happy – that's what we always try to do. Like, for example, by spinning with the hockey stick, you are really dizzy and you cannot run straight. When you do something kind of funny, that makes the older people watch, because they [usually] don't do [such a thing]. When they see something kind of funny they get a good feeling just by watching. It helps us to move. We do it for the elders, because they are watching, they are there.

According to Gamailee, the attention and amusement of the elders measured the success of the game. Not only are elders highly esteemed, they are also representatives of traditional Inuit values. One of these values was not to be lazy, in order to have a happy life. They were said to have always been busy and not to have rested for a minute. By providing and performing a game that emphasized activity, a link is laid to that traditional value. The happiness it produced in the elders was also shared by the whole community. Their happiness was perceived to inspire the players to do their best.

Children among the audience were considered neither to be competent players nor audience. Their presence, however, was only appreciated as long as they observed as far as possible the rules of conduct. Especially after the game, when they imitated the actions of the players, many people hugged younger children or watched older ones contentedly. The presence of children at the games was an opportunity to transfer traditional social skill, values, and physical capabilities.

The prize

Winning was the product of a social process rather than of the individual's efforts. The prize for the winner, then, was an important element in the organization of a game. The importance of the prize was emphasized when its amount was announced at the Fire Brigade's game as well as in other games. The prize money was the resulte of a long term process of saved honorariums. The efforts to produce a prize expressed the Fire Brigade's appreciation of the community as well as their ability to provide a game.[240] Besides marking the social process of producing a winner, the prize also acknowledged the proper practice and the skill of the players.

In addition to the social, there was also a religious aspect to the prize because related to the occasion of Christmas. Talking about the Fire Brigade's contribution, Gamailee Nookiruaq explained that Christmas was important to him because:

---

239 Adam Smith, the recreation director, pointed out that the municipal *Christmas Organizing Committee* increasingly tried to also accommodate the taste of younger people. For instance, they balanced the number of dice games, especially liked by elders, and of athletic games, preferred by younger people, during the evening.

240 I deal with the issue of the position of the provider in the following paragraph.

Christ was born and if it wasn't for him there were not to be any [Christmas] days to celebrate. That is what it is all about, nothing else. It is not for Santa. Not for gifts. It is just the reminder of the great gift that we have received from the God Father. He gave his only son to the people as a savior. [...] Giving gifts is just another example that God has given his only son, as a prize. That is the most important thing. It is, and it will be.

Gamailee referred to Christmas in terms of God's gift of salvation. He interpreted this gift in terms of a prize. He thus positioned the prize as part of the competition in the framework of Christian religion – the dominant discourse on cosmological relationships.[241] Religious and social salvation were connected. The performance of games in celebration of the birth of Jesus, contributed to the salvation of the community by transforming relations of conflict and rivalry – that were perceived to threaten the community – into cooperative relations within which competition was productive. The prize symbolized this transformative process.

The proper way of dealing with prizes was an issue of continuous discourses. One issue under consideration was what to give as a prize: money or objects. In 1999, this issue was dealt with flexibly, because what to give was basically up to the provider of a game. To appreciate whatever you received was perceived to be proper social conduct. Gamailee Nookiruaq explained the decision of the Fire Brigade to contribute a monetary prize:

I think it is always better to give them cash. It is their money. They want it. They can buy anything they want with it. It is their choice, not ours. Some people [however] say that it is better to receive material things, not the money. For example, if I won a cup, I have it. If I won the money, it is already gone.

Whereas the municipality chose money, private and business contributors often opted for objects as prizes. In particular families who provided a game, offered prizes of substantial value when measured by the monthly income of the contributing household. For instance, one family, celebrating the adoption of a son, offered a new bedspread, a new lamp and food, among smaller things as prizes for the game.

Though people indeed were satisfied with any prize they won, they did not mind when it was substantial. The generosity of the giver was acknowledged. People's attitude towards winning prizes had been the issue of discourse especially among elders. They expressed their uneasiness about what they perceived to be an increasing relevance of the value of the prize. They compared today's practices with those in the camps of their youth. For instance, Aka Keyooktak and Martha Kopalie, who participated in an interview together, observed:

Aka Keyooktak: "Traditionally, the games didn't have big big prizes, but today it is all cash prizes. Everybody seems to want to win cash. Traditionally they had very simple prizes for winning. There were prizes, but not expensive ones. Today they get prizes. The children that are growing up are going to be thinking that they get cash prizes; that it's going to be cash prizes for ever and ever. That's how they are going to think now. Traditionally they had very simple prizes. And when I was growing up, I never thought about money. I had never seen money, even when I was working as a young lady in Pangnirtung. But [even] the old people

---

241 See the chapters *Theoretical introduction and methodology* and *Christianity in Qikiqtarjuaq*.

are just more interested in winning money right now – money, money, money is the boss," she said laughing.

Martha Kopalie: "It is very different now; they are more interested in winning money. They would be asked to be woken up when it is time to play games and to win money.[242] When you wake up a young person, s/he is dressed up right away to play games, you know, to win money. For me it seems too much, trying to win money, money, money. Even with the dangerous skidoo, even ladies are going around. They don't care about themselves as long as they win."

Aka Keyooktak: "They only think about winning money, that is all they worry about, because they know that they're going to get lots of cash by winning, so all their interest is to win."

In their perception, the condition of play was at stake. The competitions became an earnest rivalry about goods and, therewith, dangerous. The prize contributed from within the community, then, did not represent a functional social process, but rather winning the prize became an individual enterprise.

Whereas these elders perceived the increasing importance of the material value of the prize as a potential threat to the Christmas celebration, Adam Smith, the Recreation Director, looked at the increase in the monetary value of prizes from a different perspective. He explained that people would spend higher amounts of money for Christmas gifts than before. Then, many people would use the prize-money to bolster the family's budget to buy groceries during the days of Christmas. Winning the prize was, from his perspective,[243] an acceptable procurement strategy.

The traditional perception and practice of prize distributions was, however, not absent in today's celebration as the following example illustrates: The Youth Committee organized a game that featured a lot of very small prizes, for instance rubber gloves and a jelly-o pudding mix. It was in particular the banality of these objects that made people excited about the game. They laughed a lot and expressed in so many words and gestures appreciation for what was given to them.

The position of provider

A generous provider had a high status in Inuit society and, if especially skilled and knowledgeable in some field, often had a position of leadership. The Fire Brigade had an institutionalized position of authority. They perceived, however, that the success of their fire prevention work was not so much a question of giving people directions on what to do to avoid a fire hazard, but basically on their acceptance by and cooperation with the local population. This more informal

---

242 All elders interviewed recall that they, when they were children, got up very early on Christmas morning. They then went around the camp to wish everybody a merry Christmas. To get up early was a matter of honor. Those children who slept in, where laughed at. To get up early in the morning was a virtue. To mention the waking up in relation to the desire to win money can be understood as a harsh criticism of the behavior of younger people nowadays. They do not get up to celebrate Christmas, but to win money.

243 He worked as staff for the municipality and was a member of the municipal *Christmas Committee* that is constituted by CSC members. The times that I participated in their meetings as a guest, the amount of the prize money or its distribution was not of critical concern. They shared with the elders the perception that some people only came for the prizes and this conduct was not appreciated. Thus, there is clearly some ambivalence involved in today's practices of prize distributions.

element of the Brigade's relationship with the community was emphasized by Gamailee when he explained the Fire Brigade's motivation to provide games for Christmas:

> It is very important for the Fire Department to do something for the community. If it wasn't for the people of Qikiqtarjuaq, if they were not listening to the Fire Department about what we want them to do and to be very careful about open flames, then there would have been more fires, for sure [...]. They listen to the Fire Department and it is very important to do something for them, because it would be a disaster if the people would not listen to the Fire Department. [...] Every time we invite them, they all support us rather than ignoring what the Fire Fighters want to do for the people.

He described the contribution of a game in terms of mutual acknowledgment of each other's position in the community. The Fire Brigade expressed its appreciation of the Qikiqtarjuaq's inhabitants' cooperation in their work, just as the participants in the game expressed their acknowledgment of the leadership position of the provider. As already suggested in the discussion of the prize, a game was an opportunity to acknowledge somebody else as a competent social partner and to present oneself as such. This also held true for the position of the provider and leader and his/her/its fellowship. Holding a position as a provider was formulated as part of a cooperative process.

The Screw Removal dice game
Various dice games were frequently played during Christmas festival and had a high turnout of players. Members of all eligible age-groups participated, and the frequent participation of elders

Picture 41 *Mayor Lootie Toomasie is writing '2000' on as many as possible slips of paper during a dice game at the school staff's Christmas party.*

was especially appreciated. According to Adam Smith, the Recreation Director, dice games were considered 'traditional' by many Inuit. To play such a game, players formed a circle, in the center of which the object of the game was placed. The game started when the organizer of the game or one of the players determined the lucky number by a throw of the dice. One or more dice made the round and each player who had the lucky number hurried to the center to work on the object until replaced by another player. The object can take various forms: the object of the game described in this chapter was a wooden board with about eighty screws fastened in it. The players had to remove the screws and the player who took out the last would be the winner. Most Inuit liked the highly dynamic and competitive game, especially if it was organized in such a way that it could gain the right momentum.[244] In order to keep the game interesting, the organizers steered the speed of the game by adding or taking away dice and sometimes adapted the object.

Description
Only a few people had yet arrived for the evening program of December the 29th,1999. Small groups of silent people with their jackets still on were sitting scattered in the gym. The children, however, were cheerfully playing and apparently enjoyed having the run of the place. More people arrived, and the gym slowly filled.

The *Recreation Committee* announced a dice game and all adults, elders and the few teenagers present immediately got up and formed a circle. The organizers waited a little longer for newcomers to take a place in the circle. Men stood next to women, old next to young, and kin next to unrelated people. People continued to join in, even after the game had started.[245] Finally, about 100 players participated and practically no one remained seated.

Adam Smith went to the center of the circle to maintain the equipment and to function as referee. Somebody had switched on a tape with Inuktitut accordion music and several players tapped their feet to the rhythm. A staff member of *The Recreation Committee* determined the lucky number. Conversations faded away and the players concentrated on the game. Two dice were handed to randomly chosen players standing across each other in the circle. They rolled the dice, checked the number and either remained seated or sped to the center to work on the object when the lucky number turned up. Their neighbors to the left picked up the dice and proceeded in the same way.

Several players developed dicing techniques that were half-seriously intended to improve their chances for the lucky number. Some blew on the dice, others threw them high up in the air, some shook them for a long time, and others made them turn over many times in their flight. Players who during the game notably often threw the lucky number received comments with a mixture of admiration, astonishment and joking reproach. If a player never got the lucky number, neighbors good-humoredly expressed pity. When players had a long time to work on

244 During a dice game played at a birthday party I was once told to be less emotionally reserved and more avid in working on the object of the game – ripping pages out a telephone book.

245 Adam Smith made explicit use of this integrative feature of dice games in setting up the evening program. He explained:

I often did the [dice games] in the beginning of every night when people were still coming. They weren't really scheduled. If I was to do a relay race in the beginning and I only have 40 or 50 people, it would be really fast. If we do a dice game in the beginning, it takes about half an hour and everybody will be there by the time we have done that game – up to 150 people. It is a lot easier to go from there. I did them as a gathering type of thing. Because then you can still play as you come.

Picture 42 *Danny Audlakiak takes over removing screws in the dice game.*

the task, people in the circle urged each other to speed up to replace him/her. Being replaced, the player hurried to his/her seat to make sure not to miss a passing dice. Neighbors took care that the dice did not pass too fast to ensure his/her renewed participation.

Though excited or sometimes bored, players always adhered to the rules of the game. For instance, a player next to me had thrown her dice far away in the rush of the game. When the dice stopped turning and only circled around its axis, I picked it up and told her the number. She tenaciously corrected me not to touch the dice before it had entirely stopped and before she could see the number herself. The object of the game was also dealt with seriously by most players. Although onlookers rarely commented on a performance, the player working on the task was the center of everyone's attention. None performed unnecessarily slowly or slovenly. If things did not work properly, players showed no embarrassment nor were they commented upon. Especially men made an effort to work speedily and competently, without showing off, however. And some also took over the responsibility to work on awkwardly positioned screws in order to pave the way for the players coming next. A few elders, however, gave an intentionally comic performance that kindled much amusement.

After about 15 minutes of play, the game lost its pace for a while, as removing the screws took a long time. Participants resumed their conversations, some got a chair to sit comfortably in the circle, and others left for a cigarette break and refreshments. Still, most participants did their best to remove the remaining about 30 screws speedily, though with little excitement. The organizers added a screwdriver to speed the process up. When only three or four screws were left, the excitement gradually increased again and the additional tool was removed. Participants motivated each other to speed up, shouting: "*atiii*! Go!" The person to take out the last screw would win – and everybody wanted to be the winner and wanted to throw the dice as often as possible. Handing over the screwdriver in the center got increasingly rough and assertive.[246] Many became even physical, jostling their rivals. There was no gallantry towards each other, not

---

246 Styles of handing over the object varied from person to person. Whereas some handed it over voluntarily and right away, others tried to keep on working as long as possible. Some of the replacing players immediately took the task out of the hands of the predecessor, others waited to receive it.

Picture 43 *Competing for the screw drivers.*

even towards elders. The excitement reached its peak when Adam raised two fingers to indicate that only two screws were left. Players sped to the center in quick succession, within seconds, pushed the rival away from the object and grabbed the screwdriver. In the midst of turbulent competition for access to the screwdriver, the referee gave the sign that the game was over. William Ilkalik, who had already walked away, had taken out the last screw. He victoriously raised his arms once and the circle broke up.

The prize was distributed together with the prizes of the following game. The names of the winners were announced, William went to the stage, signed a receipt, received an envelop containing $25 and shook hands. Hardly anyone applauded. The winner went back to his chair and meanwhile a new game was in preparation.

Discussion

Dice games, such as the screw-removal game played that evening, emphasized chance rather than competition in skills and physical fitness. Slow performances on the object were only to one's own disadvantage. That might have been the reason why elders attended who otherwise often watched the games or participated only in those especially organized for elders. In the formation of the circle, but also in the practice of the game, social distinctions by gender, age-groups, and relationships were not marked. The circle was also continuously open to newcomers.[247] In this way, the dice game had the highest integrative capacity of all competitions played at Christmas.

The structure of the game organized all participants in the circle into competitive relationships. A second circuit of competition evolved from the practice of the game. The players in the circle tended to cooperate in order to end as quickly as possible the turn of the player working on the object. The emphasis on competition was not only a strategic move. It was also highly valued, because the competitiveness generated excitement – the spice of the game. The

247 In various dice games in which the object was to complete a task, such as the screw removal game, people preferred not to join in when the task had been more than half done – probably because they felt it improper to profit from the work done by others without having contributed to it. In other variations of dice games, people joined in at anytime.

organizers took care to provide the necessary speed and suspense, for instance by choosing an adequate object and by manipulating accessibility to the dice and the game equipment.

Competitiveness was especially apparent in how many of the players took hold of the object towards the conclusion of the game. It was something of a scramble, though even there, one would not take something away from another person. To engage in a similar physical struggle over an object in daily life would be considered most inappropriate and could lead to a loss of face and further aggression. In the game, however, acts of rivalry were placed in a safe and productive context. Here, competition was part of cooperative efforts. First, the design of the game's object required the combined efforts of all players to establish the winning condition. Second, the players in the circle expected each other's best effort to speed up the procedure of throwing the dice, particularly toward the end of the game. Compliance to cooperate in this respect promoted each other's and one's own chances to win. In this way, the players cooperated to enhance the element of competition. Third, whereas the person working on the task explicitly competed against those in the circle, s/he became part of cooperative efforts as soon as s/he was replaced and had returned to the circle. The neighbors in the circle even took care that s/he would have access to the passing dice to get a chance to work on the object again. And fourth, by performing properly competitively or comically, players added to the excitement among the players.

Who would be the winner was to a high degree unpredictable as it was, to a high degree, based on luck. At the same time, the winner was the product of a social process, just as in the Fire Brigade's relay race. In both competitions, the team evolved around the object of the game. In the dice game, the players competed and cooperated simultaneously. They provided access to the object and competed for it. They provided each other the winning condition, and yet they competed for it. The game concluded with the determination of a winner and with no losers.

The Funny Person contest

The comic performances of the contestants in the *Funny Person* competition were one of the highlights of the Christmas games in 1999. The gym was packed with an expectant audience, among them men and women who had prepared a presentation or who were still uncertain if and when they should perform. People were seated in one or two rows along the walls, leaving a large square in the center as the stage. Some spectators were asked to be jury members. The jury decided on the funniest male, female, and elder actors. The winners would receive a prize of $30 each.

When the game was announced, conversations faded away and people looked around to see who was going to perform first. After about half a minute, a middle-aged man stepped forward, but not as far as to the center of the stage. He positioned his legs into horse-stand with knees bent low. He bent his body a bit and pulled his face into grimaces with his hands. Then he stretched his arms and rotated them jerkily. He concluded his presentation by standing on his left leg and scratching his right armpit, probably imitating an ape.

The next contestant was a young man who had already begun his performance before reaching the stage. He also went into a horse-stand with his knees violently shaking. Turning slowly around, he tickled the palm of his outstretched right hand with the forefinger of the other hand signifying sexual intercourse. He concluded his presentation with sticking his tongue out at the audience. The audience was very much amused. His presentation took not more than a minute, but when he returned to his seat, people applauded excitedly.[248]

---

[248] I am lacking documentation on the names of the first two participants. The following performers will be identified by name.

Picture 44 *Pauloosie Kunilusie winning the Funny Person contest.*

Next was a man in late middle-age, John Ayaruaq. People applauded in anticipation; but when he just crossed the stage and walked toward a group of people, a disappointed murmur arose. Disappointment quickly turned into excitement when they realized that he just had borrowed the jacket of Jonas Audlakiak, the 'Christmas Man'. For many years, it had been one of Jonas' tasks to discipline of the children during the Christmas festival. The audience bursted into laughter when John dressed in Jonas' jacket, went on the stage with long strides, ushering imagined children away with harsh swings of his arms and angry shouts at the audience. After about 20 seconds, he took off his costume and pulled his t-shirt over his head in such a way that only his face was protruding. He lifted up his shoulders and moved about stiffly with spread legs and bent knees, resembling an ape. Staring at the audience, he walked a few steps and then stopped, put his hands to his genitals, and rhythmically pushed his hips forward. The audience thought this was hilarious and applauded enthusiastically when he left the stage.

Now the audience had to wait for another presentation. A few people crossed the stage to enter or leave the gym, and each time, the audience applauded encouragement to them to present something. Suddenly, Pauloosie Kunilusie, a male elder, businessman, and founder of the first Pentecostal congregation of Qikiqtarjuaq,[249] walked straight to the center of the stage. He took off his pullover with determination and, with a seductive swing, threw it into the public. Whoever had been busy elsewhere hurried back to his/her seat immediately. Stone-faced and unflinchingly he took of his t-shirt and threw it over his shoulder and finally cast off his shoes. His performance produced an atmosphere of suspense and hilarity among the audience. His performance reached its peak when he also bared his bottom, taking down the back of his jogging pants and underwear. This induced fits of laughter and much alarm among the audience, particularly when he made his round, sitting down on some people's, mostly women's, laps. He pulled his pants up while walking from one to the other and took them down to sit. Everybody was torn between fleeing and remaining. Most men were laughing – and moved a few steps out of his way. Women often tried to prevent him from approaching by hiding their faces behind their neighbors back or by holding their children in front of them. Some appeared to be so mesmerized that they remained motionless on their chairs and I think I saw either a twinge of panic or a twinkle of pure amusement in their eyes. The women he approached were screaming

---

249 See chapter *Christianity in Qikiqtarjuaq.*

with laughter while half-heartedly trying to escape him. After having completed his round, excluding only the area were elders were sitting, he calmly picked up his clothing and went back to his seat. It took a while until the commotion among the audience eased down. His act would be a topic of conversation even after Christmas.

When after three or four minutes nobody came up for a performance, the organizers were about to conclude the competition. But as the audience required: "More! More! Another one!", they asked a few more times for further presentations. Neevee Pitsulak, a middle-aged woman, approached the stage. She started to dance a bit to an Inuktitut accordion tune.[250] She laughed and it seemed that she thought about her next moves. People she looked at responded by laughing. Her dance became more and more bizarre and resembled the movements of a shy young girl. She jumped and used her hands to pull her face into comical grimaces. Then she dropped to the floor and crawled on all fours and, like a dog and lifted her leg as if to pee. The audience laughed heartily. Then, she stood up again and danced while rolling her eyes and waiving her fists in rhythm to the background music. She concluded her performance by making faces. She hurried back to her seat and covered herself with a jacket as long as the applause lasted.

Shortly after, a very old lady emerged from the equipment room, where she had put on her costume secretly. Sarah Kakkee, was in fact a middle-aged women. She wore a head-scarf and a long skirt. She had stuffed her mouth with some material that gave her the appearance of a toothless old woman. Leaning on a long stick she resolutely walked to the center of the stage with stiff and shaky steps. There, she looked at the audience, proudly casting her stick away. While rotating her outstretched arms forward two or three times, her knees started trembling violently. Her arms stopped abruptly; she vigorously straightened her back by pushing on her upper back with one hand and her forehead with the other. And her arms started to rotate again until her knees were shaking once more. She repeated the procedure three times. The audience did not stop laughing. She concluded her presentation by quickly bending down. Picking up her stick, she left the stage and received with a smile the enthusiastic applause.

The last person to perform was Titusie Audlakiak, a middle-aged man. He started his performance while walking to the stage. He bent his back forward and lifted his head, his eyes staring at the audience. He placed his hands in his armpits holding his elbows in a 90° angle away from his body. His whole body appeared to be in a spasm. He walked on the stage with loud howling. There, he straightened his body, touched his legs, and, with much yammering and pointing, he expressed his concern about one of his feet. That was repeated several times, and the audience alternated between silence and laughter. After indicating that actually both his legs were affected, he fell down on his knees and walked on all fours and howled like a dog. The next moment, he got up again, surprising the audience by walking relaxed and nonchalantly. His presentation took the longest and he concluded it by walking around with bent knees like an ape and sticking out his tongue.

The jury got together and decided that Sarah Kakkee was going to win the prize for the funniest female performer, John Ayaruaq the prize for the funniest male performer, and Pauloosie Kunilusie the prize for the funniest elder. The decisions of the jury corresponded closely with the response of the audience to the performances. The winners were announced, came forward, and picked up their prizes under the applause of the spectators.

---

250 See sub-chapter *Dances*.

Discussion

The Funny Person Contest was a hilarious spectacle and it fitted very well into the aim of having a happy Christmas festival. The audience amused themselves splendidly and, responded positively to all presentations, they rewarded the performers by acknowledging their skills and daring.

A common feature of all performances – and a trigger of much hilarity – was a process of de-socializing of the actors. This process can be outlined in two steps. In the first step, the performer disengaged from his/her social identity by giving a parody of someone or by playing a role. Most performers also took the second step of making a transition from the social to the non-social. John Ayaruaq's performance is an excellent example, firstly of the performance of these steps. He started with a parody of his friend Jonah and marked the conclusion of this part by taking off Jonah's jacket. He then, taking the second step, impersonated an ape-like being that displayed an uncontrolled sexuality. Thereby, he presented his otherwise private sexuality as an object of public ridicule. He had clearly marked the distinction between his performance of imitation and his performance of the ape-like being. And none of the other actors combined the two. I would like to suggest that with the introduction of the non-social into the performance, it would have been improper to continue the imitation of another person, because it would make that person ridiculous. The actor, however could take on such a role.

The performers applied the presentation of the non-social in various degrees. Whereas Sarah did not use it at all, Neevee and Titusie did not go further than impersonating the non-sexual behavior of dogs. All other performers presented uncontrolled sexuality, just as John did. However, all, except Pauloosie, took on the shape of non-human beings in this context. Pauloosie preserved his own persona. He, therein, not only went farther than the others, but also very actively involved the audience. Though I am lacking specific data on whom he approached (besides myself), I noticed that he omitted elders. It seems that he chose persons toward whom he could express dominance.

In Inuit culture, appropriate social skills and knowledge were indicators of adulthood. Modesty is one of the most highly valued features of social conduct. There is, therefore, a high threshold to present oneself in a de-socialized way in daily life. The relatively low number of performers in the *Funny Person* contest expresses how great a challenge it was to make a fool of oneself in public. It required a considerable amount of self-assurance, and to excite the audience also required a high degree of social intelligence and artistic skill. Pauloosie's presentation showed mastery in these domains in an exemplary manner. First, he dared to link his role closely to his person and, thus, placed his person in the center of attention. He expressed in his performance that he had a social position that allowed for such a strategy. Second, he keenly observed his audience and timed his movements according to their responses. Third, he had the social knowledge of whom he could involve in his performance. The range of audience reactions showed that he had the skill to walk a fine line. His performance clearly expressed that he was a self-assured religious and social leader with ambitions, and also that he had the social ability that position requires.

In pre-Christian camp times as documented for instance by Boas, processes of de-socialization were practiced in shamanistic contexts. In order to deal with animals or spirits, shamans cast off their own social structures and crossed the boarders between the categories of beings. In the Sedna festival,[251] all adult members of the winter camp participated in processes of de-socialization. For instance, two shamans representing spirits ordered men and women

---

251 See the chapter *Theoretical background and methodology.*

into pairs that spent the night together, irrespective of their marital relationships and ways of social life. Being able to cross the border between the social and the non-social demonstrated the capacity to take on a non-social identity. This capacity was linked to the ability to deal with the domain of the non-social.

When the Christian religion became the dominant framework in which cosmological relations were formulated, the value attached to the capacity for dealing with the non-social continued to be relevant, as my analysis of the *Funny Person* contest demonstrates. A person with a high social position, such as Pauloosie Kunilusie, had much to loose with a performance of bad quality.[252] But a successful performance affirmed his social position. People with a lower social status, in contrast, had little to loose but lots to gain. They expressed their social commitment by taking up the challenge to expose themselves for the entertainment of the audience. Furthermore, they could display their social and artistic skills and be acknowledged for them.

5.6.2 Morning games
Each morning, except for Sundays, the short period of daylight was used for two or three games. The competitions were held either out on the sea-ice or at the square in front of the hamlet building. Participation was low, compared to the evening program; rarely more than 20 or 30 people turned up. After a long evening of games and late night dances, most teenagers and young adults turned over in their bed once more while their parents and a few elders performed the outdoor games in the crisp cold of a mid-winter morning. An additional audience assembled only when skidoo races were announced. Though few in number, people participated enthusiastically

Picture 45 *Ping Pong-Ball Balancing game (at Easter).*

---

252 This may be the reason why no other elders or community leaders performed.

and enjoy being outside. The prizes for the outdoor games were distributed in the presence of the larger public during the evening program.

In contrast to the multitude of evening games contributed by local organizations, businesses, and private persons, the morning program was mainly provided by the municipality. Outdoor games resembled the indoor games in their set-up and organization. Teams, pairs or individuals competed in races and games of skill and chance. Outdoor competitions differed only in so far as they utilized materials such as ice, snow, and technical equipment such as rifles, harpoons, or snow-scooters. Some competitions turned outdoor activities, such as hunting, fishing, skidoo or dog-team riding into games. Just as the set-up of the games were similar, so was the atmosphere. However, happiness and enthusiasm for playing appeared to be even more emphasized in an outdoor context.

The seal hunting competition
Hunting and fishing competitions were a regular part of each year's Christmas festival. The integration of animals into their structure, however, distinguished them from other games. In 1999, a seal hunting competition between mixed doubles was organized by the municipality in cooperation with the *Housing Association*. The municipality provided the second and third prizes and the first prize for the female partner of the winning team. The first prize for the male partner, a handmade floe-edge boat, was provided by the *Housing Association*. Since the *Housing District Office* did not agree to give cash prizes, the local maintenance crew built a floe-edge boat from plywood previously used as packing material – a very attractive prize.

Description of the seal hunting competition
To ensure that all, and not just the favorite games were attended, the municipal *Community Service Committee* (CSC) had not issued a program of Christmas events in 1999. Games that required preparation from the participants, such as the seal hunt organized for December 31st, were announced on the radio.

I learned about the competition from hunters gathering at the Co-op café. They asked me if I was going to participate. I was enthusiastic about this idea, because it would be my first trip out on the land, but I realized that I would have to find a partner. Mixed doubles were to compete in hunting seals and none of the men around the coffee table offered to take me along. I simply did not know whom to ask at this early stage of my fieldwork. Moreover, I knew virtually nothing about hunting or traveling out on the land. I discussed these issues with my host, Lizzy Anaviapik, and she offered to ask her sister's teenage son, Jimmy, if he would like to team up with me. He agreed, and when he picked me up he was riding his grandfather's skidoo and *qamutik* (sled) and brought his own rifle. I provided the gas for the trip.

The day before the hunt, a start appeared uncertain. Hunters had reported that they encountered unfavorable ice conditions on their trips and that the weather was far from ideal for breathing hole hunting. Conditions improved so far during the night that the organizers decided to give it a try. About 15 teams assembled on the sea-ice north of Qikiqtarjuaq. Jimmy and the team comprised of two of his cousins were the youngest participants. The others were between about 25 and 60 years of age. About half the teams were composed of relatives or were married couples. In other cases, the partners appeared to be well-acquainted.

While we were waiting for the start, the men stood together and talked about travel conditions and the whereabouts of seal. The women went from one skidoo to the next to chat about work, family, or the latest news. Monica, a women in her late 20s, and her cousin and namesake-brother Jimmy challenged each other in a wrestling competition, a common pastime when traveling out on the sea-ice. When the organizers announced the start, men took the front seats on their snow-scooters and women the back seats. The teams dispersed over the sea-ice. Usually, two or three of them traveled together ensuring each other's safety. Some hunters explored the areas ahead and informed us about areas of dangerous ice on the way. Jimmy, and his cousins with whom we traveled, Lucy and Pauloosie, decided not to go any further and to start looking for seal breathing holes right there to avoid any risks. They soon gave up, though, because snowdrifts covered many holes and those they could find had been abandoned long ago. My three companions decided to cease hunting and to follow the tracks of Jimmy's uncle, Jaypetee Nookiguak, who did not participate in the hunt but had gone to check his seal nets.

He had just disentangled a seal from the net when we arrived, and the young people at once helped to press the water out of it's lungs with their feet. When I asked Jaypetee if he would not participate in the competition, he smiled and answered: "no way." But he liked to go out hunting. To him, 'real' Inuit culture was best experienced out on the land, and not in the community. After about half an hour, we left and had tea with the other participants in a cabin at the camp site of Old Broughton Island. It turned out that only one seal was caught. None of the teams met the criteria for winning a prize.

Nonetheless, the CSC and Housing Association wanted to distribute their prizes. Prizes for games that did not yield a winner were usually decided by a follow-up game during the evening program. The CSC, together with representatives of the *Housing Association*, announced that the prizes were going to be awarded in two steps: The male and female winners of the second and third prizes (twice $75 and $50 respectively) would be determined by a water balloon bowling competition between the participants in the seal hunt. The entire community (above the age of 18), however, was given the opportunity to compete for the first prizes in a bingo competition.

For the balloon bowling competition, first women and then men lined up. The contestants tried to bounce a water-balloon as close as possible to a target. The contestant closest and second-closest to the target balloon would be the winners. After women and men completed their competitions, the winners' names were announced and they received their prizes.

As the bingo competition was announced, every adult and elder picked up a bingo board. Complete silence fell as people concentrated on the numbers announced in rapid succession. Elders were assisted by their neighbors to follow the rapid succession of numbers. When the first man went forward with a completed board to be checked, the tension relaxed – until his claim was confirmed and the bingo continued to determine the female winner.

The prizes were distributed then. The winning woman received $100, and the audience applauded briefly. When the boat was carried in by several men, people applauded and laughed – and so did the winner. He was the Housing foreman who himself had built the boat together with some colleagues. Neither of the first prize winners had participated in the seal hunt, but nobody minded.

Discussion

The seal hunting contest was an attention-getting, Christmas game. People were always in favor of hunting and they complimented the sturdiness of the hunter-players who braved the cold to attend a game. Furthermore, the hunt required preparation and investment of money from the contestants. The relatively high prizes reflected these efforts.

In contrast to indoor games, the seal hunt as well as other morning games were not only shaped by the organizers, but also by the outdoor conditions. The providers could not entirely control the conditions and the actual development of the game – it was even uncertain if the game could take place at all. They had to allow for such factors as the weather, ice-conditions, and in case of the hunting game, animal migrations. It was also particular to hunting competitions that the combination of hunting and playing had the potential to create a specific problem: Inuit assumed that success in hunting was not only based on skills, knowledge, and good luck, but also on proper conduct toward the animals hunted. The relationship between humans and animals was sensitive to transgressions. If the conduct of humans was offensive to animals, they were expected to withdraw from the hunters. The goal of hunting was to kill an animal in order to provide people with meat and fur. Bringing home one's catch, the hunter had the obligation to introduce it into a circuit of sharing within his household, family, and, if sufficient, also with the community. Turning the meat into a commodity and selling it is strongly discouraged. Whereas in hunting, the killing of the seal is the goal, the seal becomes a means to obtain a prize, such as the floe-edge boat, in the competition.

A few hunters expressed feeling uncomfortable with hunting in this context. Jaypetee Nookiguak's attitude towards the seal hunt competition is one example of this sentiment. Another man, in his 30s, also believed that hunting should not be a game. He explained that his step-father had taught him that seals and other animals should only be killed when people were in need of food or clothing. He felt uncomfortable killing animals for the sake of a competition, or for that of a prize. The perception of the incompatibility of hunting and playing was marginal in the community, however. Still, participants in the competition appeared to recognize the potential for conflict as they constantly maneuvered to avoid being disrespectful to animals or to spoil the game. For instance, men (and probably some of the women) prepared for their participation in the game as though preparing for a regular hunt. However, even though they were well-aware that the conditions were unfavorable for breathing hole hunting (and would render other techniques more effective), they still participated in the game. During the game, most teams started out with a serious attempt to catch seals, but as soon as they perceived there was little chance of success, most contestants just gave up their enterprise and withdrew from the competition. Giving up the hunt when outdoor conditions provide considerable obstacles was a regular hunting practice. Pursuing one's enterprise under such circumstances was discouraged as 'trying too hard'. It was not only foolish but was also considered disrespectful toward the animals. Skilled hunters did not challenge the animals and the environment, but rather took hunting conditions into consideration and planned their expeditions accordingly. Respect for the unpredictability of success in hunting is not only a matter of practical experience, but also a moral value. The players of the hunting game took this into consideration when they based their success in the hunt on good luck rather than on a prolonged search for seals for the sake of the competition. They gave in their performances precedence to their hunting ideology over playing.

This relationship between hunting and playing was also apparent in interactions between the teams. The formal structure of the game organized the participants into stable units to compete for access to seals. Though competition was an essential feature in the design of the game, rivalry was not emphasized in its performance. Rather than focusing on their teams, contestants first created various contexts of cooperation. For instance, the teams shared information on the whereabouts of the seals and the ice-conditions. In doing so, they furthered each other's chance of success. Furthermore, they traveled together to ensure each other's safety. Second, the teams were less stable than indicated by the design of the game. The teams dissolved prior to and after concluding the hunt, and contestants socialized with each other. The teams were also of no relevance in the organization of the follow-up games. The team was a means to a practical end. It did not develop a corporate identity, nor was the prize related to the team compositions. Good luck and cooperation were emphasized in the seal hunt, rather than competition and social categorization. This relation between cooperation and competition reflects regular hunting practices, underlining the primacy of hunting over playing in the competition.[253]

The relationship of cooperation to competition was also structurally addressed in the performance of other games, such as the relay race of the Fire Brigade. The teams' construction went through phases of cooperation and competition in temporal succession. At first, same sex doubles separated to join the competing teams. In the further rounds, the winning team split up to form the two new competing teams. Former partners turned into competitors, and competitors provided each other with the opportunity to participate and win the competition. The category of "the loser" did not emerge. The participants cooperated to render competition possible. Competition created a joyful game for participants and audience alike. The distribution of a prize marked the completion of the social process of producing a winner.

I want to return at this point to the issue of the prize in the seal hunt. The success of a regular hunt was represented by the killed seal; success in the game was the production of a winner of the prize. The results of the processes of catching a seal or of winning a prize were both essentially unpredictable. Though sharing this feature, the processes were not equal. When hunting was integrated into the process of playing, the product of the hunt – the killed seal – turned into the object of the process of the game. The prize marked the successful dealing with the object. The killed seal was subordinated to the logic of the game. As this was not acceptable to most Inuit, a second discourse was established that subordinated the play to the hunting ideology.[254]

The distinction of the discourses of competing for the prize in a competition on the one hand, and of seal hunting activities on the other, was also apparent in the choice and design of the concluding competitions. Whereas the second and third prizes were eventually distributed among the participants in the hunt, the entire (adult) community was eligible for the first prizes. Little relevance was attributed to the particular team composition during the hunt, nor to a hunting set-up in the choice of the follow-up competitions to choose a winner. The process of distributing the prizes had to be completed regardless of the setup of the original game. The element of community-at-play rather than hunting was emphasized in the alternative games – whereas the element of hunting rather than that of play was emphasized in the context of the hunting competition.

Hunting as a game directly addressed the relationship between the social domain of humans and the cosmological domain of land and animals. The relationship was dealt with according to traditional values expressed in the image of the *inummariit* nomadic hunters. I suggest that the proximity to this ideal by being active outdoors was also expressed to be particularly pleasant in the players' perception of the morning games. They thought it a shame that most of the younger people preferred to join in the late night dances rather than to participate in the morning games.

---

253 Competition was also part of the hunting practices in the sense that hunters competed for social status. One's status increased with hunting success.

254 This relationship between playing and hunting was also expressed in the fact that country food was never used as a prize. The social and cosmic circuit of sharing country food was part of the hunting ideology. It apparently could not be used to mark the success of the subordinate circuit of playing. The only exception in this respect was clams. Clam divers had organized a competition for clams. Clams, however, were a very recently available delicacy and were therefore apparently not dealt with in the same terms as other, more traditional, country food.

5.6.3 Discussion of the games

The research question posed in the introduction to this elaboration on Christmas games: what, then, was the relevance of the collective performance of games for the processes of community formation in Qikiqtarjuaq? The games described and discussed above are examples of some 70 games played during the Christmas festival in 1999 and about the same number of games played in 2000. We saw that, whereas the games had various setups and objectives, the moral values of cooperation and modesty, as expressed in their actual performance, were marked features in all of them. In games, people interacted with each other in various types of ideal relationships – in contrast to the some increasingly difficult social interactions in daily life in the period prior to Christmas.[255] Whatever conflicts and rivalries might have existed prior to the games, by performing games conflicts and rivalries were perceived to dissolve and to transform into productive competition in a cooperative endeavor to produce a winner.

By playing, the community organized itself into various temporary formations of ideal relationships. These formations were structured by (combinations of) gender, age, occasionally kinship and marriage, or they emphasized unity. The community-at-play functioned not by the grace of a specific organizing structure but by the grace of a proper social process consisting of interactions between individuals. The social process had the aim to produce a winner interpreting individual success as a product of proper social interaction. The audience acknowledged individual performances and the attractiveness of the game – a competition setup and its performance by players that generated happy excitement was appreciated and perceived to be a successful game. It not only expressed the social skill of the players to interact in highly competitive and/or comical situations but the happiness also expressed the high value placed on a functional community 'being together'. In the context of this ideal society, all participants as well as the provider of the game present themselves as potential social partners and position themselves socially.

The 'ideal society' referred to the image of the *inummariit* living in nomadic hunting communities. Elders, who were perceived to be closest to the *inummariit*, recollected the transition from the organization of games in camps to those in the settlement. In the new social situation of the settlement, it was not the camp leaders, but the municipality that functioned as the major provider of the collective games and the distributor of internal (e.g. money through *Raffle Ticket* sale) and external (e.g. Nunavut Government funding) property by the unpredictable processes of winning a prize. Contributing organizations, such as the municipality, considered themselves to be of relevance to the community and part of their identity was related to the provision of and participation in games. Therewith, they demonstrated that they were meaningful partners for the population and worthy to continue practices of leadership.

The games were part of the festival that celebrated the birth of Jesus Christ – an event addressed by Inuit in terms of salvation and renewal of the relationship with God.[256] Participating in this period of transformation required an ideal community devoid of conflicts and, at the same time, the ideal society was produced in the performance of the festival. Games, in particular, effected the transformation of conflict into friendly competition.

In this context, Gamailee Nookiruaq referred to the gift of salvation as a prize given by God to the people. The notion of the prize referred, just stated above, to a social process with the aim of producing a winner. The establishment of an ideal relation to God was formulated

---

255 See the chapter *Seasonality of Qikiqtarjuaq.*

256 See the sub-chapter *Christmas and New Year services.*

as following the principles of performing a game. The practice of playing games, in turn, was positioned within a Christian framework. The relationships to animals and land were also dealt with through games. We saw, however, that in the context of games, proper hunting conduct had priority over playing. Social relationships could not be established at the expense of cosmological relationships, but only in correspondence with them – and neither could be established at the expense of Christian relationships, for example by not observing the Sabbath, but only in correspondence with them.[257]

Laugrand & Oosten's (2002: 221) finding in regard to Christian Inuit hunting camps that "in playing games, the community shows its ability to deal with [...] tensions and to dissolve them in a general atmosphere of friendly competition" was a continuing feature of Inuit society and can be extended to the functioning of the modern community of Qikiqtarjuaq. Actually, in the performance of games, the formation of the community of Qikiqtarjuaq continued to be that of a nomadic hunting society as it was formulated in the image of the *inummariit*. The community rather than constituting itself as a sedentary organization, in its games constituted the reverse, it integrated features of its sedentary social condition into the 'old model'. The old model is demonstrated by the function of provider by the municipality.

5.7 Dances

Introduction
Dances were scheduled as the concluding event for each day of the Christmas festival.[258] Two dances were planned for each evening: *Inuktitut* ('like Inuit do') dances and *Qallunatitut* ('like Qallunaat do') dances. The distinction was in the type of music played and the style of dancing. The Inuktitut style referred to jig-dances performed to Scottish folk music played on the accordion. It was originally taken over from the whalers. Modern popular music was used for Qallunaatitut dances. Throughout the year, dances were held with recent music. When the organizers explicitly wanted to attract people of all ages, they would play "oldies", or pieces from the 1980s and then people often danced in pairs.

For the Qallunaatitut dances held in the hamlet gym at Christmastime, however, more recent music was played, usually of the hip-hop variety, and the style of dancing was inspired by the newest music videos shown on TV music channels. These dances were attended by older teenagers, people in their twenties, a few middle-aged women and occasionally one elder – Ipeelee Naujavik. He was actually the only elder who also participated in most of the regular dance events on Friday and Saturday evenings throughout the year.[259]

Inuktitut holiday dances were scheduled following the games in the school gym, but because of the many games played in the evening, dances often did not start before midnight. Many adults and elders felt too tired to attend, so the Inuktitut dances were often cancelled. However, in order to provide opportunities for Inuktitut dancing, one or two short sessions were squeezed in between games, and Inuktitut dances were also used for games. For example, the *shoe scramble* and *musical chairs* employed round dance formations.

---

257 See sub-chapter *Christmas feast*.

258 Dances could also be held on a Sunday after 9 pm. Then, the Sabbath was believed to be concluded.

259 Friday dances were organized for teenagers and Saturday dances for adults and elders, though the latter were not expected to actually participate.

Picture 46 *Men scrambling for shoes during the Shoe Scramble dance competition.*

5.7.1 Inuktitut dances

The Inuktitut dance on the 29th of December, 1999 was well attended. The well-known accordion music of Seemeeunie Keenainak, a Pangnirtung musician, was played from a tape. About 250 people of all age-groups were sitting along the walls and the children made the rounds, visiting people. When the dance was announced, about 30 young and middle-aged men and women formed pairs, usually of mixed gender and often not based on marriage or close kin relations.[260] Some of them were tapping their feet to the rhythm of the music; others stood motionless, awaiting instructions from the organizers for the first formation.[261] Children, who were not eligible to participate, imitated the dances and continued to visit people. The audience watched and chatted quietly and some, carried away by the music, clapped their hands and tapped their feet. The elders were sitting quietly in their chairs, most of them with a little smile.[262]

The basic dance step was a jumped forward kick with alternating feet. Men and women alike used this step, but while women moved modestly, men performed vigorously. For the first formation, a row of men and a row of women lined up facing each other. While all danced in place, the first person to the left of one row and the first person to the right of the other row danced to the center between the rows, linking arms, turned around once, and then separated to move to the other end of their rows. Then the next two dancers moved to the center, and so on and so forth until everybody had been once in the center. Then, the two rows moved closer together and the dancers of each row stood shoulder to shoulder. The first pair to the right moved a bit away and the woman had the task to catch the man while both were running around

---

260 People teamed up in a similar way as for games.

261 The initiative to change the formation also could come from the dancers themselves.

262 Elders who were physically still fit often joined the dances, though not this evening.

Picture 47 *Inuktitut dance.*

both lines of dancers. When the man was caught, the pair took themselves to the rear end of their lines, and the next pair started. When everyone had his/her turn, the dance partners were holding both of each other 's hands aloft to form a roof. The first pair to the left then danced through the roofed aisle thus formed and arrived at the rear end of their lines. This formation was danced several times. Each time that it was concluded, the two rows split and each marched half circle. When the partners met each other at the end of the half circle they held hands and the two rows formed again. After four rounds of this formation, several other variants of line and circle formations were danced.

Partners hardly looked at each other or exchanged a word. However, in my own experience during particular formations where partners were changed in rapid succession,[263] male partners tended to convey some kind of message by shaking my hand in different ways. For instance, some held my hand just a bit too long. Another pressed it twice quickly. This hidden communication added a personal note to the outwardly often neutral interaction.

After about twenty minutes of continuous dance, most women started to walk instead of using the jump-step, but men continued their vigorous dancing style till the end. Whereas women went back to their seats, smilingly touching their red cheeks, wiping sweat from their forehead, and airing pullovers, men, sweating as well, hardly displayed any signs of exhaustion and joined another dance round.

5.7.2 Qallunaatitut dances

In contrast to Inuktitut dances, Qallunaatitut dances were usually carried on through to the late hours. Younger staff members of the CSC setup the sound equipment in the hamlet gym and created a disco atmosphere by dimming the lights and switching on a few coloured spotlights. Participants had to be 16 years or older. On the average, some twenty people participated, most of them around their twenties. Occasionally also a few middle-aged women and one elder, Ipeelee Naukavik, participated. This was approximately the same configuration of dancers as during the regular Friday and Saturday dance events throughout the rest of the year. Oldies were played to accommodate a more mixed public only at the New Year dances.

---

263 For example, the inner circle of men was rapidly moving, while the outer circle of women remained standing.

The music was contributed by CSC staff, other participants, and the local radio station. Everyone could request the disc jockey to play a particular recording – mostly chosen from a repertoire of which one knew that most dancers would like – and he, then, played it at high volume. Along the walls of the gym, benches were arranged and small groups of young people sat dispersed over the whole gym. Whereas young men usually moved around a lot and hung around with several of their acquaintances, young women tended to stick together in groups, chatting (as far as possible given the high volume at which the music was played) and giggling. Rarely more than six or seven people went on to the dance floor. When the music ended, they rushed back to their seats and waited to see if theywould dance to the next piece, or not. Younger men and women usually danced in separate areas of the center square that was lit by the coloured spots. A few individuals chose to dance in the dark parts of the room, because they felt too shy to be watched by others. All of the young people very skilfully imitated the newest dance styles shown on music video clips on TV. The few older dancers mostly kept to the styles popular in their youth, for example break dancing or disco. The dance lasted into the early morning hours. Shortly after the young people went home to sleep, their parents and grandparents were getting up to prepare for the outdoor games.

Perceptions of the dances at Christmas time
The Inuktitut and Qallunaatitut dances were scheduled in such a way that everyone interested could participate in both. Dances, in particular if continued until one was hot and sweaty, were perceived to benefit a person 's physical condition and to make him/her happy. However, people tended to value Inuktitut and Qallunaatitut dances differently in this respect. Members of all age-groups appreciated Inuktitut dances, although some teenagers found them boring, as one middle-aged woman told me. Those who participated seemed enthusiastic, however. An Inuktitut dance was for the whole community – though children were, as in most other Christmas practices, not eligible to participate in the activity proper. People related or not related by marriage or kinship danced together and partners changed rapidly. The interaction between dance partners was focussed on dancing and there was little further (visible) contact between them. The little relevance attributed in pairs emphasized the commonality generated by dancing.

The perception of Qallunaatitut dances was more ambivalent. Young people were interested in the newest developments in pop music and they liked to come together to dance and hang around. The participation of older people in Qallunaat dances when oldies were also played indicated that Qallunaatitut dances were widely appreciated. In contrast to Inuktitut dances, the emphasis was more on the individual dancer and the pairs, but it was still an event for the whole community. This was different when the music played at dance events was primarily for a younger public. Most people agreed that younger people should have their dances, however elders did express concern, particularly about the late hours. Martha Nookiruaq, an elder, stated:

> They have dances all night long. Back then, they had dances and quit before midnight. In the beginning I was against [the late hours] and it irritated me at the time. They are hyper when they should be sleeping and they are sleeping when they should be awake during the day.

Not only the separation of young people from the older generations, but also the loudness of the music added to a sense of danger associated with these dances. Occasional incidents of drug and alcohol abuse or a fight between young men did nothing to diminish these concerns.

Discussion

Dances were anticipated, but often priority was given to the games – though their large number was criticised by a number of people[264] – and Inuktitut dances were cancelled as many adult and elderly people felt too tired to participate. Unlike most adults and elders, younger people had adapted their sleep-rhythm to stay awake all night and sleep in the morning. Therefore, the Qallunaatitut dances usually took place.

Organizing an Inuktitut dance instead of a Qallunaat dance for the young people was apparently not an option. The Inuktitut dance was marked as an event of the whole community. It would, then, first, not be proper to organize an Inuktitut dance specifically for young people and exclude others. Moreover, the exclusion of children from the dances proper indicated that dancers not only had to have the physical skill to dance – many children were talented dancers already at a young age, and it was appropriate for them to imitate the dancers – but that participation also required social skills. Dancers had to be self-assured and modest, enthusiastic and controlled, and they had to be capable of dancing with all members of the community, despite any tensions that might exist between them. Children were thought to still lack, for instance, self control. In many ways, teenagers were considered adults in Inuit society, and they were expected to make their own decisions and to establish their own social relations. At the same time, most of them had not acquired a social position or status, yet. Moreover, people were concerned about the social troubles a number of them tended to run into.[265] Therefore, I have wondered if people consider the youths to indeed be grown-up enough to hold Inuktitut dances properly. The fact that elders, and others, associated a sense of danger with the young people 's Qallunaatitut dances,[266] shows that (some) youths were perceived to be incapable of holding a proper Inuktitut dance among themselves.

5.7.3 Recollections of the elders of dances in camps

In their recollections of the Christmas festivals of their youth, dances were memorable events for some of the elders. Others did not remember any dances in their camps at Christmas or New Year. For example, Jacopie Kokseak recalled from Padloping that: "Back then, with inadequate space in the sod houses, we did not have dances. Later on, in the years when there were more people settled in the community and there were also more white people, there were dances." Though dances were not an obligatory part of the Christmas festivities, they were enjoyed a lot and held if there was enough space for everybody to participate. Aka Keyooktak, from a camp in Cumberland Sound, had very vivid memories of the dances during her youth:

---

264 Beside the hamlet's games, also businesses, organizations, and private people contributed games. As their contributions often were not scheduled in, the games regularly took longer than planned. See chapter *Games*.

265 J.G. Oosten told me once that when the Inuit elders attending research workshops on shamanism in 2004 referred to the 'young people ' to whom they would like to transfer their knowledge, they actually talk about people of about 45 years of age.

266 The sense of danger evolved from, for instance, the focus on the individual dancer dancing for and by him/ herself, the difficulties occasionally evolving from the dances, but also from their, for many Inuit, unfamiliar and non-Inuktitut music (see for example their negative experiences with Heavy Metal music as described in chapter *Christianity in Qikiqtarjuaq*), and the, in comparison with Inuktitut dances, somewhat melancholy atmosphere.

I remember that a lot of dancing went on. They would hold the dances in the largest *qammaq*. And because of they danced so much, it was very hot there. The kids opened the door, and the cold made it seem like smoke. It looked like smoke because it was so cold. The only source of heat was a *qullik* ('seal oil lamp'), that was the only source of heat. But the people dancing, they were sweating and were hot, they really had a good time, they really enjoyed themselves. And as soon as you opened the door, because of the coldness and the people sweating, you could feel the cold right away, there was no heat, there was no electricity, only a little *qullik*. The dances were enjoyed the most. I am sure they were hot because they were wearing skins, clothing like that, I am sure they would sweat because traditional clothing were seal pants and *kamiit* and caribou outfit, but the dances at that time were enjoyed the most.

When I asked her if the children also attended, she replied that "children did not attend. They didn't dance with the adults, maybe due to the lack of space, but after the adults finished their dancing, the kids came and pretended to dance."Also Martha Kopalie, from Kivitoo, recalled the community dances and that people came together in one house: "In Kivitoo there was a sort of cabin, where Qauma lived.[267] There, they held dances. Now, there is only one building in Kivitoo, but there used to be lots." Just as at today 's Inuktitut dances, there were no guitars, but "strictly accordion," as Mary Oonga Audlakiak recalled from the Cumberland Sound area.

Discussion of the recollections of elders
Dances in the past were a communal activity and the participation of all adults and elders of the camp was crucial, but the dance floor did not have to be large enough to accommodate the children. Dancing was thought to require abilities children still lacked. When they held their own little dance, people perceived that they imitated the dances of the adults. The children were present as audience and then subsequently exercised what they saw in a dance among themselves.

Aka Keyooktak recollected the cloud of steam that escaped the *qammaq* when the door was opened. A marked feature of the dances was that people performed intensively. It was a pleasant memory for Aka that people danced until they were hot and sweaty. We saw that this was also a feature of today 's dances. Generating body heat was also highly appreciated in daily life as beneficial for the well-being of people. Martha Nookiruaq once told me that "even when it was not Christmas, we were happy together. When our camps got together in one camp, men interacted by wrestling and building their tired muscles."[268] Also today, wrestling is a much practiced competition when out on the land. It is appreciated not only for its fun and sociality, but also because its practice produced body heat that was believed to regenerate one 's strength and endurance, then to be used on long trips. Inuit believed that through physical exercise strength and well-being can be established. When, in the past, the whole camp and, today, the whole community danced together at Christmas, community was not only established by participating in a collective practice, but also by collectively producing body heat thought to be beneficial for everybody. I wonder, if sweating also has a transcendental element to it. For example, Maressa (1986) writing about the

---

267 It was a tiny warehouse of the *Sabellum Trading Company*. It measured about 12 m², including an oven.

268 Atuat, a female elder from Igloolik, who was interviewed by Bernard Saladin d'Anglure in 1974, expressed a similar perception of the beneficial effect of competitions of strength and endurance, in her case a boxing match: "The function of the confrontations was to purify the camps of sickness and strengthen people's health and energy!" (quotation in: Saladin d'Anglure 1993: 73)

sweat bath among western Inuit groups, pointed out that through sweating people established relationships with the transcendental domain, in particular with ancestors. In Qikiqtarjuaq as well as in the recollections of elders, the features of heightened vitality and of joy associated with dancing, were emphasized. The dancers gave themselves fully to the dance. In regions in which drum dancing is popular the immersion into the rhythm of the drum – a feature also found in the Inuktitut dances – leads to states of trance. The drum dancer transgresses the border between the social and the transcendental domains without getting caught in the latter. S/he is able to act in both. The enjoyment of the Inuktitut dance may carry a transcendental element. Enjoying the dances is based on the entertainment they provide, but enjoyment is also associated with a notion of enlightenment. It is a feeling that is also evoked in religious contexts such as in prayer, when receiving a vision, when singing church songs, or when being freed from the clutches of demons. In shamanic times, the presence of the helping spirit was often associated with feelings of joy (see, for example, Laugrand, Oosten, & Trudel 2000). At this point, these are merely suggestions on the capacities of Inuktitut dancing; future research on this issue would certainly be rewarding.

5.7.4 Music and song

The above paragraphs dealt with two kinds of dancing that were to a large degree distinguished by the music played. Having discussed dance, the following paragraphs will provide a brief focus on music in order to examine the relevance of that distinction between different kinds of music has for Inuit.

Inuit listened to and produced a large variety of music. Which kind of music was played was strongly linked to the situation and the audience. The local radio station provided music for the broadest public. They played mainly somewhat older pop music, Inuktitut pop hits, folk and country & western, and occasionally also classical music. On Christian holidays or when someone died, they played exclusively country & western and gospel music. Other public occasions for music performances were dance events and music presentations. In 2000, the first *Qikiqtarjuaq Music Festival* was celebrated. Several local bands played pop style pieces composed by band members. A few resident Qallunaat contributed guitar music and singing. Two teenage and two younger Inuit girls performed throat singing.[269] Throat singing was perceived by many adult and older people not to belong to the Southern Baffin region. And whereas many people applauded the girls' performances, I was told that there were also comments by older relatives.

Music was also important in church. Traditional Anglican services made use of the organ and the Anglican hymn books. Since 2000, the Anglican Church also acquired modern band instruments to perform modern Christian songs, usually composed in pop style. The Full Gospel Church operated a band from the beginning. In place of an organ, they use a keyboard. Whereas Pentecostal Inuit (Anglican and Full Gospel)[270] also agree to sing hymns accompanied by the organ, Inuit of traditional Anglican faith tend to think that band instruments and the modern songs were inappropriate in church. At school, children learn Qallunaat and modern Inuktitut children 's songs, but they are also taught traditional songs and *Ayaya*-songs[271] by the elders.

---

269 For the performance of throat singing two persons, usually women, stay close together facing each other. They alternately produce a sound (mostly based on a word) in the throat and inhale the air the other breathed out. The rhythm of this alternation of singing and inhaling gets increasingly faster until the song ends in laughter of one of the singers.

270 See chapter *Christianity in Qikiqtarjuaq*.

271 These were made up spontaneously by the singer telling about an experience s/he had or a specific situation.

Two types of music were banned from the public domain: Hard Rock and Heavy Metal. In particular the sound and texts of the latter were thought by many to have a negative effect on young people.[272]

At home, people listened to various types of music according to their taste. Most households had a large collection of CDs with pop music, modern Christian music,[273] classical music, etc. Some younger people had CDs by Heavy Metal or Hard Rock bands and parents probably commented on them, but I never heard that they prohibited their use. People in many households could play an instrument such as guitar, accordion, or keyboards and played these at home. When hunting or fishing out on the land, some people used songs to lure the game. When ice-hole fishing, for example, Leah Noah Nookiruaq sang a fishing song with a broad smile for me, because I was not very successful in procuring fish. The song was meant to encourage the fish to bite the hook. Furthermore, adults often made up a little song for infants that were special to them and they often sang it when the child was around. And there were also a number of people who composed songs and wrote lyrics.[274]

I am not going to deal with the various kinds of music in detail, but I want to address two elements features that mark distinctions between the different types of music: instrumentation and text.

Instrumentation

The organ, the accordion, and modern band instruments were associated with particular kinds of music: The accordion with Inuktitut dance music, Anglican hymns with the organ, modern Christian songs as well as Qallunaatitut dance music and Heavy Metal with band instruments (though in performances of the latter they were known to be regularly smashed).[275]

In particular the performance of modern Christian songs in church raised mixed opinions.[276] Whereas most of those who agreed with the modern songs and instrumentation believed that these, too, were God 's creation, the opponents of these performances, usually traditional Anglican believers, believed that neither instruments nor the new songs belonged in the church.

It appears that particularly instruments with a long tradition in Inuit ways of life, the accordion and the organ, were thought proper by elders, but also by younger people, for ritual performances, such as a church service and a community dance. Modern instruments were accepted as part of Inuit life as well, but opinions about their status as proper instruments for these special occasions were mixed.

Lyrics

Another difference between Inuktitut and Qallunaatitut dance music was that, whereas Inuktitut dance music did not feature lyrics, most Qallunaatitut dance music did. I was always impressed by the intensity with which people indulged in a song, if it was to their liking. At home, they repeatedly played the same song, in English or Inuktitut, and often sang along. At the Full Gospel and Pentecostal Anglican services, the congregation repeated the same song over and over

---

272 See chapter *Christianity in Qikiqtarjuaq.*

273 A middle aged woman told me that she often listens to gospel music when cleaning the house. According to her and other Inuit, cleaning the house would be more thorough then.

274 I will discuss the issue of lyrics in a following paragraph.

275 Traditional Inuit drums are associated with northern Baffin and are said not to be a tradition in the south.

276 See chapter *Christianity in Qikiqtarjuaq.*

again, getting increasingly excited. Lyrics were also used to refer to experiences, to express one 's affection for a child, to lure game, or to convey a message or emotion to the listeners (and singers). Inuit often told me that when actively listening to the lyrics of a song they liked, or by singing the words, one would feel the effects of the words on one's emotions and thoughts. These effects could be enhanced by a catching melody. Local composers aimed to provide people with songs that would help to improve the well-being of the listeners and performers.[277]

Inuit practices of writing songs

The Fire Brigade had established a band that performed at Christmas. Their leading member was Gamailee Nookiruaq, a well-known musician in Nunavut. He wrote and composed most of the songs performed by this band. He described his procedure and aim for writing a song as follows:

> When I try to make up a song, I usually take one or two people with me to write up a song. It has to be suitable for the people to understand. [If it is a song dealing with the work of the fire department] we let the fire fighters see it first, if they like it [...]. A song is a good way to tell the people something, because they listen to the music. On top of that, they listen to the words. That is good.
>
> I had four people out there helping me with the [Christmas] song. Even one little letter if it is right or wrong ... It was going to be my special song for Christmas. That is why people knew the words by heart [later on]. I try to make real good sentences for a song to let the people understand and let them see what the song is about and to let them think if it is right or wrong. It should help the people who listen to the song, by the words. I wanted to help out whomever is feeling desperate, feeling down or kind of sad or lonely or something like that – to put them on a higher level rather than just worrying. We always sing it at Christmas. [...] A lot of times, when I try to make a new song, a new rhythm, new words it took me almost all day, some of them two days or a week. Weeks.

A song is not written lightly. Not only should the music and the lyrics be of high quality, they also should have a positive effect on people – to help people. The wish to help others and to be accepted by the people provides the composer with a leadership position in the community.[278] Moreover, each time that people listen to his song, it places part of the responsibility for their well-being on his shoulders. Gamailee Nookiruaq emphasized that the composition of a song is a social process rather than done on his own. Neither can leaders in the social and religious domains operate alone, but only in cooperation with their followers. Billy Arnaquq, the pastor of the Full Gospel Church, was another composer in Qikiqtarjuaq. He exclusively wrote religious lyrics. From his view and practice:

> A song has to be written with the heart. Otherwise well written songs have only a short duration of popularity, if they are not written with the heart. I pray for my songs, in order to be able to write them this way. Each song takes a long time of preparation to be written. Through praying the songs receive their power to establish a relationship with God. God 's hand is involved in the composition of a song. By singing the songs a pathway opens.

---

277 Inuit perceptions of Heavy Metal was an example of the destructive power melody and lyrics were thought to have on listeners. See chapter *Christianity in Qikiqtarjuaq*.

278 See the chapters *Life in Qikiqtarjuaq* and *Christianity in Qikiqtarjuaq*.

Picture 48 *The Fire Brigade performs a song written by Gamailee Nookiguak (to the right) at Christmas.*

> I integrate the Holy Spirit in writing songs, so that the Holy Spirit can have an impact through the songs – this is the only way to have an impact with the songs.

Billy Arnaquq also aimed to write songs that make a difference to people – in his case in terms of people 's relation to God. Also he emphasized that he did not write his songs by himself. He did not ask colleagues to cooperate, but sought the cooperation of God through the Holy Spirit in order to provide the song with the required quality to help people.[279]

5.7.5 Discussion of the dances

Song was clearly highly valued. Inuit perceived songs to have an impact on a person's life. Composers and writers chose words with great care and they cooperated with social and/or spiritual helpers. It was important that the words express accessible truths, and be useful and uplifting to the listeners. Inuit used the concept of 'doing something with heart' to express the quality of the composition of a song as well as the quality of listening to and memorizing the song. The notion of 'doing something with heart' referred to truth as well as to a quality of relating to a person's thoughts and emotions. In the context of religious practices it also is meant to open a relation to the cosmic domain – God or Devil. Inuktitut song and dance were rarely combined in Qikiqtarjuaq. Exceptions during the period of my fieldwork were, first, a contest at Christmas in which Inuit men and women imitated Qallunaat stars dancing and singing – an event that kindled much amusement. Second, the (very moderate) dancing during Pentecostal services that was perceived with mixed opinions. And third, the performance of the drama *Northern Lights* during the Christmas service.[280] In conversations on the drama, people expressed that the dance added power to the lyrics.

Qallunaatitut dance music, however, often did. Many Inuit knew the lyrics of their favorite English songs and sang along; I never heard anybody commenting on any particular power, for instance, a *Spice Girls* song had – though some of my female acquaintances felt that singing along made them happy. It was fun and the text soon forgotten. This was different, however, with the, often destructive or occult, lyrics of Heavy Metal pieces. They were believed to have an

---

279 Also Gamailee Nookiruaq wrote Christian songs, for instance the Christmas song he talked about.

280 See the sub-chapter *Christmas and New Year church services.*

impact on the listeners. I want to argue that the various experiences people had with Qallunaat songs contributed to their ambivalence about Qallunaatitut dancing events. Many elders were basically monolingual, so it was difficult for them to determine whether the lyrics of a new song were harmless or potentially dangerous. Based on the perception that dance could add power to words, then dancing to Qallunaatitut pop songs was potentially dangerous – at least for people who lacked the required discernment, such as teenagers. The capacity of words was not an issue in Inuktitut dances. Well-being and community was produced interacting in a dance together, and not by speaking powerful words.

5.8 Discussion of the Christmas festival

In order to deal with the question of whether the community of Qikiqtarjuaq is ritually constituted as a social unit and in what form, this study focussed on the major community festival of the annual cycle, which is Christmas – *quviasuvik* ('a time of happiness'). Perceived as a time of cosmological and social renewal, it brings together local people and guests in Christmas and New Year services, gift exchanges, feasts, games, and dances.

Being together with the largest possible social group was highly valued. At the various occasions, the community was organized into continually changing formations based on, for instance, close family relations and household membership, gender, age or simply contingency. The relationships evolving from participation did not become permanent, but dissolved after the performance.

The interactions were, in practices and perceptions, primarily marked by undivided sociality and the absence of tensions. And in whatever specific formation the community was organized, the performance of the various activities was successful, because, as it was emphasized, the participants performed properly. In particular games provided a form of supreme sociality to social interactions by combining cooperation with competition – a process marked with a prize. This suggests that the propriety of social interactions was important for the functioning of the festival. This argument is supported by the fact that children were permitted to only partially participate in the feast. Children are much appreciated in Inuit society, and their presence at the festival was enjoyed as long as they did not disturb the proceedings. Although they were provided with their own Christmas occasions, they were thought to only imitate the performances of adults. In Inuit perceptions, children still have to gain *isuma* ('mental capability') required to fully participate. This does not mean to say that children do not have, and participate in, various social relationships. They are offspring, siblings, namesakes or friends. That these relationships are actually of relevance was shown in the gift giving in which children acknowledged important relationships by their full participation.

Elders were another group that did not perform fully in games and dances. This was said to be due to their physical conditions. Elders often remained audience – an activity highly valued throughout the festival. It was important to organizers and performers alike to take care that elders would enjoy the performances. It was also important that they would watch proper performances. Elders were the closest representatives of the *inummariit* that connect Inuit with the past and express a continuation of Inuit society. In the services, the church leaders provided space for elders to present their testimonies and to lead the congregation. Also this practice expressed the leading position of elders not only in the social domain but also in respect to the transcendental domain. The *funny person* performance of Pauloosie Kunilusie is another case in point. He expressed in his performance the ability to deal with the social and the non-social domain. Whereas it were the ancestors who were the most relevant audience in the Sedna festival of the past, elders are the most relevant audience today.

Since the establishment of Qikiqtarjuaq as a settlement, the Christmas festival is, to a large degree, organized and provided for by community organizations, and in particular by the municipality. This task is important to the municipality and they make considerable efforts herein. Also other organizations of modern community life do their best to be involved and to support the festival. Why is Christmas of such a high relevance to them? To be a generous provider has much prestige among Inuit and is often associated with a leadership position. By getting involved with the Christmas festival, the municipality expresses its perception of being relevant for modern community life. Being accepted in this position by the population, the leadership position, initially only formally defined in reference to the modern community organization, is thereby not only confirmed but also formulated in an 'Inuit way' as referred to in the image of the *inummariit*.

The festival effected social renewal as well as renewal of transcendental relationships to God, the game animals, and the land. The renewal of the relationship to God was approached directly in the services and ample space was given to testimonies. The elders, in particular, took the lead, performing as leaders of the community, so that their confessions was one of the major contributions. As discussed in chapter *Christianity in Qikiqtarjuaq*, public confession deals with the wrongdoings of a person in relation to the community and to God. The renewal of the relationship with God was expressed in terms of the awarding of a 'prize'– the birth of Jesus Christ – by Gamailee Nookiruaq. With this image he emphasized that the renewed relation to God expressed itself in form of a supreme sociality provided to social interactions by games.
Relationships to animals, that were subordinated to the relationship with God, were addressed most directly in the feast. Sharing country food and consuming it together connected the participants to the hunting circuit and therewith to the animals and to the land. Qallunaat food did not have that capacity, but it was perceived to be a traditional food and it added to the enjoyment of the feast.

At Christmas, social relationships were temporarily established in various interactions between people, who (temporally) shared a location, and non-human agencies. The Christmas festival ordered Inuit social life as a hunting community in reference to the image of the *inummariit*.

Chapter 6
A community at play

The topic of play in Inuit culture and society has been extensively discussed by Briggs (e.g.1979, 1998), notably its role in conflict resolution and socialization. Less attention has been paid to the collective use of games in Inuit social life. In Qikiqtarjuaq, games are highly enjoyed. Playing constitutes an excellent opportunity to organize models of social interaction and express important ideals and values.

In the past, Inuit were a society of nomadic hunters that followed a seasonal cycle of movement, concentration and dispersion. Mauss & Beuchat (1979 [1904]) considered this seasonality to be the core of Inuit social organization. Social relations were organized in terms of a temporary framework and embedded in seasonally shared localities. Mauss & Beuchat considered summer and winter as two different modes of the same society. Hence, Inuit sociality was shaped by locality and temporality.[281]

The establishment by the Canadian Government of sedentary settlements in the mid 20th century drastically changed the social conditions of the Inuit. Although relocated from nomadic camps to sedentary settlements, Inuit perceptions of community and practices of community life have changed less than we might have expected. Inuit still perceive themselves as a hunting society and formulate their self-perceptions in cosmological terms emphasizing relations to God, land and animals.

When Inuit were converted to Christianity in the first half of the 20th century, the old practices and beliefs were replaced by new ones. Most of the rules pertaining to hunting, birth and death disappeared and with it the shamanic practices closely interwoven with it. The rules of the new Christian religion, such as respecting the Sabbath, were perceived as much lighter than the traditional rules, which were especially restrictive for women. Sedna and other non-human beings, who withheld sea game when people transgressed social and ritual rules, were replaced by the Christian God who had created animals for the benefit of human beings. Inuit perceive hunting out on the land for the animals God has created for them as the true vocation of Inuit life, and, even within the Christian framework, the relationship to land and animals is still a necessary precondition for people's well-being and spiritual health. It is therefore beneficial to maintain a nomadic life style that connects the land and the community.

South Baffin Island became an Anglican area when the Reverend E.J. Peck arrived on Blacklead Island in 1894. There was hardly any competition for the Anglican Church[282] until the 1980s, when the Pentecostal movement arrived in the North. Some Pentecostal practices, for instance the baptism in the Holy Spirit, evoke features of traditional spiritual life as can be found in the enlightenment and joy that also marks the shamanic experience. The Anglican Church first opposed Pentecostalism, but gradually took a more positive attitude towards these new practices that eventually attract many Anglicans. Today, because the Anglican Church has integrated many

---

281   See also Saladin d'Anglure 1993 for a discussion of Mauss & Beuchat in respect to the *Tivajuut* winter festival (comparable to the Sedna festival of Southern Baffin Island) in Igloolik in the beginning of the 20th century.

282   The frontier between Catholicism and Anglicans was far to the North West in the Igloolik and Nattilik area.

beliefs and practices introduced by the Pentecostal movements, the past antagonism between Anglicans and Pentecostals has lost its sting.

The Anglican Church takes care to maintain its connection to the past. The elders especially feel strongly rooted in Anglican tradition and, because the elders should not be alienated, traditional Anglican ways are also pursued by 'reborn' church leaders, provide a context in which the elders feel comfortable.

Even though Inuit are aware that Christianity was introduced from outside by the Reverend Peck, they now consider it as part and parcel of traditional Inuit culture. Peck is remembered as Uqammaq – 'The One Who Speaks Well'. The Qallunaat origin of Christianity is of little relevance to Inuit. The Anglican Church is strongly associated with the *inummariit*, the true Inuit who lived off the land before permanent settlements were created. The elders still remember this period, and more than anyone else, they represent the *inummariit*. The lifestyle of the *inummariit* today represents an ideal that strongly contrasts with the sedentary life in the community and is associated with knowledge of the land, its animals and the skills required to survive. Many traditional skills, such as the sewing of traditional clothing, knowledge of the weather and igloo building, are taught today in workshops and local Arctic College institutions.

It is acting in an 'Inuit way' that makes one an Inuk. In order to be able to act in an 'Inuit way', a person requires *isuma* ('mental capacity') – something children and Qallunaat are often thought to be lacking (see also Omura 2002). It is not so much *what* a person does – people differ from each other – but *how* it is done which is of importance. Thus, even behavior and customs that resulted from contact with Western societies, such as drinking tea, Christianity, and jig dancing have become part of the *inummariit* image – on the condition that they are perceived to be useful and that they are done in the 'Inuit way' (Omura 2002: 107).

The *inummariit* image connects Inuit to the land they inhabit as well as to their ancestors. Relationships with their ancestors are shaped in many ways. One of its most important expressions is the continuity of names: the children are renamed after their ancestors who thus live on in their descendants. This relation takes precedence over the relations between living people so that kinsmen will often address each other on the basis of the relationship between their deceased namesakes.[283] Thus the connection to ancestors remains an essential feature of Inuit identity and cosmology, as it was in the past.

In Qikiqtarjuaq, Inuit perceive that the camping life out on the land has the most close resemblance to the *inummariit* way of life. The camping seasons are still part of a seasonal cycle of concentration in the settlement and dispersion to camps, which is highly valued by Inuit. Mauss & Beuchat (1979 [1904]: 76-77) emphasized the differences in intensity of social life:

> Winter is a season when Eskimo society is highly concentrated and in a state of continual excitement and hyperactivity. Because individuals are brought into close contact with one another, their social interactions become more frequent, more continuous and more coherent; ideas are exchanged; feelings are mutually revived and reinforced. By its existence and constant activity, the group becomes more aware of itself and assumes a more prominent place in the consciousness of individuals. Conversely in summer, social bonds are relaxed; fewer relationships are formed, and there are fewer people with whom to make them; and thus, psychologically, life slackens its pace.

---

283 See for the North Baffin area Kublu & Oosten (1999).

Even though camp life represents the life style of the *inummariit* today, life in the community, with its close connection and interaction with Qallunaat people and institutions, in the winter season is a lifestyle that has become part of Inuit culture and society.

Camp life provides Inuit with an opportunity to hunt animals and connect to the land. When they return to the village, they bring the harvest with them, distributing fish and meat among their kinsmen. However, they are ambivalent about being in the community, whereas being out camping is perceived to contribute to the well-being of Inuit. The community provides an opportunity for social interactions and festivals, but it can also have detrimental effects that are thought to manifest themselves, for example, in suicides, domestic violence, and drug abuse. Therefore, organizing camps out on the land, usually on a religious basis, is an established method of healing for those in need. The community does provide all the benefits of modern life: adequate housing, shops, schools and churches. It allows for intensive social interaction and collective festivals. The most valued occasion, the Christmas festival, is considered crucial to community life all over the Arctic.[284]

Christmas has been the most important ritual in the Christian holiday cycle since the start of the Anglican mission. Missionaries did not confine themselves to the celebration of the services, but also organized the festival and provided banquets with western food for the Qallunaat and country food for Inuit. Moreover, they organized games with prizes, which immediately became very popular.[285]

Today, the celebration of Christmas that follows the Anglican tradition is conceived as an excellent framework to bring together everyone in the community. All my informants agreed that the community should not be divided by conflicting religious orientations.

In the period in which Christmas was first introduced to Inuit, Qallunaat invested considerable effort in organizing the celebration. Christian Inuit camps took over the organization of the festival when there was no direct access to a mission station. With the establishment of the modern settlement Inuit institutions have taken over the task of organizing and providing for the festival, and they have extended it from a one-day celebration to a festival of ten days. Over the years, the importance of the Christmas celebration has increased. The importance of Christmas is illustrated, for example, in the reportage of the major Nunavut newspaper, the *Nunatsiaq News*. In their December issue, Christmas has become a central topic and an occasion for adding a *Christmas Special* that informs about events taking place all over Nunavut. The special issue includes reminiscences of the old days and provides a platform for the Churches, politicians, and businessmen to express their best wishes and Christmas messages. The Christmas celebration is even deemed to be a concern of the Nunavut government, which provides the major financial

---

284 Barbara Bodenhorn (1993) already showed the relevance of the Iñupiat Christmas festival of Barrow, Alaska for the constitution of the community. Iñupiat provide a sufficiently similar and sufficiently different case for a fruitful comparison on the ritual constitution of modern Inuit communities.

285 Missionary reports on Christmas among the Inuit, published in, for instance, the Catholic journal *Eskimo* or the Anglican journal *Arctic News*, provided uplifting stories. Both ancient and modern Inuit Christmas celebrations continue to inspire publications, mostly but certainly not exclusively, by Qallunaat authors. See for instance the anthology of old and recent accounts, *Christmas in the Big Igloo: True tales from the Canadian Arctic* edited by Kenn Harper in 1983. (See, for instance: Akeesho (1974), Alooktook (1974), Boisclair (1950), d'Argencourt (1976), Eber (1989), Ernerk (1995), George (1998), Hantzsch (1977 [1909-1911]), Hoare (1964), Mary-Rousselière (1956), Philippe (1946, 1947), Rokeby-Thomas (1975), Stevenson, A. (1965), and Van der Velde (1948, 1956)

sources to local institutions that contribute to the festival. The Christmas festival has always been an issue of dynamic discourse on proper ways to celebrate it. The festival can integrate new elements, but care has to be taken that it is performed properly. Both individuals and institutions are expected to contribute to the celebrations.[286] While organizations provide prizes, food, games etc., individuals participate in services, games, banquets, gift-giving etc. Generosity is a prime expression of sociality in these contributions. By providing prizes, people contribute to the well-being of the community. The qualification of Christ as the ultimate prize, expresses the value of the prize as a gift.

In Qikiqtarjuaq, as in the winter camps of the past, religious life intensifies in winter, and festivals are celebrated by the entire community. When people concentrate in the settlement in the fall after the camping period, old and new conflicts between people emerge. It is also a period of more frequent dangerous encounters with non-human beings. The Christmas festival is anticipated as a period of being happy together and for social and cosmological renewal. A variety of religious and social activities are organized during the ten days of the Christmas celebration; services, gift exchanges, feasts, games, and dances all contribute to resolving the tensions that have arisen between individuals and reshaping the community's social life, and are expressed in the following.

People relate directly to God during the religious services. The elements of confession and conversion are prominent in the testimonials of the elders. The community re-establishes itself as a religious community in relation to God. People invest in their relations by exchanging gifts, and social relations are objictied in the gifts themselves. People can privilege specific relationships, and the relationship between giver and receiver is often made explicit by providing the name of the giver. The feast connects the community to the game, and sharing and consuming food together creates community. Food sharing is considered to be fundamental to the *inummariit* way of life. No one should leave hungry, everyone should be free to take country food home and no one should be excluded. The community's vitality is enhanced by dancing. Inuktitut dances are especially enjoyed by the elders. Whereas in the past, ancestors observed the Sedna festival, today it is most important that the elders enjoy the games and dances, as they represent a link to the *inummariit* and to the past.

Games provide one of the most striking features of the festival. The games are intended to allow people to show their physical and social skills and for the enjoyment of all participants. People interact in games and prove themselves as skillful partners in cooperative performances. The games are often designed so that the participants have to rely on the other participants to gain a result. The winner can only become victorious through the contributions of others. This structure expresses a fundamental Inuit value that every success ultimately depends on social relationships. The ideal that is expressed is cooperation. The community does not represent to Inuit a corporate unit encompassing and transcending the participants; it represents much more the potential for cooperation. Competition is a structural feature of play, and play constitutes an ideal form to shape and express productive competition. Ideally, this competition is enjoyable for the participants as well as the spectators. Everyone should enjoy the proceedings, and the

---

286 Nicole Gombay (2005, in press) and Nabuhiro Kishigami (2000, 2004: 85) discussed how Inuit deal with modern institutions on different levels, suggesting that the management of various identities and sets of rules are strategies employed. They found, in agreement with my own results, that institutions are integrated in daily life on 'Inuit terms'. The Christmas festival would provide an interesting field for further study with respect to how leadership is dealt with there.

element of competition should also end with the game-playing. Winners and losers should end the game with a smile, and the winner should express his/her gratitude to the community and the other participants.

These activities and interactions do not lead to further obligations, but they create the conditions for cooperation in the coming season. When, in the following spring, people disperse to their campsites, some of these potential relations will be established – but all of them have had that potential.

The translation of 'Christmas' to *quviasuvik* ('a time of happiness') expresses the joy experienced by human beings in shaping and constituting the social and cosmological relations of their society. In this process they not only present themselves to transcendental agencies, primarily God and the *inummariit*, but especially in traditional dances and games, they may also represent the ancestors whose names they are carrying. Being joyful appears to have a spiritual dimension. We saw in the stories on conversion that light and joy were associated with the presence of God. In the past, the shaman, as well as the helping spirit, was believed to emanate light by which the shaman could see. Rev. Peck, collecting long lists of helping spirits, emphasized the connection between enlightenment and enjoyment in the shaman's work with the spirit (Laugrand & Oosten & Trudel 2000: 108). Relations with transcendental agencies, then, can be encompassed in the enjoyment. Thus the notion of play, so fruitfully developed by Jean Briggs, acquires a special meaning: it constitutes a modality which allows the community to connect itself to transcendental agencies, and to establish a sense of community and cooperation between the participants. All involved are well aware, though, that these relations are fragile and can only be fully realized in play.

Abbreviations

ATTS Arthur Turner Training School (Anglican)
CBC   Canadian Broadcasting Cooperation
CDLC Community Land and Development Committee (Qikiqtarjuaq)
CSC   Community Service Committee (Qikiqtarjuaq)
DAB   Development Appeal Board (Qikiqtarjuaq)
DEW   Distant Early Warning System
DSD   Department of Sustainable Development (Nunavut)
FLAC Finance, Legislative and Administrative Committee (Qikiqtarjuaq)
HTO   Hunters and Trappers Organization (Qikiqtarjuaq)
NSDC Nunvut Social Development Council
NTI   Nunvaut Tungaavik Incorporated
QIA   Qikiqtaaniq Inuit Association (Nunavut)
RCMP Royal Canadian Mounted Police
SAO   Senior Administrative Officer
WA   Women's Auxiliary Group (Anglican)

Appendices

Appendix 1

Ministers who served or visited Qikiqtarjuaq, camps, and work locations (Kivitoo, Padloping, Cape Dyer DEW line, Durban Island) to perform baptisms and wedding ceremonies:

Date	Minister
1960	W.A. Graham (visiting)
1960-1964	S. Wilkinson (visiting)
1963-1964	R. Paradis (visiting)
1967	Lay reader Pauloosie Angmarlik; he performed baptisms incidentally till 1977
1967-1971	Whitbread (became Archdeacon in 1970, since then visiting)
1972-1975, 1984	Gardener (local minister?)
1975-1983	J. Allooloo (local minister)
1984	Pauloosie Qaqasiq (visiting)
1985-1987	Joshua J. Aneak (local minister?)
1988	Benjamin Arreak (visiting)
1988-1990	B. Nakoolak (local minister?)
1990-1994	Iola Metuq (local minister)
1994	Benjamin Areak (visiting)
1994-1995	L. Nakoolak (visiting?)
1995	B. Arreak (visiting)
1995-1996	L. Mike (visiting)
1996-1997	J.J. Aneak (visiting)
1997-2000	L. Mike(partly visiting)
1999	D. Aupalak (visiting)
2000	A. Tigulak (visiting)

Visiting ministers or bishops were related to either the Pangnirtung or Iqaluit parishes.

Appendix 2

List of Christmas games 1999[287]

Outdoor games

Date	Title	Features	Winner[288]	Organizer
24.12.99	Water Balloon Toss	Pairs of man and woman line up. The partners toss a water balloon back and forth until it breaks. Each round they increase the distance. The remaining couple wins.	M, F	CSC
24.12.99	Skidoo Race with Jerry Cans on Garbage Bag	First men than women line up with machines. All of a group start at same time. Who is back first wins.	M, F	CSC
27.12.99	Ptarmigan Hunt	The winner is who brings back with a ptarmigan first.	M, F	CSC/HTO
27.12.99	Ice Weighing Contest	Participants try to get a piece of ice of the same weight as the piece displayed by organizers	M, F, E	CSC
28.12.99	Skidoo Race	Individual contestants start in different classes. The fastest wins.	M, F	CSC
29.12.99	Dog Team Race	A race with teams of 7 dogs. (cancelled)	One	CSC
29.12.99	Ice Hole Opening	Open a hole through the ice as fast as possible.	M, F	CSC
29.12.99	Cod Fishing	The first person to catch a cod wins.	M, F	CSC
29.12.99	Ping Pong Relay	Game played with two teams. Ball has to be carried on a spoon, hold with the mouth.	M, F	CSC
30.12.99	Seal Hunting Contest	Teams of one man and one woman are the competing units; both have to catch a seal. The teams meet and then start to hunt towards the north at the same time.	M + F	CSC/ Housing
30.12.99	Snow Sculpture Contest	Snow sculptures are judged.	Not specified	CSC
30.12.99	Darts at Water Balloons	Three darts thrown; number of balloons busted. If same number, than who busts balloon first with one throw each.	M, F, E, Ch	CSC
31.12.99	Jigging	Trying to fish a cod as fast as possible.	One	HTO
31.12.99	Caber Toss	Toss log. Longest distance wins.	M, W	CSC
31.12.99	Three Legged Races	A man and a woman are tied together and have to run. Fastest team wins.	M, W	CSC
01.01.00	Seal Hunt	Catching two seals first.	M, W	HTO

---

287 This list is based on the contests that I have documented, which are about 90 % of the games played during the community Christmas festival. The list also includes games that were organized at institutional celebrations to which I was invited.

288 Some games especially allocate a prize for elders *E*. The letter *M* stands for man, the letter *W* stands for woman, and *Ch* for child.

Indoor games

Date	Title	Features	Winners	Organizers
16.12.99	Styrofoam on a Thread	Dice game, with needle and thread, put styrofoam pieces on thread.	One	Arctic College Christmas
16.12.99	Hand Clap	Played in a circle, one neighbour claps the next on the hand, who his too late or makes a mistake is out.	One	Arctic College Christmas
16.12.99	Place Hat on Somebody	Players sit in circle, with backs toward each other, put on hat on neighbour, when music stops wearer of hat out.	One	Arctic College Christmas
17.12.99	Go through Hula Hoop	Game played in circle, when music stops the wearer of the hula hoop is out.	One	Wolf Cubs Christmas
17.12.99	Santa Claus Relay	Two teams, race, players wear Santa Claus beards.	One	Wolf Cubs Christmas
18.12.99	Gift Draw and Giving on	Everybody contributes gift, name is drawn, gift chosen, next person may take another person's gift or take a new one.	All	Teacher's Christmas
18.12.99	Wool Game	Dice game, make ball of wool.	One	Teacher's Chrismtas
18.12.99	Pick a Thread	Dice game, pick as many threads as possible.	One	Teacher's Christmas
18.12.99	Draw	People drew numbers, certain numbers win prizes.	Several	School's Christmas
21.12.99	Hot Dog Eating Contest	As many hot dogs as possible in certain time.	M, W	Northern Store
22.12.99	Best Decorated House Judging	The decoration of the exterior of the house with Christmas lights and other items is judged.	1., 2., 3.	Northern Store
23.12.99	Balloon Scramble	Part of Midnight Madness Sales at Northern.	Several	Northern Store
23.12.99	Scavenger Hunt	A piece of paper was hidden in gym, finder wins.	One	CSC
23.12.99	Arm Wrestling	Pairs compete in arm wrestling. Several rounds till winners determined.	M, W, Ch	CSC
23.12.99	Styrofoam Throw	Individuals compete with each other, throw a styrofoam piece as far as possible.	M, W, Ch	CSC
24.12.99	Grand Prize Draw	Prizes distribution with a draw.		Northern Store
24.12.99	Collecting Signatures	Players received paper with names: they have to go to the persons to collect their signatures.	M, F, E	CSC
24.12.99	Elastic Face Game	Players must get elastic band of face without using hands.	M, W, E	CSC
24.12.99	Over-Under Relay	Two teams game, team lines up with every second person bending and every first person spreading legs, contestants have to race through by jumping and crawling, and then line up again.	M, W	CSC
24.12.99	Collecting Signatures	Players receive paper with names: they have to go to the identified persons to collect their signatures.	M, F, E	CSC

Date	Title	Features	Winners	Organizers
24.12.99	Elastic Band Shooting	Competition between individual players with the objective to shoot an elastic as far as possible.	M, F, E	CSC
24.12.99	Move through a Hula Hup	Game played in a circle; contestants have to move through a hula hup ring; the person holding it when music stops is out of the game.	One	CSC
24.12.99	Three Way Tie up Pop Can Collection	Three individual competitors pull on connected ropes each of which is tied around each player's hip to reach a pop can.	M, F	CSC
24.12.99	Christmas Lights Draw	Everybody who has Christmas lights as decoration may participate in the draw.	One	CSC
27.12.99	Longest Yarn in Bag	Everybody pulls yarn out of bag – the longest wins.	One	CSC
27.12.99	Pin the Snowmobile to Qikiqtarjuaq	Player is blindfolded and tries to pin a paper-snowmobile as close as possible to Qikiqtarjuaq on a map.	M, W, E, Ch	CSC
27.12.99	Children over 2 Walking Race	Race between individual competitors.	Ch	CSC
27.12.99	Children under 2 Crawling Race	Race between individual competitors.	Ch	CSC
27.12.99	Hot Broom	Played in a circle, a broom is given from one person to the next until music stops. The person holding the broom is out.	M, W, E	CSC
27.12.99	Draw	Enter one's name, written on a piece of paper, to a draw	One	CSC
27.12.99	Draw	People enter their names to the draw through the radio	One	clam diver
27.12.99	Candy Throw	Organiser throws candy, people try to catch them or pick them up from the floor.	Ch, E	CSC
28.12.99	Women's Pool Tournament	Pool; each player has three attempts.	F	Co-Op
28.12.99	Bench Stretch	Player kneels on a bench. Contestant must reach as far as possible and place a marker. No part of the body may touch the ground.	M, F	CSC
28.12.99	Musical Chair	For each contestant except one chairs were placed down. Players moved around the; as music stops players had to sit down, the one without seat was out	M, F, E	CSC
28.12.99	Candy Throw	The provider throws candy in the crowd. Everybody scrambles.	Ch	P. Kunilusie
28.12.99	Balloon Game	Balloon dance.	M, W, E, Ch	CSC
28.12.99	Balloon Game	Balloon dance.	E, Ch	CSC
28.12.99	Dice Game with Yarn	Played in a circle. Yarn has to be rolled up.	not defined	CSC
29.12.99	Screw Removal Game	Dice game played in circle. Screws have to be removed from a board.	M, W	CSC
29.12.99	Pop Can Bowling	Individual contestants have to hit the can or they are out.	M, W, E, Ch	CSC

Date	Title	Features	Winners	Organizers
29.12.99	Ping Pong Blow relay	Played in pairs. Player kneels down and blows ball into direction of partner at other side of the gym	M, W	CSC
29.12.99	Lip Sync Competition	Kareoke	1., 2., 3.	CSC
29.12.99	Traditional Clothing Contest	Contestants present traditional clothing (newly sewn)	1-4 prizes	CSC?
30.12.99	Dice Game with Yarn	see above	not specified	CSC
30.12.99	Dice Game Draw	Dice game played in a circle. Pieces of paper with number on them are rolled into a ball. Who gets such a paper while unrolling the ball receives the associated prize.		Mary Killiktee
30.12.99	Aeroplane	Contestant is lifted and fully stretched, helper holds feet, two others hold each a hand. The contestant has to hold stretch as long as possible. Easier variant for women and children.	M, W, Ch	CSC
30.12.99	Big Ball Balance	Played by two contestants, people balance on big ball and try to touch the partner in such a way that he falls.	M, W, Ch	CSC
30.12.99	Russian Kick	Object has to be kicked with certain jumping technique.	M, W, Ch	CSC
30.12.99	Basketball Shootout	Three shots. The person with most goals wins.	M, W, E, Ch	CSC
30.12.99	Community Gift Bingo	Every participant brings a small gift. Bingo is played. Winners receive gifts (for man, for woman).	M, W	CSC
31.12.99	Ataata, Anaana, Irniq, Paniq ('Mother, Father, Son, Daughter')	All participate at the same time. Each player draws paper with a family-role written on it. When the music stops families (F, M, S, D) get together, who is left over is out.	4 winners	Co-op
31.12.99	Soccer Shootout	Individual contestants. Three shots with football through hula hoops. The person with most goals wins.	M, W, E, Ch	CSC
31.12.99	Colour Game	individual participants, meaning of colours: yellow 'sit down', brown 'spin', etc., last person doing action is out	M, W, Ch	CSC
1999 (date unclear)	Dress in Aumauti	Two team competition. Each member of the team has to dress and undress as fast as possible in an amauti (women's jacket with large hood to carry babies).	M, W	DEA
1999	Pull a Thread	Dice game played in circle. Contestants had to pull as many threads as possible out of a heap during their turns.	One	DEA
1999	Hockey Shootout	Individual contestants shoot puck with hockey stick at a target. Who gets closest wins.	M, W, E, Ch	CSC

Date	Title	Features	Winners	Organizers
1999	Shoe Scramble	Pairs of man and woman. The woman takes a shoe of and throws it in the center. The men dance in circle passing all the women. When the music stops, men have to get a shoe and fit it to the right woman. The last pair is out.	The remaining pair	CSC
1999	Number of People Group	Individual players move around slowly. Music plays. When the music stops, organisers say a number. People have to form groups of the correct number. Those who are too late are out. Several rounds of elimination.	Two winners	CSC
1999	Have the Right Child	All participants had to grab a small child. Who was holding the child the organizer had in mind was the winner	One	Pauloosie Kunilusie
1999	Dice Game with Draw	Dice game, with wool, pieces of paper with number, draw for material prizes	Several	Pauloosie Kunilusie
1999	Dance Game	Pairs of man and woman. Shortage of one man. Men assemble in middle, hold out one arm, women walk around, when music stops women have to find partner.	M, W	CSC
01.01.00	Volleyball Pop Can Relay	Played with two teams. A ball has to be carried on pop can while racing.	M, W, Ch	CSC
01.01.00	Look Like Opposite Sex Contest	Participants dress like the opposite sex. A jury judges the best costume and performance.	M, W	CSC
01.01.00	Elders Speak English Qallunaat Speak Inuktitut	Each participant has to repeat words. Jury judges decides on best performance.	Qallunaat and E	CSC
01.01.00	Dice Game, Writing a Word on Paper Slips	Dice game in circle. One has to write as many words as possible on slips of paper during one's turn.	not defined	CSC
01.01.00	Funny Faces	Individual perform in funny and strange ways, jury judges the most funny.	M, W, E	CSC

Bibliography

Akeesho, Atsainak
1974   Christmas in a hunting camp. *Inukshuk* 23: 8.

Alooktook, Ipellie
1972   Community Christmas. *North* XIX(6): 24-27.

———
1987   Christmas is for everyone. *Inuit Monthly* III(9): 36-39.

Anonymous
1977   Information on the parishes. *The Arctic* News: 3.

Adams, Colin
1972   Flexibility in Canadian Eskimo social forms and behavior: A situational and
        transactional appraisal. *Alliance in Eskimo society: Proceedings of the American Ethnological
        Society, 1971.* Ed. Lee Guemple, 9-16. Vol. suppl. Seattle/London: American Ethnological
        Society, University of Washington Press.

Amit, Vered
2002   Reconceptualizing community. *Realizing community: Concepts, social relationships and
        sentiments.* Ed. Vered Amit, 1-20. (European Association of Social Anthropologists).
        London/New York: Routledge.

Baffin Regional Health Board
1995   *Community profile 1994,* Iqaluit.

———
1999   *Community profile 1998,* Iqaluit.

Balikci, Asen
1970   *The Netsilik Eskimo.* Garden City N.Y.: The Natural History Press.

Bilby, Julian
1923   *Among unknown Eskimo: An account of twelve years intimate relations with the primitive
        Eskimo of ice-bound Baffin Land, with a description of their ways of living, hunting customs
        and beliefs.* Philadelphia: J. B. Lippincott.

Blaisel, Xavier, and Knötsch, Cathleen
1995   *Contextualization and Christianization in Cumberland Sound, Baffin Island (1880s-1920s):
        Shamans, lay readers, and priests in the Arctic – Rival contenders for heirship to the throne.*

Paper presented at the annual CASCA conference, Université du Québec à Montréal, May 27-29, 1995.

Blaisel, Xavier, and Oosten, Jarich G.
1997   La logique des échanges des fêtes d'hiver inuit. *Anthropologie et Sociétés* 21(2-3): 19-44.

Boas, Franz
1888   The Central Eskimo. *6th Annual Report of the Bureau of American Ethnology for the years 1884-1885.* 399-669. Washington.

————

1901   The Eskimo of Baffin Land and Hudson Bay: From Notes Collected by Capt. George Comer, Capt. James S. Mutch, and Rev. E. J. Peck. *Bulletin of the American Museum of Natural History,* 15.

————

1900   Religious beliefs of the Central Eskimo. *Popular Science Monthly* 57: 624-632.

————

1907   Second Report on the Eskimo of Baffin Land and Hudson Bay: From notes collected by Captain George Comer, Captain James S. Mutch, and Rev. E. J. Peck. Bulletin of the American Museum of Natural History, 15(2): 374-570.

Bodenhorn, Barbara
1993   Christmas present: Christmas public. *Unwrapping Christmas.* Ed. Daniel Miller, 193-216. Oxford: Clarendon Press.

————

2000   'He used to be my relative': Exploring the bases of relatedness among Iñupiat of northern Alaska. *Cultures of relatedness: New approaches to the study of kinship.* Ed. Janet Carsten, 128-148. Cambridge: Cambridge University Press.

Boisclair, J.-B.
1950   Christmas in the Far North. *Eskimo* 15: 13-14.

Briggs, Jean L.
1979   *Aspects of Inuit value socialization.* National Museum of Man Mercury Series, 56. Ottawa: National Museum of Man.

————

1997   From trait to emblem and back: Living and representing culture in everyday life. *Arctic Anthropology* 34(1): 227-235.

————

1998   *Inuit morality play: the emotional education of a three-year-old.* New Haven a.o.: Yale U.P.

2000   Conflict management in a modern Inuit community. *Hunters and gatherers in the modern world: Conflict, resistance, and self-determination.* Eds. Peter P. Schweitzer, Megan Biesele, and Robert K. Hitchcock, 110-124. New York/Oxford: Berghahn Books.

Brody, Hugh
1976   Inummariit: The Real Eskimos. *Inuit Land Use and Occupancy Project.* Ed. M. Freeman, 223-228. Ottawa.

Burch, Ernest S., Ellanna, Linda (Eds.)
1994   *Key issues in hunter-gatherer research.* Providence/Oxford: Berg Publishers.

Carsten, Janet (Ed.)
2000   *Cultures of relatedness: New approaches to the study of kinship.* Cambridge: Cambridge University Press.

Cohen, Anthony P.
1985   *The symbolic construction of community.* London: Tavistock.

Collignon, Béatrice
2005   Inuit place names and sense of place. *Critical Inuit Studies: An anthology of contemporary Arctic ethnography.* Eds. Pamela Stern & Lisa Stevenson, chapt. 12. Kincoln: University of Nebraska Press [manuscript in press].

Damas, David
1963   *Iglulingmiut kinship and local groupings: A structural approach.* National Museum of Canada Bulletin, 196. Ottawa: National Museum of Canada.

1964   The patterning of the Iglulingmiut kinship system. *Ethnology* 3(4): 377-88.

1988   The contact-traditional horizon of the Central Arctic: Reassessment of a concept and reexamination of an era. *Arctic Anthropology* 25(2): 101-138.

2002   *Arctic migrants – Arctic villagers: The transformation of Inuit settlement in the Central Arctic.* Montreal a.o.: McGill-Queen's University Press.

d'Argencourt, Lea
1976   Merry Christmas. *Inuit Today* 5(11): 38-40.

Dickerson, Mark O.
1992   *Whose North? Political change, political development, and self-government in the Northwest Territories.* Vancouver: UBC Press.

Dorais, Louis-Jacques
1997   *Quaqtaq: Modernity and identity in an Inuit community.* Toronto a.o.: University of
        Toronto Press.

Eber, Dorothy
1989   *When the whalers were up North: Inuit memories from the Eastern Arctic.* Montreal a.o.:
        McGill-Queen's University Press.

Ernerk, Peter
1995   1950-1960 Repulse Bay Christmas. *Nunatusiaq News* (Iqaluit), Merry Christmas-Special,
        p.22.

Freeman, Milton M.R.
1976   *Report: Inuit land use and occupancy project.* 3 vols. Ottawa: Department for Indian and
        Norther Affairs.

Frobisher, Martin
2001   *The third voyage of Martin Frobisher to Baffin Island, 1578.* Works issued by the Hakluyt
        Society, 3rd series, no. 6. London: Hakluyt Society.

George, Jane
1998   George Oneak remembers Christmas in Old Fort Chimo. *Nunatsiaq News* (Iqaluit), 18
        Dec., n.p.

Goldring, Phillip
1986   Inuit economic responses to Euro-American contacts: southeast Baffin Island, 1924-
        1940. *Historical Papers/Communications Historique,* 146-172.

Goldring, Philipp, Payment, D., and Preiss, P.
1989   *Auyuittuq National Park Reserve: Resource description and analysis.* Winnipeg: Natural
        Resource Conservation Canadian Parks Service Prairie and Northern Region.

Gombay, Nicole
2005   Shifting identities in a shifting world: Food, place, community, and the politics of scale
        in an Inuit settlement. *Environment and Planning D: Society and Space.* [Manuscript, in
        press]

Graburn, Nelson H.H.
1964   *Taqamiut Eskimo kinship terminology.* Ottawa: Northern Coordination and Research
        Centre.

Guemple, Lee
1971a   Introduction. *Alliance in Eskimo Society.* Ed. L. Guemple, 1-8. Proceedings of the
        American Ethnological Society, no. 1971, Supplement. Seattle, London: American
        Ethnological Society.

1971b   Kinship and alliance in Belcher Island Eskimo society. *Alliance in Eskimo Society*,
         Ed. L. Guemple, 56-79. Proceedings of the American Ethnological Society, no. 1971,
         Supplement. Seattle, London: American Ethnological Society.

Hall, Charles F.
1865   *Arctic researches and life among the Esquimaux: Being the narrative of an expedition
         in search of Sir John Franklin, in the years 1860, 1861 and 1862.* New York: Harper &
         Brothers.

Hantzsch, Bernhard A.
1977   *My life among the Eskimos: The Baffin journals of Bernhard Adolph Hantzsch 1909-1911.*
         Saskatoon: University of Sasketchewan Press.

Harper, Kenn
1983a   *Christmas in the Big Igloo: True tales from the Canadian Arctic.* Yellowknife: Outcrop
         – The Northern Publisher.

────
1983b   Writing Inuktitut: An historical perspective. *Inuktitut* Sept.: 2-35.

Hawkes, E. W.
1916   *The Labrador Eskimo.* Canada Department of Mines, Geological Survey Memoir 91,
         Anthropological Series 14. Ottawa: Government Printing Bureau.

Hoare, E.
1964   Christmas in the Arctic. *The Arctic News,* n.p.

Irimoto, Takashi and Yamada, Takako (Eds.)
2004   *Circumpolar ethnicity and identity.* Senri Ethnological Studies No. 66. Osaka: National
         Museum of Ethnology.

Kishigami, Nobuhiro
2000   Contemporary Inuit food sharing and hunter support program of Nunavik, Canada.
         The social economy of sharing: resource allocation and modern hunter-gatherers. Papers
         presented at the 8th International Conference on Hunting and Gathering Societies
         (CHAGS 8), National Museum of Ethnology, Osaka, in October 1998. Eds. George W.
         Wenzel, Grete Hovelsrud-Broda, and Nobuhiro Kishigami, Senri Ethnological Studies,
         53, 171-192. Osaka: National Museum of Ethnology.

────
2004   Cultural and ethnic identities of Inuit in Canada. *Circumpolar ethnicity and identity.*
         Eds. Takashi Irimoto and Takako Yamada, Senri Ethnological Studies No. 66, 81-93.
         Osaka: National Museum of Ethnology.

Kublu, Alexina and Oosten, Jarich G.
1999   Changing perspectives of name and identity among the Inuit of Northeast Canada. *Arctic identities: Continuity and change in Inuit and Saami societies.* Eds. Jarich Oosten, and Cornelius Remie, CNWS Publications Vol. 74, 56-78. Leiden: Research School CNWS.

Kuhnlein, H. V. et.al.
2000   *Assessment of dietary benefit/risk in Inuit communities.* Centre for Indigenous Peoples' Nutrition and Environment (CINE), Ste-Anne-de-Bellevue, QC.

Kumlien, Ludwig
1879   *Contributions to the natural history of arctic America, made in connection with the Howgate polar expedition, 1877-1878.* Smithsonian Miscellaneous Collections Vol. 23; No. 5; Bulletin of the United States National Museum; Nr. 15. Washington.

Lanting, Erik
1999   Identity in Tasiusaq. *Arctic identities: Continuity and change in Inuit and Saami societies.* Eds. J. Oosten and C. Remie, CNWS Publications Vol. 74, 135-144. Leiden: Research School CNWS.

Laugrand, Frédéric
1997   *Siqqitiqpuq: Le process de la conversion et la réception du Christianism par les Inuit de l'Arctique de l'Est-Canadien (1890-1940).* Unpublished PhD dissertation Université Laval.

———

2002   *Mourir et renaître: La réception du christianisme par les Inuit de l'Arctique de lÉst canadien (1890-1940).* Québec: Les Presses de l'Université Laval/Research School CNWS.

Laugrand, Frédéric, Oosten, Jarich G., and Trudel, François
2000   *Representing tuurngait.* Memory and History in Nunvut. Vol. 1. Iqaluit: Nunavut Arctic College.

Laugrand, Frédéric, Oosten, Jarich G., and Kakkik, Maaki
2003   *Keeping the faith.* Memory and History in Nunvut. Vol.2. Iqaluit: Nunavut Arctic College.

Lawson, N. J.
1984   *Native peoples and National Parks: The case of Ayuittuq National Park Reserve and the proposed Ellesmere Island National Park reserve, N.W.T.* Unpublished PhD dissertation Trent University.

Lyon, George F.
1824.   *The private journal of Captain G.F. Lyon of H.M.S. Hecla, during the recent voyage of discovery under Captain Parry.* London: John Murray.

MacDonald, John

1998   *The Arctic sky: Inuit astronomy, star lore, and legend.* Toronto/Iqaluit: Royal Ontario Museum/Nunavut Research Institute.

Maressa, J. Maqiuq

1961   *The Eskimo sweat bath.* Hohenschäftlarn: Klaus Renner

Mary-Rousselière, Guy

1956   Christmas igloo. *Beaver* winter: 4-5.

Matthiasson, John S.

1992   *Living on the land: Change among the Inuit of Baffin Island.* Peterborough, Ont.: Broadview Press.

Mauss, Marcel and Henri Beuchat.

1979   *Seasonal variations of the Eskimo: A study in social morphology.* Translated from the French by James J. Fox. London: Routledge & Kegan Paul [1904].

McElroy, Ann

1977   *Alternatives in modernization: Styles and strategies in the acculturative behavior of Baffin Island Inuit.* HRAFlex Books, ND5-001, Ethnography Series, Vol. 11. Self-published.

McGhee, Robert

1996   *Ancient people of the Arctic.* Vancouver, BC: UBC Press; in association with Canadian Museum of Civilizations.

———

1970   Speculations on climatic change and Thule Culture development. *Folk – Dansk Etnografisk Tidschrift* 11-12: 173-84.

Müller-Wille, Ludger

1987   *Gazetteer of Inuit place names in Nunvik (Qc).* Westmount (Qc.): Avatag Cultural Institute.

Nelson, Edward William

1900   The Eskimo about Bering Strait. *Eighteenth Annual Report of the Bureau of American Ethnology, 1896-97*: 19-518. Washington: Government Printing Office.

Nicholson, L. H.

1959   The problem of the people. *The Beaver*, outfit 289. 20-24.

Nunavut Land Claims Agreement

1993   *Agreement between the Inuit of the Nunavut settlement area and her Majesty the Queen in Rights of Canada.* Ottawa: Department for Indian and Northern Affairs.

Nuttall, Mark
2000   Choosing kin: Sharing and subsistence in a Greenlandic hunting community. *Dividends of kinship: Meanings and uses of social relatedness.* Ed. Peter P. Schweitzer, 33-60. London, New York: Routledge.

Omura, Keiichi
2002   Construction of inuinnaqtun (real Inuit-way): *Self-image and everyday practices in Inuit society. Self- and other-images of hunter-gatherers.* Papers presented at the 18th International Conference on Hunting and Gathering Societies (CHAGS 8) National Museum of Ethnology, Osaka, October 1998. Eds. Henry Steward, Alan Barnard, Keiichi Omura, 101-111. Senri Ethnological Studies, 60. Osaka: National Museum of Ethnology.

Oosten, Jarich G.
2001   Ritual play at an Inuit Winter Feast. *North Atlantic Studies* 4, no. 1&2: 17-24.

Oosten, Jarich and Remie, Cornelius (Eds.)
1999   *Arctic identities: Continuity and change in Inuit and Saami societies.* Leiden: Research School CNWS.

Oswalt, H. Wendell, and James W. VanStone
1955   Partially acculturated communities: Canadian Athapaskans and West Alaskan Eskimos. *Anthropologica* n.s.: 23-31.

Oswalt, Wendell H., and James W. VanStone
1960   The future of the Caribou Eskimos. *Anthropologica* 2, no. 2: 154-176.

Parry, William E.
1824   *Journal of a second voyage for the discovery of a Northwest Passage from the Atlantic to the Pacific: Performed in the years 1821-22-23, in His Majesty's ships Fury and Hecla.* London: John Murray.

Payment, D.
1996   Persistence and change in the spiritual traditions of the Inuit of Pangnirtung and Qikiqtarjuaq (Broughton Island) since the 1890s. *Western Oblate Studies* 4: 143-59.

Philippe, Jean
1946   Christmas among the Eskimos. *Eskimo* 3: n.p.

———
1947   White Christmas. *Eskimo* 7: 3.

Purich, Donald
1992   *The Inuit and their land: The story of Nunavut.* Toronto: James Lorimer & Co Publishers.

Rasing, Wim C. E.
1994   *Too many people: Order and nonconformity in Iglulingmiut social process.* Recht en Samenleving, 8. Nijmegen: Katholieke Universiteit, Faculteit Rechtsgeleerdheid,

Rasmussen, Knud
1929   Intellectual Culture of the Iglulik Eskimos: Report of the Fifth Thule Expedition, 1921-24., vol 7. Copenhagen: Gyldendalske Boghandel.

———
1931   The Netsilik Eskimos: Social life and spiritual culture. *Report of the Fifth Thule Expedition 1921-24*, 8(1-2). Copenhagen: Gyldendalske Boghandel.

Redfield, Robert
1971   *The little community, and Peasant society and culture.* Chicago: University of Chicago Press.

Remie, Cornelius H. W.
1990   Landclaims en politieke emancipatie bij de Inuit in Noord-Canada. *Antropologische Verkenningen* 9, no. 4: 50-64.

———
1989   The struggle for land among the Inuit of the Canadian Arctic. T*he struggle for land world-wide.* Nijmegen Studies in Development and Cultural Change, Vol. 1. Eds. G. Peperkamp and C.H.W. Remie, 19-29. Saarbrücken/Fort Lauderdale: Breitenbach.

Rokeby-Thomas, A.
1975   Christmas 1938: The last Christmas in the Arctic was to be the happiest of all. *North* 22: 52-57.

Ross, Gillies W.
1975   *Whaling and Eskimos: Hudson Bay 1860-1915.*W. Gillies Ross. Publications in Ethnology, National Museum of Man, 10. Ottawa: National Museums of Canada, National Museum of Man.

Saladin d'Anglure, Bernard
1989   La part du chamane ou le communisme sexuel inuit dans l'Artique central canadien. *Journal De La Société Des Américanistes* LXXV: 133-71.

———
1993   The shaman's share, or Inuit sexual communism in the Canadian Central Arctic. *Anthropologica* 39, 59-103.

Schledermann, Peter
1975   *Thule Eskimo Prehistory of Cumberland Sound, Baffin Island, Canada.* Ottawa: National Museum of Man Mercury Series, Archeological Survey of Canada Paper 38.

Schweitzer, Peter P. (Ed.)
2000   *Dividends of kinship: Meanings and uses of social relatedness.* London: Routledge.

Schweitzer, Peter P., Biesele, Megan, and Hitchcock, Robert K. (Eds.)
2000   *Hunters and gatherers in the modern world: conflict, resistance, and self-determination.* New York/Oxford: Berghahn Books.

Sonne, Brigitte
1990   The acculturation of Sea Woman: Early contact relations between Inuit and Whites as revealed in the origin myth of Sea Woman. M.O.G., *Man and Society* 13: 3-34.

Stern, Pamela and Stevenson, Lisa (Eds.)
2005   Critical Inuit Studies: An anthology of contemporary Arctic ethnography. Lincoln: University of Nevada Press [in press].

Stevenson, Alexander
1965   Quviasukvik – the time for rejoicing: Arctic Christmas thirty years ago. *North* 12(6): 28-31.

Stevenson, Marc G.
1997   *Inuit, whalers, and cultural persistence: structure in Cumberland Sound and Central Inuit social organization.* Toronto [a.o.]: Oxford U.P.

Steward, Henry, Barnard, Alan, and Omura, Keiichi (Eds.)
2002   *Self- and other-image of hunter-gatheres.* Papers presented at the 8th International Conference on Hunting and Gathering Societies (CHAGS 8) National Museum of Ethnology, Osaka, October 1998. Senri Ethnological Studies, 60. Osaka: National Museum of Anthropology.

Therrien, Michèle
1999   'All Qallunaat predicted our extinction': Some Inuit points of view on identity. *Arctic identities: Continuity and change in Inuit and Saami societies.* Eds. Jarich Oosten, and Cornelius Remie, CNWS Publications, Vol. 74, 28-35. Leiden: Research School CNWS.

Thomas, D. K., and C. T. Thompson
1972   *Eskimo housings as planned culture change.* Ottawa: IAND Publication.

Van der Velde, Frans
1948   Christmas near the magnetic pole. *Eskimo* 11: 2-4.

———
1956   Christmas in Pelly Bay. *Eskimo* 8-12.

van Londen, Selma
1994   *Meesters van de lange nacht: Ecologie en mythologie van de Inuit.* Unpublished PhD dissertation Utrecht University.

Wenzel, George W.
1981   *Clyde Inuit adaptation and ecology: The organisation of subsistence.* Ottawa: National
        Museum of Man.

____

1994   Recent change in Inuit summer residence patterning at Clyde River, East Baffin Island.
        Key issues in hunter-gatherer research. Eds. Ernest S. Burch, Linda J. Ellanna, 289-308.
        Providence/Oxford: Berg Publishers.

Wenzel, George W., Hoversrud-Broda, Grete, and Kishigami, Nobuhiro (Eds.)
2000   *The social economy of sharing: Resource allocation and modern hunter-gatherers.* Papers
        presented at the 8th International Conference on Hunting and Gathering Societies
        (CHAGS 8) National Museum of Ethnology, Osaka, in October 1998. Senri
        Anthropological Series, 53. Osaka: National Museum of Ethnology.

Williams, J. F.
1965   *Department of Northern Affairs and National Resources Northern Administration Branch:
        Investigation and Report on Development of Settlement at Broughton Island – Northwest
        Territories. Project No. 65/204-3.* Ottawa: Department of Northern Affairs and National
        Resources.

Web Pages

Anonymous
>   *How Great Thou Art.*
>   (Available at http://igeb.org/spiritua/howgreat.html) Accessed 23 May 2003.

R. Armbruster
>   *Spiritual tide rising in Qikiqtarjuaq, Nunavut!.*
>   (Available at www.canadaawakening.com/new_page-1.htm (see also pages 2, 3), Fall
>   2002) Accessed 3 February 2003.

Department of Sustainable Development (DSD)
>   *Tasks.*
>   (Available at http://www.gov.nu.ca/Nunavut/English/departments/DSD/, 2000)
>   Accessed 16 May 2003.

Environment Canada
>   *Monthly Data Report 2000, Qikiqtarjuaq (Nunavut).*
>   (Available at http://www.climate.weatheroffice.ec.gc.ca/climateData/monthlydata_
>   e.html, 21 June 2002) Accessed 25 September 2003.

Nunavut Social Development Council (NSDC)
>   *Report of the Nunavut traditional knowledge conference. Igloolik, March 20-24, 1998.*
>   (Available at pooka.nunavut.com/~research/docs/TK%20Conference.htm, 1998)
>   Accessed 23 July 2003.

RCMP
>   *Origins of the RCMP.*
>   (Available at http://www.rcmp.ca/history/origins1_e.htm, 23 March 2004) Accessed 21
>   April 2004.

J. Spillennar
>   *Arctic Mission Oureach.*
>   (Available at http://www.acticmissions.com) Accessed 14 January 2003.

Statistics Canada
>   *Community Profile Qikiqtarjuaq, Nunavut (2001).*
>   Available at http://www.statcan.ca) Accessed 24 April 2003.

L.S. Wilson
>   (Available at http://www.lswilson.ca) Accessed 22 September 2003.

Summary in Dutch/
Nederlandse Samenvatting

In het verleden vormden de Inuit een samenleving van nomadische jagers. Sociale relaties waren afhankelijk van tijd en plaats. Mauss & Beuchat (1970 [1904]) beschouwden de spreiding in de zomer gevolgd door concentratie in de winter als twee verschillende fases van dezelfde gemeenschap. Sociale relaties waren vervlochten met relaties tot transcendente wezens. De Inuit in mijn onderzoeksregio werden ruim honderd jaar geleden tot het Christendom bekeerd door de Anglicaanse zending. In de 20ste eeuw veranderden de sociale condities drastisch door de ontwikkeling van permanente nederzettingen door de Canadese overheid. De centrale vraag van deze studie is: Hoe nemen Inuit het sociale leven in een moderne nederzetting waar en hoe passen zij hun nomadisch bestaan aan aan de condities van een permanente nederzetting? Dit probleem wordt uiteengezet in het inleidende hoofdstuk *Theoretical background and methodology*.

Deze studie is gebaseerd op 13 maanden veldwerk (1999-2001) verricht in Qikiqtarjuaq, een dorp in noordoost Canada in de provincie Nunavut. Deze nederzetting heeft rond 500 inwoners en bezit vele moderne diensten en voorzieningen. Uit de beschrijving van het leven van de gemeenschap in hoofdstuk 2, *Life in Qikiqtarjuaq*, blijkt dat ondanks de verandering van de nomadische levenswijze naar een leven in permanente nederzettingen, de perceptie van de Inuit van de samenleving en hun levenswijzen minder veranderd is dan ik had verwacht. De Inuit zien zichzelf nog steeds als jagers en formuleren hun zelf-percepties in kosmologische termen die de relaties met God, het land en de dieren benadrukken.

Inuit beschouwen de jacht 'op het land' op de dieren die God voor hen gemaakt heeft als de ware roeping van Inuit. Ook binnen het Christelijke raamwerk zijn de relaties met het land en de dieren noodzakelijke voorwaarden voor lichamelijk en geestelijk welzijn. Het is daarom goed om een nomadische levenswijze te behouden die 'het land' en de samenleving verbindt.

De relaties tussen mensen en transcendente entiteiten worden binnen het dominante Christelijke raamwerk geformuleerd. Dit raamwerk is onderwerp van dynamische veranderingen. Hoofdstuk 3, *Christianity in Qikiqtarjuaq*, behandelt het Inuit Christendom zowel vanuit het perspectief van de kerkelijke instituties als ook vanuit het perspectief van Inuit geloofsvoorstellingen en praktijken.

Tot de jaren '60, toen de Pinksterbeweging zich naar het Noorden uitbreidde, was er nauwelijks concurrentie voor de Anglicaanse kerk. De Pinksterbeweging bracht nieuwe charismatische praktijken met zich mee, zoals het 'dopen in de Heilige Geest', die lijken op elementen uit het traditionele spirituele leven, zoals de beleving van vreugde en verlichting die de sjamanistische ervaring kenmerkt. In eerste instantie was de Anglicaanse kerk fel gekant tegen de Pinsterbeweging, maar zij nam geleidelijk een meer positieve houding aan ten opzichte van de nieuwe gebruiken die ook voor veel Anglicanen aantrekkelijk waren. Tegenwoordig heeft de Anglicaanse kerk veel praktijken van de Pinksterbeweging overgenomen, maar ze draagt er nog steeds zorg voor de relatie met haar eigen verleden te bewaren. Speciaal de ouderen voelen zich sterk geworteld in de Anglicaanse traditie en willen daarvan niet vervreemd worden. Traditioneel Anglicaanse gebruiken worden nagestreefd door *reborn* kerkleiders om met name de ouderen zich thuis te laten voelen.

Hoewel de Inuit zich ervan bewust zijn dat het Christendom van buitenaf is geïntroduceerd, beschouwen zij het toch als eigen aan de traditionele Inuit cultuur. De *qallunaat* (blanke mensen) oorsprong van het Christendom is weinig relevant voor de Inuit. De Anglicaanse kerk wordt sterk geassocieerd met de *inummariit*, de 'ware' Inuit, die van het land leefden voor de tijd van permanente nederzettingen. De ouderen herinneren zich deze tijd nog en zij zijn meer dan ieder ander de representatie van de *inummariit*. Deze levenswijze is verbonden met kennis van het land, de dieren en de voor het overleven benodigde vaardigheden. In het dagelijks leven is het het belangrijkst om te leven als een *Inuk*, volgens de *inummariit* wijze van handelen en denken. Het is niet belangrijk *wat* iemand doet – mensen verschillen van elkaar – maar *hoe* iemand iets doet. Hierdoor kunnen gedrag en praktijken uit de Qallunaat wereld, zoals het Christendom of het drinken van thee en nieuwe dansvormen, onderdeel worden van het beeld van de *inummariit*.

Het beeld van de *inummariit* verbindt Inuit zowel met het land dat ze bewonen als met hun voorouders. Relaties met de voorouders worden op velerlei wijze gevormd. Een van de belangrijkste dingen is de continuïteit van de namen; kinderen worden vernoemd naar hun voorouders die hierdoor voortleven in hun nageslacht. De relatie tussen de voorouders heeft voorrang op die tussen levende mensen. Verwanten spreken elkaar vaak aan met termen die bij de relaties van hun voorouders horen. De connectie met de voorouders blijft een essentieel onderdeel van Inuit identiteit en kosmologie.

Tegenwoordig benadert het verblijf in jachtkampen voor Inuit het meest de *inummariit* levenswijze. Het maakt deel uit van de seizoensgebonden cyclus van concentratie in de nederzetting en spreiding naar zomerkampen die de samenleving van Qikiqtarjuaq ondergaat. Deze wordt gezien als bevorderlijk voor het welzijn. De moderne seizoencyclus word besproken in hoofdstuk 4, *The seasonal cycle of Qikiqtarjuaq*. Inuit waarderen deze cyclus zeer. Het verblijf in de kampen wordt ervaren als bevorderlijk voor het welzijn. Aan het samenleven in de nederzetting, onder andere tijdens de winter, worden ambivalente waarden toegekend. Enerzijds zien Inuit nadelige effecten van het verblijf in Qikiqtarjuaq, die zich kunnen manifesteren in huiselijk geweld, zelfmoord en drugsmisbruik. Een veel gehanteerde remedie is het organiseren van een tijdelijk verblijf in een kamp op het land voor wie hulp nodig heeft. De organisatie van deze kampen heeft meestal een religieuze achtergrond. Anderzijds geeft het verblijf in Qikiqtarjuaq toegang tot moderne voorzieningen als scholen, winkels en kerken alsmede de mogelijkheid tot sociale interactie en grote gemeenschappelijke rituele feesten.

Kerstmis is het belangrijkste feest van het jaar. Alle inwoners nemen deel aan het tiendaagse feest. Tijdens het feest wordt participatie in de gemeenschap zeer positief gewaardeerd. Dit roept de vraag op of de gemeenschap van Qikiqtarjuaq geconstitueerd wordt door middel van rituelen en zo ja, in welke vorm. En verder hoe deze gemeenschap is ingebed in de seizoensgebonden variatie van het samenleven.

In hoofdstuk 5, *Quviasuvik- Christmas, 'a Time of Happiness' in Qikiqtarjuaq* staan deze vragen centraal. Sinds het begin van de Anglicaanse missie is het kerstfeest het belangrijkste ritueel in de jaarcyclus van Christelijke feestdagen. De missionarissen beperkten zich niet tot het verzorgen van de kerkdienst maar organiseerden ook een feest met een westers banket voor de *Qallunaat* en met vooral *country food* (wild en vis) voor de Inuit. Zij organiseerden ook wedstrijden met prijzen, die onmiddellijk erg populair werden. Tegenwoordig wordt de viering van Kerstmis volgens de Anglicaanse traditie beschouwd als een uitstekend raamwerk om iedereen in de gemeenschap samen te brengen.

Het Kerstfeest is verlengd van één dag tot een viering van tien dagen. In Nunavut is het Kerstfeest zelfs voor de overheid van belang. Zij geeft geld aan locale instituties, die vervolgens bijdragen aan het feest en voorzien in prijzen, eten en wedstrijden. Ook van individuen wordt verwacht dat zij aan het feest bijdragen. Zij doen bijvoorbeeld mee aan de diensten, wedstrijden, banketten en het geven van geschenken. In deze bijdragen is de mate van vrijgevigheid een belangrijke uitdrukking van socialiteit.

Het Kerstfeest wordt beleefd als een periode van gelukkig samenzijn en als een tijd van sociale en kosmologische vernieuwing. De variëteit aan religieuze en sociale activiteiten – diensten, uitwisseling van geschenken, banketten, wedstrijden en dansen – dragen alle bij aan het oplossen van sociale spanningen en geven vorm aan het hernieuwde sociale leven: Tijdens de diensten staan mensen in direct contact met God. De elementen biecht en bekering spelen een belangrijke rol in de getuigenissen van de ouderen. De gemeenschap hervindt zichzelf als een religieuze gemeenschap in relatie tot God. Bij het uitwisselen van geschenken investeren mensen in hun relaties en sociale relaties worden gematerialiseerd in de objecten die men geeft en krijgt. Het banket verbindt de mensen met elkaar en de gemeenschap als geheel met het jachtwild door het delen en gezamenlijk eten van voedsel. Het delen van voedsel wordt beschouwd als een fundamenteel kenmerk van de *inummariit* levenswijze. Niemand vertrekt met honger, iedereen mag eten mee naar huis nemen en niemand wordt buitengesloten. Bij het dansen verbinden mensen zich met elkaar in een verhoogde vitaliteit. Met name de *elders* genieten van de *inuktitut* ('like Inuit do') dansen. Zij vertegenwoordigen de band met de *inummariit* en het verleden.

De wedstrijden zijn het meest opvallende onderdeel van het feest. Ze worden georganiseerd met het doel alle deelnemers plezier te bezorgen. In het spel kunnen de deelnemers hun fysieke kracht en sociale vaardigheden laten zien in interactie met elkaar. Vaak zijn de wedstrijden zo ontworpen dat het succes van de deelnemers afhankelijk is van de samenwerking met andere deelnemers. De winnaar kan alleen winnen door de bijdrage van anderen. Deze structuur vertegenwoordigt een fundamentele Inuit waarde; ieder succes hangt tenslotte af van sociale relaties. Het ideaal dat wordt uitgedrukt is coöperatie.

Voor Inuit betekent de gemeenschap niet zozeer een collectief dat het individu omvat en overstijgt als wel een mogelijkheid tot samenwerking binnen een verzameling individuen. Competitie is een kenmerk van wedstrijdspelen en spel is de ideale gedaante voor het vormen en tot uitdrukking brengen van productieve competitie. Idealiter houdt deze competitie in dat deelnemers en toeschouwers genieten van de spelen en dat de competitie ophoudt bij het einde van het spel. Zowel winnaars als verliezers worden geacht de wedstrijd te beëindigen met een glimlach, waarbij de winnaars hun dankbaarheid laten zien aan de gemeenschap en de andere deelnemers. Deze activiteiten en interacties verplichten verder tot niets maar scheppen de voorwaarden voor toekomstige samenwerking. Als in de erop volgende lente de mensen vertrekken uit Qikiqtarjuaq en zich verspreiden over de jachtgronden zullen alleen enkele van de tijdens de wedstrijden ontwikkelde relaties resulteren in concrete samenwerkingsverbanden maar in potentie zou dit met alle relaties kunnen gebeuren.

De vertaling van Kerstmis door *quviasuvik* ('een tijd van geluk') drukt de vreugde uit die de mensen hebben in het hernieuwen en vormgeven van de sociale en kosmologische relaties die de grondslag zijn voor hun gemeenschap. Vreugde blijkt tevens een spirituele dimensie te hebben. In religieuze ervaringen, zoals bekering, worden licht en vreugde verbonden met de aanwezigheid van God. In het verleden werd zowel de sjamaan als ook de hulpgeest geassocieerd met licht en vreugde. In die vreugde kunnen relaties met transcendente wezens worden omvat. In het spel kan de gemeenschap zich verbinden met transcendente wezens en tevens een gevoel van gemeenschap en coöperatie tussen de deelnemers scheppen. Maar allen die meedoen zijn er zich van bewust dat deze relaties breekbaar zijn en alleen in het spel volledig tot uiting kunnen komen.

Curriculum vitae

Anja Niole Stuckenberger was born on 18 February 1971, in Bochum, Germany. She studied Cultural Anthropology, Psychology, and Linguistics at the *Westfälische Wilhelms Universität Münster* (Germany), where she received her M.A. with honors in 1997. Afterwards she prepared her PhD project at the the *Rijksuniversiteit Leiden* (The Netherlands) and studied Inuktitut at the *Institut National de la Langues Orientales* in Paris (France). She was employed as a PhD candidate at the *Department for Cultural Anthropology* at the *Utrecht University* from 1999 until 2004. As part of her project, she carried out 14 months of fieldwork in Qikiqtarjuaq, Nunavut (Canada) from 1999 until 2001. From 2004 until 2005 she taught at Utrecht University. Currently, she holds a Postdoc position at the *Institute of Arctic Studies* that is part of the *Sloane Dickey Center for International Understanding* at *Dartmouth College*, Hanover (NH), USA.